D0437942

Warped 10/2010

AT HOME
ON THE
STREET

AT HOME

ON THE

STREET

People, Poverty, and
a Hidden Culture of
Homelessness

Jason Adam Wasserman
Jeffrey Michael Clair

LYNNE
RIENNER
PUBLISHERS

BOULDER
LONDON

Published in the United States of America in 2010 by
Lynne Rienner Publishers, Inc.
1800 30th Street, Boulder, Colorado 80301
www.rienner.com

and in the United Kingdom by
Lynne Rienner Publishers, Inc.
3 Henrietta Street, Covent Garden, London WC2E 8LU

Library of Congress Cataloging-in-Publication Data
Wasserman, Jason Adam.
  At home on the street : people, poverty, and a hidden culture of
homelessness / Jason Adam Wasserman and Jeffrey Michael Clair.
Includes bibliographical references and index.
ISBN 978-1-58826-725-2 (hardcover: alk. paper)
ISBN 978-1-58826-701-6 (pbk.: alk. paper)
  1. Homelessness—United States. 2. Homeless persons—United States.
I. Clair, Jeffrey M., 1958– II. Title.
HV4505.W26 2009
362.50973—dc22   2009023438

British Cataloguing in Publication Data
A Cataloguing in Publication record for this book
is available from the British Library.

Printed and bound in the United States of America

 The paper used in this publication meets the requirements
of the American National Standard for Permanence of
Paper for Printed Library Materials Z39.48-1992.

5 4 3 2 1

Contents

Preface

We never started out to write a book on homelessness. In fact, we were well into our research before the idea of writing anything occurred to us. We began this as a project while teaching a course on visual sociology. At the time, our only aspirations were to make a short documentary, hoping that the process of making it with our class would afford us a teaching opportunity. We picked homelessness for convenience, because we had several colleagues who had researched it, and they provided us with quick interviews and local contacts. It was many weeks into the project that a writing opportunity seemed plausible. After interviewing local service-providers and our colleagues, and after various hesitations, we actually went out and talked to some people who were homeless, men who we had noticed were routinely gathered in a vacant lot next to the train tracks. What they told us just did not fit with what we had heard from the experts. And so, sitting in Jeffrey Clair's van after an early trip to that vacant lot, we turned a one-semester classroom project into what ended up being a four-year ethnographic study.

Having allowed ourselves to experience things on the street—by staying there for consecutive days and nights and by cultivating intimate relationships with those who live there—we hope to add new insights and dimensions to the sizable body of research on homelessness. To do so, we intentionally try to avoid coming to typical social science conclusions, which warrant and even demand neatly categorized and overly generalized understandings. Rather, we call attention to complexities and apparent contradictions and have tried to flesh them out while leaving them realistically complex and contradictory.

This study was approved by the institutional review board at the University of Alabama at Birmingham, the academic home for both of us during the study. The protocol was a complex one, as ethnographies quite often are. In lieu of written consent, we got consent on film from those interviewed and also permission to use first names or nicknames. We explained the risks of being seen and possibly identified, including added stigma, but also possible location by authorities or unwanted contact with family members. Some people opted not to participate in formal interviews or to be on film for these reasons, while others consented to do so and often even implored us to film them, seeing it as an opportunity to share their voices. What this means is that, in this text, names have been changed only for those people who were observed in public, consensual settings, but who did not participate in formal interviews and therefore did not participate in the formal consent process giving us explicit permission to use their first names or nicknames.

Our data collection methods included not only recording and transcribing formal interviews, but also keeping field notes of each research experience. While quotations from formal interviews are verbatim, those captured in our field notes were recorded soon after our time in the field, but nonetheless from memory. Still, we believe that they are accurate reflections of the sentiments of the people from whom they came. As we describe in more detail in Chapter 2, we used a grounded theory methodology whereby we coded our interviews and narrative data, along with some relevant pieces of media.

As a supplement to this text, we have made sections of our data available for free download on the web, both in raw and coded forms. Our original research goal was to create a documentary film, and that film has become an integral part of our data collection. The downloadable data and the film can be accessed by visiting either www.athomeonthestreet.com or www.americanrefugeesfilm.com. Both of these provide the reader an important window to our gracious participants and the analytic process of our research.

We have numerous people to thank. Many of the faculty and graduate students in the Department of Sociology at the University of Alabama at Birmingham supplied us with donations that we took to the streets during our fieldwork. Others were called on for rides while we were staying on the street and did not have our own transportation. Still others provided consult on a variety of issues throughout our investigation that was invaluable to shaping our insights. Clair was awarded a small faculty development grant that was extremely helpful to our procuring research tools such as videotape and allowed us to hire assistants to aid with the transcriptions of some of our recorded interviews. Brian Hinote, Ken Wilson, Max Michael, Chris Taylor, Jeff Hall, Mark

LaGory, Ferris Ritchey, and Kevin Fitzpatrick were important sources of counsel throughout the process. We also thank Michael Rowe and Timothy Pippert for their reviews of an early draft of the manuscript. Their comments were critical to the final product, and since both are respected researchers and experts in the area, we are humbled by their participation in this work. Finally, we thank Lynne Rienner Publishers and in particular our editor, Andrew Berzanskis, who allowed us to culminate our insights and helped us find our voice.

While coauthors often thank each other for collaboration on a project, our collaboration was intricate well beyond the norm. We both agree that this book and the research that preceded it would not have been possible without each other. We both brought talents and experiences to bear on each aspect of the project, but the synthesis of our personalities and perspectives is really the basis for whatever success we might be able to claim. In short, we fit together in a way that made all of this possible. Trust and respect underlie every good partnership, but our similarities connected us, while our differences rounded out our team into something special. There was no part of this project that was done by either of us alone, and, under bridges and along train tracks, we formed eternal bonds of friendship.

In the end, however, we owe our biggest debt to our participants, both those who are homeless and those who serve them in various ways. Too often, those of us who document the lives of others credit ourselves with having done more than we do. Although we describe the lives of those on the street and the tireless work of the many people who labor on their behalf, it is their ongoing experiences and efforts that form the basis of this book. Even where we are critical, we respect a great deal all those who try, often thanklessly, to improve our society. Most especially, we respect and often stand in awe of those who live on the street, in circumstances that most of us cannot fathom and will never know. Above all, it was the openness and sharing of those we met that made this book possible, and we hope desperately to have done justice to their experience.

1

Introduction: Homelessness in the United States

When coauthor Jason Wasserman was ten, his mother took him to a local soup kitchen to serve people who were poor and homeless in the community. The experience was intended as a lesson in appreciating all his family had, and it still furnishes vivid memories. He can remember the uncomfortable feeling—guilt, tension, and vulnerability. Feeling sorry for the people in line, he remembers disliking one of the other volunteers who yelled at someone for trying to get a second helping of food before everyone else had eaten. He was raised in a solidly middle-class family with a grandfather, who as far back as he can remember, had lectured him about financial responsibility. So on the way home, when his mother asked how he thought those people had ended up that way, his answer was simple. "Bad investments," he responded with confidence.

People always laugh at this story, at the humorous misconception of a child. But the general feeling toward homelessness is equally, although more subtly, absurd. The culture of the United States is saturated with an intense individualism, a bootstrap vision of social mobility. We see our country as a land of opportunity, where anyone who tries hard enough can be successful. But inverting that logic yields a rather dark worldview. If working hard leads to success, then, by deduction, those who are unsuccessful simply are not hard workers.[1] The policies that follow from this conclusion allow us to construct problems such as poverty and homelessness as individual not social in nature. We therefore can ignore them; they are not *our* problems. At ten years old, the answer Wasserman offered was the product of precisely this individualist ideology, which he had been socialized to accept at the most fundamental of levels.

Such visions of homelessness result from deeper fundamental disconnections between "us" and "them" that manifest in all sorts of societal oppositions.[2] The us-them dichotomy is a way of seeing the world, one that underlies the most difficult social problems of our time, including issues of class, race, nationality, and gender. Of particular interest here, the us-them dichotomy emerges in discourse to separate those who are homeless from those who are not, and then again, with narrower focus, to distinguish those who use services and participate in programs from those held to be all the more lowly, the people who stay on the street.

The social separation inherent in the us-them dichotomy is both physical and conceptual. The former consists of political, economic, and cultural practices that systematically disadvantage and disfranchise certain groups. It is not a coincidence that African Americans are far more likely than their white counterparts to be poor and homeless.[3] Conceptually, we most often define individual identity by group membership and the contrast between our groups and those of others. Homelessness is not purely an economic disadvantage but also a stigmatized social identity that is given meaning according to its conceptual distance from "the norm."

In contrast to this atomistic view, which sees groups in rather rigid ways, we could have a dynamic vision of society in general and homelessness in particular. This vision might suggest our interrelatedness, the insufficiency of "us" and "them." In some very large cities, real estate demands force proximity of the rich and poor and shrink this social distance, but generally our relationship to those who are homeless is broken, partly because we fail to recognize our coexistence.[4] Where we do engage homelessness, we mostly sit passively by and allow service providers and government programs to represent "us," the normal, legitimate community. Not surprisingly, we often are unsuccessful in resolving any issues, either for those who are homeless or society at large.

This book will explore the relationship between the "us" and "them." We focus both on legal institutions and homeless-service providers as the arms of society that most actively engage homelessness, paying particular attention to differences between those who live on the streets and those who utilize shelters and service programs. Those individuals who are street homeless often reject what is being made available by the social service system. Alternatively, we also might say that service institutions have proved incapable of reaching this group in a meaningful way. Either way, those on the street highlight not only the overall failure of our society to provide for the poor but also the failures of specific institutions charged with that task. The former leaves us with the suggestion that we ought to provide more services to those who are poor and homeless, but the latter adds an important nuance that questions exactly what kind of services we ought to offer and how we ought to organize the institutions that provide them.[5]

Project Background

Our roots in homeless research, or rather our lack thereof, warrant some explanation. We utilized a grounded research approach, meaning that we began with few preconceptions about homelessness and allowed insights to emerge from raw observations, as opposed to testing a priori hypotheses. Since neither of the authors had any prior research experience in homelessness, or much prior academic interest in it for that matter, this method was as much necessity as choice. In fact, we began this research when teaching a sociology of film course, where we had hoped to organize the class around making a documentary film. We picked homelessness as the topic for that film because other faculty in our department had done homeless research, and we thought they could provide our initial interviews and then put us in touch with all the right people in the community. We laugh about it now, more than four years later, but at the time we anticipated finishing the project by the end of the sixteen-week semester.

We imagine our field research began like countless other projects. For their varied epistemological dispositions, ethnographers surely all share a common prearrival anxiety. By definition, the researcher is not "one of them," and this usually is an uncomfortable situation. We had several false starts before finally making it out to the streets, using weather and various other excuses for repeatedly putting the initial visit off another few days. The day of our first visit a thousand things ran through our heads and occupied our conversation as we left to go "make contact." Would two white, middle-class academics be accepted by a group of poor, mostly black men? Would we be resented? Would we be safe?

As we were getting into the car for our first field excursion, a man approached us who appeared to be homeless and somewhat intoxicated. He did not speak coherently, but extended his hand to greet Wasserman. As they shook hands, he moved in as if he was going to give Wasserman a hug. Wasserman instinctively stiffened his arm to block the attempt, and the irony of the moment became crystal clear. The idea that we were going out to look for people who were homeless, to make contact with them, like it was some sort of trip, was absurd. We were not leaving our world to visit theirs. The "us" and "them" dichotomy that permeates culture and even research on homelessness was for us a casualty of a simple early awakening: people who are homeless are everywhere.

When we arrived that first day at Catchout Corner, a locally famous gathering spot for people who are homeless, we had no idea what to expect, no idea what we were going to say, and certainly no idea that four years later we would still be making these trips. Catchout essentially is a vacant lot that serves as the venue for dozens of men who are poor, most of whom are homeless, waiting for random jobs that pay under the table. The lot was empty that day because of the rain, but four or five men were gathered under the train viaduct just a few yards away. Clair explained to them who we were and what we were doing there. His explanation was as good as it could have been, but by traditional research standards we did not really *know* what we were doing there.

We knew that we were trying to make a short documentary film on homelessness as a class project. We knew that the service providers and researchers we already had interviewed could not explain why someone would live under a bridge rather than in a shelter, and we knew that lots of people—a seemingly increasing number—were living that way. Also, we knew there had to be a reason. And mostly, we knew that we were disillusioned with "experts"; we both deeply believed that if you want to know about someone, you should start by talking *with* them, not talking about them. "What do you want to know?" the men asked. "We just want to know what your life is like." It was the best we could do. We had only one specific question: why did they not go to the shelters? Other than that, we just kind of wanted to know it all.

Keeping our visit short, we stayed just long enough for them to tell us that they felt a "peace of mind" on the streets—a relaxing mental state that comes with no responsibility or social constraints—and that they hated the shelters because they were dirty, unsafe, confining, and degrading. We asked if we could come back and talk to them, and they said that Sunday afternoons would be a good time because that was when a lot of folks gathered to socialize. Although our first visit was brief, we learned a lot. We learned that the service providers' conception of those on the street did not mesh with our impressions of what they themselves were saying. We learned that there was a wealth of knowledge on the street that had escaped most of society, even the experts running social services, and that these men could teach it to us if they wanted-ed. We learned that this was not going to be any small-scale class project. And we learned that by default we would be doing grounded theory, not because we particularly were philosophically disposed to the technique, but because we were completely ignorant of the subject and felt like the street, as opposed to the academic literature, was the right place to begin to educate ourselves.

In other words, we did not learn much about those who are street homeless on that first trip, but we learned a great deal about ourselves (and the experts we already had contacted). We became aware that we knew almost nothing about the lives of those people, and even on that first day, we learned that the next several years of our lives would be spent trying to whittle away at that ignorance.

Over the four years we actively conducted fieldwork, we met hundreds of people. As we became increasingly integrated into settings like Catchout Corner, we gained a reputation that often preceded us. Eventually, introducing ourselves to strangers on the street often would elicit something like, "Oh yeah, I heard about you guys." True to the method, we allowed our observations and what our participants said to direct the course of our research. This led to all sorts of experiences we never anticipated. After being invited into private camps, we spent consecutive nights on the streets. We interviewed police officers and graffiti artists, who, because of their "professions," have contact with those on the street. We ate at soup kitchens and "street meals" and stayed in a shelter anonymously. We conducted formal interviews and raw observation. We crawled under viaducts and over laid-up train cars, climbed chain-linked fences, sat in plush chairs at the city council, in the pews of inner-city churches, and on the sidewalks of inner-city streets. This book is the integration and analysis of all of those experiences.

Homelessness in American Culture: Some Foundational Generalizations

The tradition of rugged American individualism can easily be located at the heart of our political and economic institutions. Drawing on political theorists such as John Locke and economists such as Adam Smith, US culture has a long history of believing in the power of the individual to define his or her own social position. Popular icons such as Horatio Alger portray the ideal that anyone who works hard enough will be successful, a supposition that predicates the "American dream" itself. But caught between the American dream and a much different reality is the problem of homelessness.

The gap between aspiration and achievement betrays a complex and contradictory social structure. This social structure produces misery as much out of its ideals as the materialistic barriers to achieving them; it is a misery as much embodied by institutions as enacted by them. US capitalism is characterized not just by the *existence* of competition but also by the *belief* in competition as a mechanism for social progress. Moreover, in order to define success, the system must believe in and rely on poverty as a natural and just state, as an outgrowth of corrupt individuals, that is to say those who are lazy and deviant. Poverty is US capitalism's grand punishment and a threat that is supposed to motivate citizens to participate and to succeed. As such, the privilege of wealth is considered nothing more than one's just reward for properly cultivated motivation and thus not really a privilege at all, but an ex post facto right.

Every day we live out this vision, seeing such a system as reality itself, stripped of any human design. We ignore the way in which social structure both constrains to produce poverty and enables to produce wealth. Without recognition of these processes, which are external to the individual, we are left only with the conceptualization of poverty and homelessness as natural law and a just state of affairs. Kenneth Kyle makes this point, writing:

> Some people assume that in the natural order of things, individual merit underlies personal achievement. ... One can speak of the deserving and the undeserving in absolute terms. When used as a filter for viewing individual fortune and achievement, those individuals who are more successful (certainly the "homed") are more valued than those who are less successful—clearly the homeless. The presentation of such dichotomous relationships without explaining the underlying moves making these dichotomies possible bolsters an unproblematic view of these and similar social relations.[6]

Poverty and wealth operate materially as punishment and reward in the US capitalist system, but the punishment paradigm extends far beyond the economic sphere, pervading politics and culture and often characterizing social relationships, including society's relationship to those who are homeless. Local governments jail those who are homeless, religion threatens damnation, and service providers often require submission to treatment programs in exchange for the reward of food and shelter.[7] As a society, how we deal with those who are homeless typically wavers between subtle paternalism and heavy-handed authoritarianism. Since this fails to respect the fundamental humanity of people who are homeless, the way we interact with them individually tends only to replicate essential features of the structural oppression that predicates their suffering in the first place.

We founded this project on the rejection of homelessness as a justified outcome of natural law and suggest that a cultural belief in the necessity of poverty and deprivation partly generates those conditions. While we do not have a deterministic view of social structure per se, the hegemonic forces backing this American ideology pervade even those who are harmed by it. That is to say, it oddly is the ideology of those who are poor as much as those who are wealthy.

While debunking the salience of the "us" and "them" dichotomy certainly is a valuable enterprise, it contains its own inherent dangers. Commonality with the disfranchised and "abnormal" is a recurring theme in sociology and anthropology. The thrust of much ethnographic research is that, in the end, socially distant groups often are not that different.[8] To be sure, debunking myths of difference with more robust depictions of the disfranchised is a worthy pursuit. But for all of its aiming at depth and "thick descriptions," the construction of ethnographic texts often mandates the transformation of individuals into characters and, even worse, into caricatures. That is, the complex and contradictory nature of real human beings often can become erroneously linear and consistent when ethnographic participants become ethnographic themes. While we offer similar abstractions, we hope to have left in tact as many realistic contradictions as possible. Still, the reader is well served by considering Loic Wacquant's warning about the "pitfalls of urban ethnography." Critiquing three ethnographies about people submerged in urban poverty, he writes:

> In all three studies, the inquiry substitutes a positive version of the same misshapen social figure it professes to knock down, even as it illumines a range of social relations, mechanisms, and meanings that cannot be subsumed under either variant, devilishly or saintly. But to counter the "official disparagement of 'street people'" ... with their [B]yronic heroization by transmuting them into champions of middle class virtues and founts of decency under duress only replaces one stereotype with another.[9]

Whether or not the authors targeted fit Wacquant's assessment, the ultimate conclusion is important. Romanticized figures are no less dishonest than villains. Besides that, we ought not attach too much value to ourselves, to assert that being "just like us" is an especially preferable way to be.[10] We will argue that just as we cannot counter the problematic outcomes of structural inequality by reproducing those sorts of structural inequalities in our political and economic systems, we also cannot do so by reproducing them symbolically in our rhetorical depictions.

The significance of homelessness as a social issue is difficult to overstate. In a broad sense, homelessness stands as a challenge to widely held beliefs about opportunity and success in the United States, and it highlights the importance of structural obstacles and inequality in our society. More practically, addressing homelessness is literally a matter of life and death, as it is associated with all sorts of health outcomes such as addiction, mental illness, chronic and acute disease, malnutrition, and violence. While much academic research has shown the need to focus on structural causes of homelessness, people who are homeless seem to be increasingly perceived and treated within a paradigm of individual sickness.[11] This individualist/structuralist tension has been fundamental in social science, though various disciplines have had little success in illuminating it to the culture, as betrayed by the ongoing individual-treatment approaches of homeless services. But also problematic is that the social sciences seem locked in this dichotomy to the extent that critique of the individualism within shelters deductively entails a structuralist opposition. We hope to show that it is a false choice and present some new ideas.

A Brief History of Homelessness in the United States

In their seminal work, David Snow and Leon Anderson note, "Homelessness in one form or another has existed throughout much of human history."[12] For our purposes here, we will identify shifts in the nature of homelessness in US history from the industrial to postindustrial eras, since these bear direct relation to the current population.[13] While brief, this account provides critical context to the nature and structure of contemporary homelessness, particularly in light of continuing stereotypes of those who are homeless as lazy alcoholics and skid row bums. It additionally provides a national backdrop to the more specific history of Birmingham, Alabama, where we conducted our research.

Just after the Civil War, the need to build railroads, clear forests, and mine coal created a job sector that was migratory in nature.[14] In this period, being a hobo was a glorified lifestyle, portrayed as adventurous; this was a generation of postagrarian cowboys roaming the wide-open spaces.[15] They would ride the rails from town to town, following labor opportunities. It was an exciting life, one that while certainly not encouraged by the establishment was most definitely the material of many childhood fantasies. But as this type of work vanished, the exciting life of these wayfarers came to a halt. Beginning in the 1890s, economic recessions and shrinking job sectors led to new categories of non-working people who were homeless—tramps and bums.[16] With the loss of migratory work, largely unproblematic travelers became stagnant nuisances from the perspective of residents in the cities where they settled.[17]

While "poor laws" can be traced back to the Middle Ages, a particularly illustrative response to the increasingly static homeless population was a wave of vagrancy legislation beginning around 1881.[18] These laws made it illegal for "unsightly" people to be seen in public. Current conceptions of homelessness are most directly rooted in the negative attitudes that developed in this period, when homelessness transformed from a semilegitimate nomadic lifestyle to a public nuisance that offended the sensibilities of wealthier citizens.[19]

Throughout the twentieth century, the number of people who were homeless rose temporarily during the Depression, but otherwise remained relatively small. Furthermore, the growth of postwar suburbia meant that urban homelessness was relatively hidden. However, in the mid-1970s the number of manufacturing jobs sharply declined and inflation began to outstrip income growth. At the same time, we saw the closing of over 1.1 million single-room occupancy units.[20] Homelessness is strongly related to political and economic conditions and therefore has been increasingly experienced by families, women, and younger men.[21] A remnant of earlier times, the image of the older, alcoholic skid row bum is no longer accurate (if it ever was).

Beginning in the 1990s, urban redevelopment projects brought upper- and middle-class individuals back from the suburbs and into downtown areas where they are in close contact with those who are homeless.[22] This exacerbated already strained social relationships. In the wake of the postwar flight to the suburbs, downtown areas became nighttime ghost towns that hid those who were homeless. While this likely caused society to underestimate the seriousness of the problem, it also provided refuge to those on the street. The gentrification of city centers is forcing middle and upper classes to face homelessness in the areas where they now live. This may ultimately have positive effects (as suggested by the contact hypothesis), but it currently is stimulating a new wave of vagrancy legislation strikingly similar to the so-called ugly laws of the late 1800s.[23]

Ironically, while homelessness at this writing seems more related than ever to social structural conditions, perception and social responses have remained rigidly individualistic. Those who are homeless are stigmatized as dangerous, mentally ill, drug addicts.[24] To be sure, children no longer dream of that life. Kim Hopper sums it up, stating that the annals of US homelessness are "a tangled tale of contempt, pity, and, curiously, blank disregard."[25]

Birmingham: An Archetype of Contemporary Homelessness

The city of Birmingham was a creation of US industrialization after the Civil War. It therefore embodies the significant broader historical aspects of homelessness in the United States. Birmingham predominantly is known as the location for some of the most violent civil rights confrontations of the 1960s. In fact, many know the city for little else. This weighs heavily on those who live there and particularly those leaders of business and local government wishing to draw in capital. For our purposes, Birmingham's social, political, and economic history, including its civil rights struggles, made it an archetype for the study of contemporary homelessness.

Prior to 1871, Birmingham was known as Elyton, at the time a town of little significance when compared with Montgomery and Mobile, Alabama. This was fortunate, since it was spared widespread attack by Union armies. After emerging relatively unscathed by the Civil War, Birmingham grew quickly. The convergence of train lines made the city an industrial hub, and it soon was nicknamed the "Magic City," because it developed so rapidly that it seemed to appear out of thin air.[26]

Unlike other areas of Alabama, particularly the southern part of the state known as the "Black Belt" for its rich soil, Birmingham was not ecologically well suited for the development of agriculture and had few of those famous southern plantations. Instead, the city's economic interests were squarely pinned to industrial production. As "Yankee" capital flooded into the city during Reconstruction, steel manufacturing generated an economic boom that cemented Birmingham as "the climax of a movement for economic modernization in Alabama."[27] During this period, Birmingham got its next nickname, "the Steel City."

While postwar industrial booms stimulated the economy, this ought not imply prosperity for the people of Birmingham. Industry ownership resided in the North and anti-union practices kept wages in the city comparatively low. In 1960, average per capita incomes in Birmingham were less than half that of other US cities of comparable size.[28] Moreover,

white workers disproportionately occupied higher-paying skilled manufacturing jobs, whereas African Americans largely were relegated to
lower-paying, unskilled jobs.[29] Antagonism between these two groups
also undermined attempts to organize unions.

Like many other manufacturing cities in the United States, growth
slowed during the Depression, picked up again after World War II, and
then began a more permanent decline in the early 1970s.[30] These transitions have contributed significantly to economic struggles, the city witnessing the erosion of manufacturing jobs and resulting declines in real
wages. As of 2009 there is comparatively little manufacturing. Instead,
the University of Alabama at Birmingham is the single largest economic
force in the city and the second-largest employer in the state, next to the
government itself.[31]

Prior to the civil rights movement, Birmingham had perhaps the
most violently enforced segregated race structure in the entire country.
While many people know about the famous and tragic Sixteenth Street
Baptist Church bombing, this only cemented another nickname for the
city, "Bombingham." In fact, there had been around fifty house bombings
between 1947 and 1965 as the African American population outgrew the
capacities of its neighborhoods and began to move closer to white
areas.[32] Other classic images of fire hoses and police dogs turned loose
on mostly young civil rights activists continue to haunt the city. While
legal segregation eroded with the *Brown v. Board of Education* decision
in 1954, like much of the country, Birmingham remains largely segregated by race, though primarily as a function of poverty that continues to
disproportionately affect African Americans, who are thus relegated to
the oldest and most dilapidated sectors of the city.

Race relations in the city in the early 2000s likely were not much
different from those anywhere else. Certainly racism still persists, as it
does everywhere in the United States, but as intensely antagonistic
toward civil rights as it was during the 1960s, there is evidence to suggest that Alabama generally and Birmingham in particular have come a
long way. Although George Wallace stood in the doorway of the regis-
trar's office at the University of Alabama in symbolic defiance of an
order to desegregate the school, he won his final bid for governor of
Alabama in 1982 with a vast majority of the African American vote.[33]
In 1979, Birmingham elected its first African American mayor, which
was indeed an achievement, though it likely had as much to do with
white flight to the suburbs as it did with any real racial progress.[34]
Racist demonstrations and outright attacks amounted to a pervasive
fear campaign conducted with relative impunity until the 1960s. But in

1992, counterdemonstrations against a neo-Nazi march were so large that the parade route had to be completely fenced off and the comparatively small group of racist demonstrators had to be protected under armed guard from an enormous, angry, and multiracial mob.

The religious community has been a staple of Birmingham culture throughout its tumultuous history as both an organized institutional participant in the life of the city and a spiritual refuge.[35] The social activism of African American pastors during the civil rights movement too often was eclipsed by the celebrity of national figures, but religious leaders had been active in the civil rights movement in Birmingham before that movement really appeared there.[36] Fred Shuttlesworth, later a notable homeless activist in Cincinnati, for example, was beaten mercilessly by the Ku Klux Klan in 1957 for trying to enroll his children in an all-white school.[37] While African American churches were launching pads for the demonstrations of the 1960s, since then they have been much less active in social issues, and the white churches (as is the case elsewhere, there is ongoing de facto segregation in churches) mostly followed their parishioners to the suburbs. But though there is less practical engagement of social problems by the city's religious institutions, Birmingham still can be accurately described as an intensely religious place, and as in the past, religion is still a significant way of making sense of the world.[38]

In the years prior to his death in 1968, Martin Luther King, Jr., prophetically noted the ongoing class struggles on the horizon. Influenced by more radical activists such as Stokely Carmichael and other members of the Student Nonviolent Coordinating Committee (SNCC), King had become persuaded that the legal equality achieved by the civil rights movement would be undermined by ongoing poverty, which would effectively prevent the integration of African Americans into the community. The Birmingham metropolitan area validates this worry. As with many other urban centers, the city of Birmingham witnessed dramatic declines in its population as its mostly white middle class moved to the suburbs.[39] According to census data, in 1960 there were nearly 341,000 people living within the city limits and 60 percent of them were white. As of this writing there are around 220,000 with about 75 percent being African American. More than one-quarter of the city's residents live below the poverty line compared with just 13 percent nationwide.

These transitions have been not only the latent byproduct of housing patterns but also were produced by decisions of those in the suburbs that have crippled Birmingham's economic viability. The city of Hoover, for example, formed its own separate school district and actively annexes other wealthy areas in Jefferson County in frequently successful efforts to keep its tax revenue out of the city limits. While there is an active downtown redevelopment project that has been widely supported and is quickly revitalizing the city center, this has not returned prosperity to the people who remained downtown during the suburban flight southward, but rather pushed them into the older neighborhoods north of the city.

Constituent features of homelessness in the United States include the decline of manufacturing, the segregation of class and race both in past patterns of suburbanization and in the gentrification of redeveloping city centers, and the interplay of religious belief and social circumstance. This closely parallels the history of Birmingham and of countless other midsized US cities struggling to establish a new contemporary identity in the postmanufacturing economy.

Introducing Some Key Participants

No amount of writing can ever exhaust the true humanity and complex personality of an actual individual. At best our presentations can create characters that decently approximate the living persons they describe. In this section we present some of the major players in our research, people who will emerge in the discussions throughout this book. We offer these characterizations here nervously and hope to avoid caricaturizing the people described.

Lockett

On our first visits to Catchout, we were received with guarded hospitality. For some, this reserve dissipated faster than for others, and Lockett was one person who took to us rather quickly. In the early days, he was more willing than others to give us access, to show us around the places nestled seamlessly into the cityscape, the kinds of places you cannot see from your car.

Lockett was like that kid in school who could not be quiet—the one who, no matter the repercussions, just had to crack a joke for the approval of his peers. Ironically, his friendly nature got him in trouble with the others from time to time; we sensed that they saw it as careless. While most of them would eventually become as open as Lockett, early on they were doing their homework, studying us, probing about our lives, and looking for anything disingenuous. Being gregarious on the street was a good way to get taken advantage of, and the early pervasive rumors that we were cops or profiteers were a shield intended to defend against that possibility. We had to prove ourselves.

Lockett had an emotional side as well, one he wisely kept hidden from the other guys on the Corner. But in private moments with us, he would erupt in an almost therapeutic exposition of things he normally held inside. He confessed the impact his mother's death had on him or regret for things he had done and "bad" habits he had developed. But these moments were largely eclipsed by a jolly personality with a dry sense of humor. "Professor! I got my papers today, I'm going to Iraq," he offered with a completely straight face. "Are you serious?" we asked. "Yeah, they're dropping me behind enemy lines. I'm a secret weapon," he said, holding it for a few seconds before he broke down laughing. "Don't film that, Jason—that's a lie!" he said to Wasserman who was taping the interview.

Like anyone else, Lockett was not uniformly jovial. At times he could be withdrawn and in a bad mood. He also experienced bouts of addiction, and his relatively kind demeanor translated into a great deal of control relinquished to the drug dealers who sometimes worked off the Corner. In one telling moment, early in our research, Lockett cornered Wasserman and pleaded for fifteen dollars. He claimed that if he did not get it, the dealers would think he was "a pussy." In the end, Wasserman did give him some money, though not without lingering questions of conscience about doing so. That darker moment also troubled Lockett's conscience. For the next two years, he continually reminded Wasserman that he still intended to pay him back the money. Despite seeming like something of a lost cause in certain moments, by the end of our research, Lockett was off the street, married, and working.

Hammer

If Lockett was the class clown, Hammer was the older kid who looked out for you. A former boxer who had logged twenty-three years in prison, he exuded the hardened qualities you might expect from someone at the intersection of the boxer and ex-convict demographics. Like many of the others we would meet, Hammer displayed an intelligence that had been severely underdeveloped by a lack of formal education, and he often was visibly frustrated by a vocabulary that could not keep pace with his thoughts.

Hammer warmed up to us on our first overnight excursion, after some drug dealers asked us to leave the Corner because they felt we threatened their business. While we obliged by going to spend the night at a camp several blocks away, we made it a point to return to the Corner that night for a quick hello and spent the whole next day there. We felt like we had to show that we were not intimidated. Everyone later told us we gained respect by doing that, but it seemed particularly important to Hammer. Maybe this was a holdover from his prison days, where they say taking on a tough guy is one of the few ways to get respect. But from that moment on, Hammer was committed to us and to our research. The day after our altercation with the drug dealers, Hammer sat in the empty lot with us and expressed outright anger that we were asked to leave. "This is our corner. This ain't their corner. They go home at night! I'll take you to some spots that'll blow your fuckin' mind." "Wouldn't it be trouble if we went there?" we asked. "Not if you go with me. Ain't nobody fuckin' with me out here." His tone made this sound more like a demand than a prediction. After that day, with the former boxer in our corner, we had virtual carte blanche access to the area. The word was out that we were legitimate and anyone who did not believe that could take it up with Hammer. No one ever did.

Like Lockett, Hammer had bouts with addiction. But unlike the case with Lockett, Hammer's strong personality kept him from becoming an "errand boy" to the dealers. Still, when he was high, Hammer could be an intimidating figure. He was not directly threatening, but he would undertake long diatribes about demonic evil in the world. We later discuss this in the context of southern religion.

Motown

While Hammer and Lockett, in different ways, were extroverted, Motown had a subtle personality, but one that exuded class and self-respect. He was a tall man, something exaggerated by his good posture. Motown walked with a natural dignity characteristic of royalty, steady, upright, and slow, but with intent. His receding white hair was always neatly combed and while his hands and feet were tattered from a hard, physical life, they did not denigrate the elegance of his demeanor. While Motown was a fixture in those first months at Catchout, his calm nature in the midst of other demanding personalities pushed him to the periphery of our early focus. But as initial excitements wore off and we settled into the scene, our discussions with him gained depth.

Motown's disposition enabled him to recede into his own mind, and this was an asset on the street. "You gotta be a strong person out here. I seen the streets drive people crazy," he told us. One of his favorite methods for staving off that insanity was music, hence his nickname. Motown always had a radio with him, and it became our custom to bring him batteries for it. In more social moments, he would serve as DJ for the group, playing old soul music and most often singing along. More privately, he would sit in a chair, playing his radio in what could best be described as meditation.

All of this is not to suggest that Motown was perpetually zenlike. He was capable of rising to the situation. You have to be tough at Catchout. Once, when personal issues kept us out of the field for a comparatively long period, it was Motown who met us at the car on our next arrival, demanding we explain ourselves. But once we did, Motown settled back into his usual character, with manners and dignity that belong at a catered affair instead of Catchout Corner.

Carnell

Carnell was a cut-up like Lockett, but while Lockett had an underlying sweetness to his character, there was something dark and caustic lurking in Carnell. One sensed an inner torment, but it was hard to put your finger on it. Sometimes he would engage us in good-natured and often thoughtful conversation. Other times he would barely acknowledge us or anyone else. A psychologist would probably diagnose him with a mood disorder, but in these down moments, he did not outright ignore his environment, he just disengaged from it. We had heard stories about Carnell's extremely violent temper and some bizarre past behavior that accompanied it. Legend had it, for example, that Carnell used to carry around a sword. While that would suggest a diagnosable psychological problem, over four years we never saw anything significantly abnormal, particularly considering his abnormal circumstances. When we asked Carnell about these stories, he would just smile and deflect the questions. He may have been embarrassed, but also it seemed that he knew the value of a tough reputation on the street. In some ways he perpetuated a dominant veneer, for example warning about how violent the streets could be, but for the most part, he was perfectly content to let legends lie.

Carnell was thoroughly cynical about our project and homelessness generally, and we had a hard time convincing him that our research had any worth at all. "There isn't anything to know about out here. It ain't nothing special. I mean it can be wild, but I don't understand what you want to know about." Despite the lack of value our research had in his eyes, he often made significant contributions to it, routinely giving us a lot to think about. Leaving the Corner one day after a religious woman had shown up to preach to the group, we confessed to Carnell, "Man, that woman said some real bizarre stuff." He put us in check, "Different strokes for different folks. She tripped ya'll out, but ya'll trip me out. Know what I'm sayin'?"

Like Hammer, Carnell was intelligent, but he was more articulate and clever. We once observed him trying to convince another man that "black and white don't exist." While he did not have an academic vocabulary, as he talked, it was clear that his thoughts went beyond the I-don't-see-color cliché to a deeply philosophical, social constructionist view of race and ethnicity. "What color are you?" his debate partner challenged, "'cause I'm black." Carnell wouldn't budge, "There is no black; they made that shit up."

Big E

Big E was Carnell's cousin and was one of the more religious men at Catchout. Although a religious fatalism was widespread, Big E was particularly effusive about it. "What would it take to end homelessness?" we asked a group one time. "God's gonna have to come down and touch some hearts," Big E replied, rejecting other's suggestions about various public policy solutions. While we met him on our first visits to the Corner, by the time we officially ended our fieldwork, he had been one of the few to successfully utilize the shelter programs to get off the street.

While they were related, unlike Carnell, Big E showed a great deal of interest in our research. After several months he wanted to see the film and was concerned about how we might portray them. At the same time, he expressly appreciated our approach. For example, one of our standard interview questions was, "A lot of people think you guys are all just a bunch of no good bums. What do you think about that?" This may shock researchers who often treat participants with kid gloves, but in our estimation, there was no point in ignoring the obvious. Big E particularly seemed to appreciate that approach. After our first interview with him, he came over to us: "Hey, I liked the questions you asked me, man. You didn't beat around the bush about shit."

Potato Water and Matty

Though he would later move across town, we met Potato Water during one of our early visits to Catchout. His nickname was conferred because of his love of cheap vodka. Like everyone else there, he seemed initially drawn to participating in our research because we were paying five bucks an interview (as we later discuss, we were quickly encouraged by those on the Corner themselves to abandon that practice), but Potato Water stood out for all sorts of reasons. He was the only white man around, a barrier he told us it had taken him three years to fully overcome. He was tall and lanky, with scraggly hair on his head and the kind of facial hair that results from neglect rather than design. But we got the impression that this would not be far-off his look if he was not living on the street. He had a classic southern populist demeanor, a cracker-barrel, commonsense approach to life. Potato Water had gone to college for three years and was an avid reader who nearly always had a book with him. He was an admitted alcoholic, but managed negative judgments about it by noting that he worked hard. "I'm an alcoholic, but I'm a functioning alcoholic," he put it. And like most of the others, he had not stayed in a shelter in over four years, "To me, [the shelter is] like a prison-type scene, man."

It was on our first overnight stay on the streets that we met Matty. We walked into the camp to find him relaxing on a bed, eating microwave popcorn, and watching television.[40] If it had not been for the fact that his space had no walls and an interstate overpass for a roof, it could have been any house in middle America. He was a highly organized person, as we would continue to learn over the next several years. That night we marveled at his folded laundry, neatly organized in a dresser near his bed, but we would learn this was not idiosyncratic.

In the early days of the project, we never imagined that we were building stable, longitudinal relationships, but nearly two years later, we found ourselves walking along the train tracks just east of downtown looking into the dense brush for signs of habitation. After the police scattered everyone from Catchout Corner in the fall of 2005, Potato Water and Matty's camp had been overrun with people that, not for the first time, had nowhere else to go. When this caused their highly organized living space to fall into disarray, Potato Water and Matty forged a new camp, secured with secrecy and the fact that it rested on an island where a north-south train line met an east-west track. The vague directions we were given left us hiking up and down the tracks and calling their names out into the woods, hoping for a response. We ran into several of their neighbors, others living on the street nearby, but perhaps because they were suspicious of us or because they did not want to anger Potato Water and Matty by divulging the location of their camp, they just vaguely pointed us down the line, "Over that way, somewhere." And maybe this hunt seems like a telling of a chore, and an obstacle to our research, but scouring the unseen underbelly of the cityscape filled both of us with excitement and curiosity. It seemed to us that it was exactly what sociologists ought to be doing, getting their hands dirty and dodging the train yard bulls in the process.

Steve

Steve runs one of the most prominent shelters in the city. A tour of the crumbling building immediately validates the pleas of shelter directors for more funding. Steve reflected the standard view of homelessness as largely a function of addiction and mental illness, not so much in his rhetoric as the fact that his shelter was primarily focused on treating these. But Steve also possessed a reflexive capacity that made him sensitive to, if not critical of, such an approach. Held back from a revolutionary change partly by his board of directors, partly by funding, and partly by statistics that suggest that addiction and mental illness are in fact strongly correlated with homelessness (although causal inferences are questionable), Steve nonetheless was willing to consider criticisms of the service industry. Further, he demonstrated an understanding of social structural influences that often are overlooked in the individualized treatment paradigm of the shelter. During a citywide service provider meeting, other shelter directors responded very defensively to a critical remark. True to his character, Steve stood out among the group, "We've been doing some things for a long time, and there's a good reason for some of those, but I think we should all step back and think about ways we can improve the things we do." While most shelter directors would issue categorical statements about controversial propositions like wet shelters, which allow drinking alcohol, Steve's opinions, even when definitively oppositional, were always couched in sincere considerations such as, "Well, I have mixed feelings about that."

Another clear contrast to some of the other service industry workers was the geniune emotion that Steve would display. Many of his shelter director peers understandably had become desensitized through constant contact with homelessness or had been promoted to positions that facilitated detachment. Like everyone else, Steve was a professional who could rattle off research and detail policy issues, but he consistently grounded what he said in real examples. When he did, we sensed a personal pain revealed in reflective pauses where he struggled to explain the inhumanity he dealt with everyday.

Lawton

We had made the rounds of local homeless-service providers and gotten mostly the "standard company line" about homelessness and funding needs from them. With little variation, they were all "on-message." But in what was comparatively daring and conspiratorial, a couple of them suggested in hushed tones that we talk to Lawton, a local pastor and advocate for the homeless. Steve, for example, made a characteristic, self-reflexive admission, "He can say things I can't."

From what we had seen, faith-based services in our city tended to be the harshest and most judgmental of those who were homeless (see Chapter 10), so we were skeptical when we met Lawton at his church. When he arrived, the white-haired man in his sixties, wearing plain blue Dickies work pants and a plain white shirt, got out of his pickup truck and threw open the industrial garage door entrance on the front of the church. "This is the world's largest church door," he chuckled, "'cause everyone's welcome; we don't have any criteria."

Lawton has a calm and pleasant way about him, which did nothing to prepare us for the radical things he would say. Without relinquishing a bit of his ingrained kindness, he decried the local and federal government and the inhumane negligence of the upper and middle classes, unconscious of their privilege:

> The quality of life offenses [that the city is trying to pass] are a sign of our sickness. You see, a human being's appearance or possessions should not offend you. You should be able to know and relate to their character; there are many homeless people who have great character. So that is a sign of our sickness; so they want to try to use violence to force the homeless outside of [the city] boundaries.

Lawton is a deeply religious man, unwavering in his faith and with convictions about social injustice that in his estimation were warranted directly by biblical wisdom. But he also had what we call in the academy a robust "sociological imagination." Through his spiritual prism he noted connections between national and local politics.

> George Bush is very embarrassed today because of the United States' moral failure to care for prisoners of war [at Abu Ghraib]. And God is not happy about that. God is not happy about that. The Birmingham City Council and the mayor of the city of Birmingham, if they continue in the direction they are going, are

going to have photos and pictures and suffering and pain and abuse and violence that is going to embarrass Birmingham again [like it did during the civil rights movement] because we do not know God in this city. We don't know how to relate to the poor, we don't know how to care for the poor, we don't know how to build justice, we don't know how to establish transportation, we don't know how to build housing, we don't know how to care for communities, we don't know how to care for our children, and all [the city officials] are hyped up about is getting rid of some people who are suffering tremendously. And it is wrong. And I will continue to say it's wrong.

In a climate where homeless services revolved around the individual's admission of their personal pathologies, either real or those designed to appease the service provider, Lawton stayed resolutely focused on social structural issues. And while a macrolevel vision, particularly as sociology has it, usually means distancing oneself from the immediate suffering of individuals, Lawton's compassion and anger about systemic issues was unaltered as he worked tirelessly with the real individuals swept up in that system. Friedrich Schiller once wrote:

Cherish triumphant truth in the modest sanctuary of your heart; give it an incarnate form through beauty, that it may not only be in the understanding that does homage to it, but that feeling may lovingly grasp its appearance. And that you may not by any chance take from external reality the model which you yourself ought to furnish, do not venture into its dangerous society before you are assured in your own heart that you have a good escort furnished by ideal nature. Live with your age, but be not its creation; labor for your contemporaries, but do for them what they need, and not what they praise. Without having shared their faults, share their punishment with a noble resignation, and bend under the yoke which they find it as painful to dispense with as to bear.[41]

The radicalism of Lawton's politics matched equally by kindness of his demeanor is the quintessential expression of this difficult challenge that Schiller lays before us.

Chapter Descriptions

Our work is presented here in eleven chapters. In Chapter 2 we discuss the process of starting our research and gaining access to a highly distrustful population. We also describe our analytic methods and wrestle with some ethical questions concerning research in general and ethnographies like ours in particular.

Chapters 3 through 7 concern mainly those who are homeless. In Chapter 3 we attempt to define those who are homeless in general and those who are street homeless in particular. As the street homeless population is heterogeneous in all sorts of ways, explicating exactly who the street homeless are as a salient group is no small task. Our participants are all individuals held together in a group by particular circumstances. Moreover, whether someone is street homeless often depends on what point he or she is at in his or her life. Since our research lasted more than four years, the status of some of our contacts changed. Some of our participants started out on the street and then went through shelter programs. Some have stayed in housing; some have ended up back on the Corner. Others made it off the streets without services. But most have stayed on the streets the whole time.

Chapter 4 examines causes of homelessness as debated in the literature and then also based on our observations in the field. Primarily this discussion concerns the extent to which homelessness is the result of individual behaviors such as drinking and drug use or mental illness, or structural conditions such as increasing economic inequality.

In Chapter 5 we discuss the organization of street homeless communities. This includes how they maintain relationships with one another and with mainstream society.

Chapter 6 turns from organization and relationships toward attitudes and values. Here are examined the dispositions of those on the street toward homelessness itself, as well as toward politics, social issues, and religion.

Chapter 7 considers issues of identity on the street and the way that self is protected and asserted throughout the course of being "down and out." Those who are street homeless often have strikingly resilient personalities and creative spirits that allow them to manage a host of hardships that most of us will never face. This is not to say they all are romantic figures, but rather to note the existence of such characteristics that counter the pervasive opposite stereotype that they all are dysfunctional, dependent, and deplorable.

Chapters 8 through 10 examine various groups involved with the homeless in different ways. As homelessness is routinely described as a social problem, service programs are postured as solutions, either explicitly or by implication. Our study suggests that these solutions frequently contain their own problematic features that often work at cross-purposes even with their own goals of getting those who are homeless off the street. In Chapter 8 we examine the way that businesses and government work together to legislate against those who are homeless, particularly by managing city space and increasingly shrinking the public sphere, both physically and conceptually. The former includes legislation and policies that ban those who are homeless from public spaces. The latter concerns redefining questions of "who counts" as a citizen.

In Chapter 9 we examine social services that purportedly aim at getting those who are homeless off the streets. These can be seen as a kinder alternative in contrast to the harsh demeanor of business and government, but shelter programs make problematic assumptions and judgments that often ostracize a salient portion of the homeless population, those who stay on the street. We flesh out these features of the dominant model of service provision.

In Chapter 10 we examine religious approaches to homelessness. Church groups are very active in providing services at a variety of levels of organization, from running full-fledged shelters to providing meals out of the backs of their cars. Still, discussions of the ways that religious groups interact with those who are homeless are largely absent from the literature. We find that religious groups approach homelessness in a variety of ways, but that these generally parallel the heavy-handed authoritarianism of government or the paternalistic charity of social service programs.

In Chapter 11 we conclude by offering, not solutions on how to end homelessness, but rather insights about how to begin to think about it in new ways. Rather than working toward an oversimplified clarity on the subject, we choose to acknowledge its complexity and diversity and suggest that we can begin to approach homelessness as a concept and those individuals who are homeless only by finding our way to a new concept of individuality, new models of organization, and a new sense of the appropriate character of our social relationships. All of these are examined through the concept of friendship, something we all know, but which unfortunately rarely informs our conscious thinking about social relationships, particularly in matters of public policy.

Notes

1. Wagner notes in *Checkerboard Square* that the notion of a "work ethic" serves to maintain lower-class productivity while the wealthy are conspicuously focused on leisure.
2. Kyle, *Contextualizing Homelessness*.
3. See, for example, Arnold, *Homelessness, Citizenship and Identity*.

4. See Lee et al., "Revisiting the Contact Hypothesis," suggesting that increased contact diminishes stigmas of those who are homeless.

5. See Culhane, "The Quandaries of Shelter Reform," for a related discussion.

6. Kyle, *Contextualizing Homelessness*, p. 27.

7. See Arnold, *Homelessness, Citizenship and Identity*; Lyon-Callo, *Inequality, Poverty, and Neoliberal Governance*; and Mathieu, "The Medicalization of Homelessness and the Theater of Repression."

8. Wacquant, "Scrutinizing the Street"; see, for example, Anderson, *Code of the Street*; Duneier, *Sidewalk*; Newman, *No Shame in My Game*.

9. Wacquant, "Scrutinizing the Street," p. 1520.

10. Burt, *Over the Edge*, suggests the similarity is exaggerated at best, based on the various ways in which those who are homeless tend to be deviant and on homelessness itself as a non-normative experience.

11. Arnold, *Homelessness, Citizenship and Identity*; Hopper, *Reckoning with the Homeless*; Lyon-Callo, "Medicalizing Homelessness"; Lyon-Callo, *Inequality, Poverty, and Neoliberal Governance*.

12. Snow and Anderson, *Down on Their Luck*, p. 7.

13. More detailed historical treatments can be found in Arnold, *Homelessness, Citizenship and Identity*; Depastino, *Citizen Hobo*; Failer, *Who Qualifies for Rights*; Feldman, *Citizens Without Shelter*; Hopper, *Reckoning with the Homeless*; Kusmer, *Down and Out on the Road*; and Kyle, *Contextualizing Homelessness*.

14. Arnold, *Homelessness, Citizenship and Identity*; Axelson and Dail, "The Changing Character of Homelessness in the United States"; Kusmer, *Down and Out on the Road*.

15. Anderson, *The Hobo*; Axelson and Dail, "The Changing Character of Homelessness in the United States"; Depastino, *Citizen Hobo*.

16. Axelson and Dail, "The Changing Character of Homelessness in the United States"; Rossi, *Down and Out in America*; Snow and Anderson, *Down on Their Luck*.

17. Arnold, *Homelessness, Citizenship and Identity*; Axelson and Dail, "The Changing Character of Homelessness in the United States"; Snow and Anderson, *Down on Their Luck*.

18. Axelson and Dail, "The Changing Character of Homelessness in the United States"; Phelan et al., "The Stigma of Homelessness"; Rossi, *Down and Out in America*; Schweik, *The Ugly Laws*.

19. Axelson and Dail, "The Changing Character of Homelessness in the United States"; Rossi, *Down and Out in America*; Snow and Anderson, *Down on Their Luck*.

20. Arnold, *Homelessness, Citizenship and Identity;* Gibson, *Securing the Spectacular City*; Mathieu, "The Medicalization of Homelessness and the Theater of Repression"; Mossman, "Deinstitutionalization, Homelessness, and the Myth of Psychiatric Abandonment."

21. Axelson and Dail, "The Changing Character of Homelessness in the United States"; Nunez and Fox, "A Snapshot of Family Homelessness Across America"; Rossi, *Down and Out in America*; Shlay and Rossi point out, in "Social Science Research and Contemporary Studies of Homelessness," that there is still a preponderance of single males despite increasing rates among other groups.

22. Bickford, "Constructing Inequality"; Gibson, *Securing the Spectacular City*; Mathieu, "The Medicalization of Homelessness and the Theater of Repression"; Waldron, "Homelessness and Community."

23. See Schweik, *The Ugly Laws*; Kusmer notes in *Down and Out on the Road* that the workfare policies of Mayor Rudy Giuliani in New York City mirrored the work penalties attached to vagrancy convictions in the 1800s.

24. See, for example, Failer, *Who Qualifies for Rights?*; Feldman, *Citizens Without Shelter*; Hopper, *Reckoning with the Homeless*; Lyon-Callo, "Medicalizing Homelessness"; Lyon-Callo, *Inequality, Poverty, and Neoliberal Governance*; Mathieu, "The Medicalization of Homelessness and the Theater of Repression"; Snow et al., "The Myth of Pervasive Mental Illness Among the Homeless."

25. Hopper, *Reckoning with the Homeless*, p. 26.

26. See www.birminghamal.gov, retrieved May 11, 2009.

27. McKiven, Jr., *Iron and Steel*, p. 8.

28. LaMonte, *Politics and Welfare in Birmingham, 1900–1975*.

29. McKiven, Jr., *Iron and Steel*.

30. See Scribner, *Renewing Birmingham*.

31. See McWilliams, *New Lights in the Valley*.

32. Eskew, *But for Birmingham*.

33. Lesher, *George Wallace*.

34. Franklin, *Back to Birmingham*.

35. Fallin, Jr., *The African American Church in Birmingham, Alabama, 1815–1963*.

36. Ibid.; also Manis, *A Fire You Can't Put Out*.

37. Manis, *A Fire You Can't Put Out*.

38. Fallin, Jr., *The African American Church in Birmingham, Alabama, 1815–1963*.

39. Scribner, *Renewing Birmingham*.

40. The owner of the stone company that bordered their camp under the interstate had run an extension cord out to them, giving them electricity.

41. Schiller, *On the Aesthetic Education of Man*.

2

Accessing a
Hidden Population

Doing ethnographic research requires intimate contact with participants. For our study, this included those who were homeless as well as
other types of people involved in various ways with homelessness, such
as service providers, police officers, politicians, and community leaders.
Because ethnography is an intimate research approach, establishing relationships with participants is the key for success. The purpose of this
chapter is to detail how we gained access to our participants and developed relationships with them. We then describe briefly our method of
data collection and analysis. Finally, as ethical questions emerge from
the actual process of conducting research, in which access is gained and
maintained, we discuss moral quandaries that pervade ethnography in
general and our project in particular.

Accessing the Field:
Lessons in Eternally Getting Started

As noted, our early field excursions were wrought with anxieties and
uncertainties. We had already spoken with service providers and our
academic colleagues and decided we needed to get the story straight
from the source. But we had no idea how we would be received or how
much honest information we would get from a group that is deviant by
definition and both physically and socially clandestine. But access is
never an all-or-nothing poposition, and ours would expand and contract
continually.

Access as a Process

While we were immediately impressed with how forthcoming the participants were with us, and therefore felt like we were off to a good start,
additional facades would continue to erode over the next four years. We
fought early suspicions, for example, that we might be cops. This did
not keep people from sitting around and talking with us, but certainly as
we overcame that fear, people became less and less guarded. In very palpable ways, we refined misrepresentations and misconceptions every
time we went into the field. There were times when we felt like we were
settling in, to be sure. When the field becomes comfortable for ethnographers, they essentially are put to sleep. When immersed in routine,
awareness is dulled. But times we felt lulled by familiarity were short
lived, usually ending with abrupt moments of reawakening that made
the field new again: a gun, a fight, a scathing critique, an emotional con-
fession, or the unveiling of something that revolutionized the concepts
we had been building.

Atkinson and Silverman point out that "interaction is a joint accomplishment by the participants rather than the determined outcome of the
researcher's professional agenda."[1] The social order that emerges from a
research interaction can never be attributed to researcher "direction."
Rather, such order can be seen to be "built through the contingent, embodied, ongoing interpretive work" of both participants and researchers.[2]

Strong rapport with participants is all the more important for
research involving sensitive topics and marginalized populations. It
makes sense that among those on the street there existed a common cau-
tion about us as outsiders. The key to our successful research with them
was their willingness to "embark on a risky course of action."[3] Their
decision to let us in was based on trust and the rapport that preceded it.
Only when our participants felt validated and could perceive some
degree of similarity with us did relationships become stable enough to
bear the weight of deeper, more honest investigation.

Access is not a single moment in time but a dynamic process eter-
nally negotiated, and with every breath is fluidly expanding and con-
tracting. Insofar as we cannot, as researchers, fully experience homelessness, access is a process of getting closer or further away from those
who do.[4] Popular perception tends to view access as a one-time hurdle.
In other words, access is often confused with "entry" and used to represent some specific moment in time, where researchers break down barriers to a population and move from outside to inside the social space.[5] In
contrast, developing rapport and generating workable relationships with

those on the street was a dynamic, ongoing process. A researcher may feel very close to a subject and believe she or he is getting relatively honest interactions, and then may move closer to that subject, uncovering information that previously was convincingly concealed. Similarly, a researcher initially may be very close to a subject, and then later the subject may begin to erect barriers, increasing the distance between her- or himself and the researcher. Initial contact with a group is certainly important; first impressions always are. But while interactions do become more stable as identities of both researcher and subject become increasingly concrete over time, initial access is not necessarily stable and in no way guarantees later success.

Most of the time, our early observations were not later proved wrong, but rather refined into more complex and robust understandings. Examples are plentiful. We always arrived with armloads of donations of food, toiletries, clothes, tents, or whatever we could afford.[6] On our first outings we were struck by the way that the men at Catchout Corner shared the supplies we brought. But as the months wore on, we realized that while some people were genuine, others would profess to share while at the same time using sleight-of-hand tricks to hoard things. The sharing ethos was not false pretension, but it varied across different personalities and fluctuated in relation to environmental conditions. Motown and Big E never hoarded, but Jeff always did. Others were somewhere in the middle. When work was plentiful or the public feeling generous, hoarding behavior receded, but it swelled when work, food, and clothes became scarce.

Our assessments of individual members of the street community also exemplify the refinement of simplistic early observations. Earnest was in his sixties and the oldest member of the community at Catchout, having been on the streets for more than twenty years. Our initial impressions were that Earnest was a patriarch of sorts, a respected elder who wielded influence in the community. As time went by, we realized that while the others respected Earnest as their elder, they did so in a more patronizing, appeasing sort of way, but did not listen to his advice or take seriously his opinions.

In this way our initial interpretations of life on the streets were continuously refined into more complex and accurate understandings. We had to be malleable. This often meant being conscious of staying in the moment, suspending judgments acquired through the imprints of our upbringings and disciplinary training. Our strategy for staying in the moment was to become part of the group to whatever extent possible, and this yielded a variety of strategies that we came to practice regularly.

We always took field notes after our stays on the street, never during. On days when we decided to bring out a camera, only Wasserman wandered and filmed, while Clair stayed as one of the group. Our movement back and forth between being associated with our hosts and our discipline were somewhat minimized in this way. To whatever extent possible, we did our recording and analyzing backstage. We did nothing front stage we would not do in our everyday lives.

We were not naive enough to think that at any point we had finally "gotten it"; if we had ever believed such a sweeping and definitive epistemic premise, we would have been forever frustrated, since we were constantly confronted with new knowledge. Ravindra Svarupa Dasa once said in a lecture:

> I saw a headline in one of these science magazines … and it was about some new discovery, and it said, "We used to think … but now we know." But I was startled because I remember when they used to "think," they said they "knew." Why are they saying, "Now we know"? Because now what you know, in the future is going to be what you used to think. Maybe they should say, "We used to *know*, but now we *think*." [It's] a little more honest.[7]

While we do not subscribe to a nihilistic relativism, we believe that the nature of knowing others is a process of continual unfolding, where we can refine and improve what we think but never reach an endpoint with our knowledge. Every time we entered the field, we started over. Things we learned previously became preconceptions that later were refined into new and different understandings.

Power as Shared and Dynamic

Common interpretations of the interactive dynamic between researcher and subject (those of institutional review boards, for example) conceptualize power as solely belonging to the researcher.[8] After all, in most instances, the researcher is more educated than the population that he or she investigates. But this is an insufficient and elitist view of knowledge. While researchers may possess one kind of knowledge, they certainly lack some sort of substantive understanding about the research area, or they would have no reason to conduct research in the first place. Moreover, power does not come solely from knowledge, at least in the field. Field researchers are keenly aware that participants have a great deal of power over issues of access.[9] Research participants can restrict access or deny it all together and often set the terms and conditions by which the research can proceed. For example, we had been warmly received and spoken with openly by the group at Catchout. But in order to get more formal interviews on camera, on our fifth outing or so we discussed our earlier idea of paying five dollars apiece for them. The group roundly shot down this idea. They pointed out it would not be good protocol because we would be giving a benefit only to those willing to be on camera while nonetheless accessing space that belonged to everyone. They suggested instead that we bring food and other donations and allow people to partake of them freely, thereby treating everyone on the Corner equally regardless of the extent to which they wanted to participate in the research. It was a good suggestion and became our practice over the next four years.

Access to the general field aside, individual subjects control the degree to which they are open and honest with a researcher throughout the research experience. Frustrations of fieldworkers often are the result of their own powerlessness in the researcher-subject interaction. After many months of fieldwork at Catchout Corner, we were pleased with the level of acceptance we had achieved. We were always welcomed warmly when we showed up to the Corner. But our visits had always been on Sunday afternoons, and when we entered the field on a Thursday, and on the first day of the month (the day on which government checks are issued), we met a very different atmosphere. Unknown to us, a small but powerful group of drug dealers conducted business at Catchout during the week. Because they worked in a nearby park on the weekends, we had never encountered them before. There was an immediate and palpable tension. Some of the men at the Corner, who were fond of us, were also customers of these dealers. The dealers adamantly, although not openly, wanted us to leave, since they felt our presence jeopardized their business. A series of "side" conversations resulted in Lockett's suggestion that we leave. As consolation, Potato Water and Jeff invited us to their camp to spend the night, and we took them up on their offer.

On that day we were presented quite explicitly with an access issue. After we left, we immediately began to think through the situation and how to handle it. We left because we did not want to create conflict, which could have been damaging to our research and also dangerous. However, the drug dealers were not our population of interest, and we felt no ethical obligation to respect their boundaries. If asking us to leave had come from the men who were homeless themselves, the situation would have been radically different, but they were exceedingly apologetic and felt terrible about the whole thing. Even though the men who actually lived on the street had not wanted us to leave, we worried about our credibility in their eyes, given that we had lost this power struggle with the dealers.

We decided that we needed to assert ourselves in order to protect our reputation, something that is highly important on the street. So later that night we walked back to the Corner and went over and talked to the group, including the drug dealers who had made us leave a few hours earlier. This was a gamble, and there was immediate tension. We mitigated that tension by telling everyone that we were walking to the store for some food and just wanted to say hello. That way, it was clear to them that we were not going to stay and were not interested in conflict, but that the dealers had not gotten rid of us and that we were not afraid.

The next day we went back to the Corner and sat down with the group. Again, there was uncomfortable tension, but this time no one asked us to leave. Instead, it was the dealers who walked off the lot and spent the day under the adjacent viaduct. The men who lived at Catchout were torn as to whom to sit with, but they split their time between the dealers and us. This was awkward, but it made it clear to us that we had become more welcomed and respected than just a day earlier. Our gambit had worked. Some, more brazen men like Hammer, who had not been there the day before, immediately apologized for the previous day's incident. In this one twenty-four-hour period our access contracted and expanded based on our self-presentation.

Had we fully acquiesced, we likely would have lost a great deal of respect and easily could have compromised our project altogether. Consciously and rationally approaching this access crisis, however, allowed us to turn it into something positive. For many weeks the incident was a hot topic of discussion both in our absence and presence. We gained integrity by not being intimidated; people told us that. We gained trust by showing a level of commitment that they did not expect us to have. These gains culminated several months later, when the main drug dealer walked up to the group during one of our visits and said, "I'm not shaking anyone's hand but Professor's." It was a clear sign of respect and acceptance.

In this situation, among others, power was not entirely in our hands. In very real physical terms, it was not ours at all. But our presentation allowed us to gain acceptance among those who held the power, the men on the street and the drug dealers. There was not a finite moment when this occurred; it was predicated by months of research, compromised the day we were asked to leave, and rebuilt that night, the next day, and for many months after.

Negotiable Identities as Keys to Access

The issue of access can be understood as a function of identity, both identities that are often intentionally portrayed by the researchers and those ascribed to them by participants, whether the researchers want them or not. For our project the salience of our identities varied from group to group. Often Clair's credentials as a professor were beneficial. Among those on the street, there was an air of pride about being in the company of a college professor, of being his informant, his teacher. Wasserman's role at the time as a graduate student and as younger than most of the participants sometimes gave him "little brother" status. Similarly, among service providers, Clair's professional credentials garnered respect and legitimacy, whereas because of Wasserman's status as a student, providers and other professionals seemed to have a sense of "helping out," the way one would feel obligated to help a child with their homework.

While our professor and student statuses were beneficial, our affiliation with the local university ironically had to be downplayed. The university hospital is the place where those on the street deemed "mentally ill" are forcibly taken when the police determine that they are a danger to themselves or others, and so there was some trepidation and avoidance when we first showed up at Catchout Corner.[10] The university was in this sense seen as part of the establishment that helped generate inequities. What we thought would be an identity advantage was in reality something to be overcome among those on the street.[11] But this was certainly not the case among the various service providers and city officials with whom we spoke.[12] As one might imagine, university credentials were exceedingly helpful, in these situations. In fact, in addition to our own, we nearly always initiated contact through other professors, thereby adding credentials to our identity by affiliation. Among a third group, our university credentials were entirely irrelevant. Members of Food Not Bombs—the anarchic organization dedicated to promoting peace and community through a variety of actions, including feeding people in public spaces (see Chapter 11)—were uninterested one way or another in our institutional affiliation. Relevant characteristics for them predominantly rested on Wasserman's history of involvement in the local underground music scene, a symbol of acceptable motivations and integrity uncompromised by institutional constraints. These three populations illustrate the fluid nature of identity. While our university affiliation is just one characteristic out of many at play, the population largely determined the salience of different pieces of our identities: positive, negative, or irrelevant.

Another way in which identity was key to access concerned sharing deviance. Conscious of the judgmental way in which they are generally regarded, stories of our own deviance went far in connecting us to those on the street. In terms of sharing deviance, one particular life event played a monumental role in maintaining relationships with our participants and building credibility. In 2005, as Clair was returning home, his son called him and said that a large pickup truck with floodlights was doing "doughnuts" on the grass near where their home is located, causing a lot of damage. As Clair got close to the home, he saw a truck matching the description coming the other way. He flashed his lights and called 911 as he approached the now-stopped truck. To his surprise, the driver of the truck rammed Clair's van, pushing it out of the way, and began to flee. Clair followed the truck, talking to 911 operators and continuously updating them on the truck's location. When the police finally responded, they arrested Clair for misdemeanor reckless endangerment![13]

The entire episode was a horrible experience—frustrating, emotionally draining, and completely unbelievable. Ironically, however, in terms of our research, it was wholly positive. The somewhat consuming nature of the entire process following Clair's legal battle gave a legitimate reason for some absences from one spot or another, since by that time we had more contacts than we could keep up with. Someone would say, "Hey, haven't seen you guys in a while. Thought you left us for dead." "Yeah, man, I've been dealing with that legal stuff," Clair would explain. All would be well, "Yeah, they're fucked up, ain't they." We were not lying; it did pull us away from our research. Rather than being a devastating blow to our relationships with participants, however, it allowed us to maintain relationships with them when we were not able to dedicate large amounts of time to any one group.

More important, those proceedings formed the basis of countless discussions and bonds of shared deviance. While they were usually quick to point out that Clair's encounter was minor compared with the kind they were used to, it nonetheless provided a way to connect to the participants. "Now you see what it's like," someone would say. Clair's stories about going through the court system to fight for his innocence allowed him to connect in a very real and in-depth way with our participants, the majority of whom had their own firsthand experiences with the criminal justice system. Our participants who lived on the street were shocked and, in a way, comforted by Clair's fate, as if it meant that the cops and courts can victimize anyone, not just poor black people.

The story spread on the streets like wildfire.[14] We would tell a couple people in one area and the next day, all the way across town, someone else would run up to Clair, saying, "Professor! I heard they got you!" They joked with Clair about it, but they, more than anyone else in his life, understood that it was no joke. On occasion someone would put it rather bluntly: "That ain't right. They don't mess around at that jail down there. But now you'll see what we go through."[15]

Sharing other idiosyncrasies and embarrassing moments also personalized and humanized us in the eyes of our participants. This was particularly true for those on the street. Wasserman's vegetarian diet was the subject of much amazement and good-natured teasing. Clair's stories about the tribulations of raising teenage boys were always a source of laughter, as well as his in-depth knowledge of gangster rap, with which our mostly African American population was continually impressed. As a single man at the start of the project, our participants who were homeless kept up with Wasserman's dating life and later his engagement and marriage. Clair was teased about his long, skinny Capri 120 cigarettes, even to the point where no one would bum one. Small talk about sports and sex comprised large portions of our discourse on the street. All of this small talk served a very important purpose in that it formed real interpersonal connections with our participants. They came to know our identities and biographies, just as we came to know theirs. One might easily say that our participants on the street engaged in ethnographic exploration of us as much as we did them.

The value of small talk seems lost on many service providers and researchers. At a meeting of homeless-service providers who were discussing starting a "no-strings-attached" café for those who were homeless, this became patently obvious. The proposed café was a response to a survey where 20 percent of respondents had listed food as one of their needs. The goal was a place that would be welcoming and friendly, a place were one did not have to enroll in a program or talk to a case manager in exchange for food. Most of the service providers in attendance simply could not work their way out of their roles of managing people with social problems. Their immediate reaction was to figure out how to get social workers in a position to "just talk" to those who came to eat at this hypothetical café and how to "make available" social program information. This suggestion betrays the way that the individual humanity of service providers can be eclipsed by their institutionally dictated roles. In other words, they remained nearly exclusively service providers in their relationships with those who were homeless and rarely acted simply as people in relationships with other people.[16] However, when dealing with any group of people, whether researching or "serving" them, one cannot always "be on." People want and need to be treated like people, not like cases. *Cases* are just objectified problems; *people* talk mostly about money, sports, sex, celebrities, and other people.

Brooke Harrington suggests, "Those labeled as unfamiliar, different, or unsympathetic to the group's identity are likely to be treated with suspicion and hostility."[17] Certainly this is often the case. For example, our race and class was a hurdle to overcome with the men at Catchout. As one man said: "You guys are great. We love having you around. If you weren't white, it'd be perfect." Our dress, our vehicles, and our education were initially obstacles because they were differences.

However, after a certain level of trust had been gained, differences became a positive thing. For example, we had been granted a relatively high degree of access to the behaviors and thoughts of the men at Catchout. We began to get the impression that there was nothing they would say to one another that they would also not say to us. But the opposite was not true. In other words, the men became willing to say things to us that they would not say to the others.[18] On the street, a tough image is very important.[19] Weaknesses in this image might be exploited or at least generate added conflict with the others. But this type of self-presentation did not always characterize private conversations we had. Away from the group, the men confessed feelings about things that would have been taken as weakness by the group. Our counsel was sometimes sought in private matters, and our opinions on some topics carried more weight than those of the other men (although our opinions on certain other topics carried much less weight). Clearly our identity as educated outsiders was sometimes a hindrance, particularly at early stages in the access process, but at other times it allowed us access to a fuller vision of many of these men, leading us beyond the presentation they gave within the general group dynamic.

An ethnographer cannot simply select an identity; the group must validate it. While we attempted an authentic presentation of self in a number of ways—past deviance, interests in music, self-awareness of our privilege, antiauthoritarian—these were not automatically accepted as authentic in the eyes of the group. Various instances seemed to signal these things for our participants. This mostly took place through the accumulation of minor events that illustrated our authenticity in these matters. For example, a song might come on the radio, which we would know, illustrating that we indeed knew about the things we claimed to know about. As our level of comfort and acceptance increased, voicing different opinions became a sign of authenticity. For example, a man nicknamed "Jesus" once posited that God had a plan for everyone and that the solution to homelessness could come only from God's will. Having attained a level of acceptance that allowed for it, Wasserman disagreed with him and asserted that often there were socially construct-ed barriers to individual autonomy. A pleasant discussion ensued, ending with Jesus retaining his position, but remarking that Wasserman had, "given him a lot to think about." Sometimes the researcher indeed should refrain from offering opinions, especially those contradicting the views of those he or she is researching. But in other cases acquiescence can interfere with authenticity. We adopted a strategy of polite honesty and appeared to be seen as authentic as a result.

While retaining authenticity required exposing our own opinions even when the participant might disagree, being too forceful in this could result in quick rejection. This was clearly evidenced when we attempted to bring another researcher into the field. Feeling that we had established a good deal of trust, we decided that in order to increase our time in the field, it would be beneficial to have another member on the research team. We selected a graduate student who had expressed an interest in the population and in doing ethnography. Of added benefit was that he was a young, African American male. However, during his first visit with the group, he began challenging the men and forcibly asserting his opinions about their lives.

One man named L. A., for example, talked about how he was asked by the Coalition of the Homeless to speak to the city council concern-ing some proposed vagrancy legislation. He had decided not to go because he was going to be given only three minutes, and, as he put it, "Three minutes isn't enough time for me to tell those son-of-a-bitches what I think about 'em." Our new researcher immediately asserted in a forcible tone, "You still have to *try*." L. A.'s reaction was very hostile: "I don't have to do nothin' but get my kids into school this week!" he screamed. He was clearly offended by this stranger's imposition of what was right for him. The researcher we had invited clearly had come with an *activist* rather than *interested* attitude toward the men, and they vehemently resented his leap to the former without being grounded in the latter. Had the same statement come from us, it might not have been received with such hostility, given the identity groundwork that preced-ed it. As a result, this was the one and only outing for our would-be team member.

* * *

In the end, the biggest aid to access is the ability to reflexively consider situations in which one finds oneself. Thinking through various situations and interactions allows the researcher to make the appropriate adjustments and to approach different participants in different ways. All of us play different roles in different social settings, and this is no less true for the social interactions of the ethnographic process. We could not have approached our participants on the street in the same way that we approached service providers or city council members. This is not to say that we were disingenuous with any group or dishonest in our self-presentations. Still, language, conversation topics, reliance on credentials, and the like were all employed in different ways and at different times on an interactional basis.

Data, Sample, and Method

Sampling is always important when evaluating presented work. Our strategy consisted of a mixture of techniques. By virtue of its predetermined hypotheses, quantitative research employs highly structured sampling techniques. Our research is antecedent to the derivation of testable hypotheses. Therefore, our sampling techniques necessarily were structured by different criteria. Testing theory calls ideally for random sampling techniques; generating theory calls for theoretical sampling.[20] This means that as concepts and theoretical propositions emerged from our research, we intentionally sought out participants who could elaborate those ideas. We also used the snowball sampling technique first introduced by James S. Coleman.[21] The basic idea behind this sampling technique is that potential respondents are selected from some sort of existing network. In our case, our first contact was with local homelessness researchers who helped the city do periodic counts. Serving as our seed participants, they then recommended others who would probably be willing to participate in the study. These early referrals put us in touch with shelter service-providers, who in turn recommended other people in the community engaged in the issue of homelessness. This basically was a process whereby existing sample members helped recruit future sample members. Eventually, we began to run into the same set of answers both about substantive issues and regarding possible participants.[22]

Similarly, the narrow parameters of quantitative research call for a particular composition for research samples. For our research, the issue of "who counts" was virtually nonexistent. Rather, anyone could be incorporated into our sample because our data analysis procedures sorted information conceptually rather than by demographics. Though a subsequent comparative analysis might show group differences in views of homelessness, with the grounded theory method, such information emerges from the coding process rather than a priori structuring of the sample. General categories for organizing participants in the sample can be useful for determining who said what, but are applied post facto. Our final analysis found several general groups to be relevant, though not definitive. For example, most of those on the street have previously attempted to use services, and most will do so again; distinctions between those who are street homeless and those who are consistent service users are fluid, with individuals moving in and out of either loosely defined group. But those whom we characterize as street homeless have qualitatively different dispositions than those using the shelters, even if their attitudes sometimes vacillate.

In order to obtain the broadest range of information and perspectives on the topic, we also employed what is called a maximum variation sampling technique.[23] This meant asking respondents to recommend people they specifically believed had different perspectives. While most of the service providers put us in touch with like-minded people, we did eventually get referred to some respondents with wider ranging, more diverse viewpoints. Ultimately, however, our interest in the views of the powerful as well as the disfranchised had us seeking any interview we could get.

Our sample of those on the street can be described as both stable and ever changing. There were the regulars who had occupied the streets for years as well as those who cycled in and out of homelessness. The respondent-driven sampling technique proved most effective in generating a sampling frame allowing us to produce findings that we feel are as unbiased as possible with qualitative work. As a testament to the grounded process, at various points in the book, we refer to moments when our initial perspectives were confronted and revised based on emerging information.

While the organic nature of ethnographic fieldwork resists the delineation of sample size, we feel that some estimation can be useful, as long as it is understood as contextualized by the qualitative nature of our research. Qualitative research, particularly of the unstructured variety, yields qualitatively different data, even from respondents in the same study. For example, while reading a magazine in a local coffee shop, Wasserman watched an older man with a tattered backpack and a blanket thrown over his shoulder come in and fill out a job application.

His hands shook from tremors as he filled it out, and it was clear that he had not bathed in some time; his white hair ran wild. It was a striking and painful moment to watch this man hope and try, knowing all the while that he had not a prayer of getting the job. They never spoke, and Wasserman never saw him again, but the man certainly participated in our research. We take being a participant to mean making a contribution to our understanding. Other traditional definitions make, in our opinion, little sense for ethnography. Wonderful insights sometimes were generated by a passing moment with a stranger, while at other times formal interviews or even recurrent contact yielded relatively little. Thus, our numbers should illustrate the breadth of study but do not speak directly to the quality of our data. The latter is better judged by our findings.[24]

Based on a review of our field notes, we can identify thirty "focal points" for our research.[25] Of these, eight were gathering spots for those on the street; eleven were homeless services of some kind, including shelters, soup kitchens, drug treatment, and psychiatric outreach; four were focal points of authority, including a police precinct, the City Action Partnership (CAP) office (a separate security force in the downtown area), the city council, and the police on the street; three were regular "street meals"; two were neighborhood associations; and two were community forums where homelessness was discussed.

A review of our field notes yields a street homeless sample of seventy with whom we had direct, sustained contact. Of those, we had in-depth or recurring contact with thirty-four. That is, there were thirty-four people living on the street with whom we conducted in-depth interviews or spent multiple sessions in the field. Of the thirty-four with whom we had recurring contact, we estimate that we had a dozen or more contacts with eighteen of them. With many, we spent several consecutive days and nights in their camps.

Of those homeless who were sheltered, we had direct contact with forty-six, conducting sixteen direct, in-depth interviews. This does not include the numbers we observed eating at soup kitchens, particularly during our stays on the street when we joined them. We estimate that number to be in the hundreds. Additionally, at street meals, we observed hundreds of people, and while we did not necessarily have direct or sustained contact with them, we nonetheless watched and listened to them. None of these are included in our estimates, given above, of those on the street or in shelters, because it was impossible for us to decipher where they lived or whether they were homeless at all.

We counted direct contact with fifty-five service providers, conducting direct interviews or having in-depth recurrent contact with twenty-two of them. This includes program directors and staff as well as volunteers. It also includes members of Food Not Bombs, who hosted street "picnics" (see Chapter 11). Later we will discuss the ways in which they, and others with a radical approach, do not fit ideologically with typical service providers, but this is not problematic for our enumeration purposes here.

We estimated contact with at least eight people we categorize as "authorities." This includes police officers, CAP officers and their director, and a city council member.

Finally, we had in-depth and recurrent contact with ten other people who do not fit the above categories but who had meaningful interactions with those on the street and therefore generated relevant data. These include a photographer who conducted a project on those who were homeless; two graffiti artists who have spent a great deal of time in train yards and have befriended many of the homeless living there; three local homelessness researchers; two members of neighborhood associations who, in that capacity, were active in debates about homeless issues; and one nonhomeless drug dealer who conducted his business at or near homeless gathering spots.

Our data was collected by a variety of means. Field notes were recorded after each interview and field experience, even if encounters were filmed. Interviews and usable portions of film were transcribed and coded, as were collected media and selected literature. Because our methodology works through a coding process, similar to that of traditional grounded theory, we need make no distinction in our findings between our field notes and interview transcripts. Since emergent themes develop from the coding process, these two types of data can be seamlessly integrated in our analytic schema.

The coding process of grounded theory proceeds in a hierarchical fashion beginning with narrative data, which for our project mainly consisted of interview transcripts and field notes. These data are coded line by line to crystallize key concepts that otherwise remain diffuse in extensive text.[26] Codes are then used to illuminate conceptual categories and, ultimately, themes.[27] We should note that the coding process ought not be mistaken for a simple grouping process. Instead, the technique of constant comparison, in which codes and categories emerging from some parts of the data are compared with other data, creates a dialogical dynamic between codes, categories, and themes, where concepts are continually refined throughout the analytic process.[28]

Ethics and Ethnography: Some Personal Reflections

Ethnographers often are in a precarious position.[29] They do not enjoy a security of distance from their subject or structured protocol.[30] They must throw themselves into quite a bit of chaos to practice their craft. Moreover, they seek the secrets of culture, often among disadvantaged groups. The Western imperialism of ethnography's beginnings largely has been eclipsed by the socially conscious researcher, but ethical questions remain endemic to ethnography by virtue of inescapable status differences between researcher and subject.[31] Such dynamics always carry exploitative potential, even where researchers intend to help.[32] In our research as well, we encountered a variety of ethical questions, some endemic to research itself and some characteristic of researching those who are homeless. We consider these in this chapter because they frame how we approach research in general (a question of our methodological mindset) and how we approach our particular research situation (a pragmatic question of negotiating between the field and the academy). What follows in this section are our reflexive struggles with relevant ethical questions. As such, we mostly identify moral questions with which we wrestled, rather than providing many cogent answers to them.

Many methodological problems double as ethical ones. First, if a researcher's epistemology precludes the consideration of findings as absolute truth, then they must be careful not to represent them as such. This would be tantamount to fabricating research. Since we do not hold a nihilistic view of knowledge, we do not believe this is the case, but still we recognize that the lens through which we make our observations may be different from that of others. This is an important qualification. Second, the researcher's presence can problematically alter what happens. If effect of presence on the field is significant, then reports from the field might be invalid. But the absence of a viable, ethical counterplan creates a dilemma. That is, the only alternatives are not to do research or to do it in secret, and neither is very appealing.[33] We reject the first from utilitarian considerations that, on the whole, research does more good than harm, and the second threatens the rights of those studied. Instead, we mitigate the effect of presence in various ways, such as having long sustained contact with participants, being extremely open and honest, and in other ways described above. In the end, this may not fully address the problems endemic to the presence of the researcher. But while troublesome, it seems to be as good as it gets.

Ultimately, however, throughout our research we were always outsiders with the intention of describing a subject mostly to other relative-

ly high-status outsiders.[34] This raises questions about the ultimate potential effect of our work. We would like to think that our research will produce benefits for our oppressed participants. Above all, our goal has
always been to improve their lives.[35] But by disseminating our findings
about those on the street to other outsider-elites, we could be exposing
them to the danger of more oppression. If we describe the migratory
habits and community-forming practices of those on the street, the
powers-that-be could use this to thwart the establishment of homeless
encampments. Local authorities do "homeless sweeps," seemingly randomly. Will this book aid in their efforts? Will it assist them in further
debasing the community-building patterns on which those who are street
homeless rely for physical and sociopsychological resources (i.e., the
sharing of food and clothes, referrals for temporary work, and so on)?
Here again, we cannot allay our own fears. We hope and believe our
work will benefit our participants (both those who are homeless and
nonhomeless), but we cannot be certain that our well-intended efforts
will not supply tools for further oppression. Again, we call attention to
this for its own sake, not because we can offer any solution. We cannot
predict the future, but we worry about it.

Our participants shared our concern about potential negative consequences from our research. With good reason they wanted to know
about our analytic framework and clearly believed that what we reported
could potentially pose long-term risks for them (as we discuss in more
detail below). Barrie Thorne has pointed out that assumptions that reaf-
firm a "blaming the victim" or a "deficiency" approach to oppressed
segments of society can affect public policy and tend to reinforce existing inequalities.[36] Many of those on the street, although they would state
it differently, intuitively knew of the potential consequences of letting
the wrong outsiders in.

Questions about interacting with particular kinds of populations raise
other critical issues.[37] Much research is aimed at oppressed populations.
However, as described above, researchers mostly are outsiders and often
belong to elite groups and organizations. They are professors at universi-
ties, often with decidedly comfortable lives. Access to oppressed populations, who often are highly distrustful, must be carefully negotiated and
usually remains precarious.[38] The ethical question here concerns the
extent to which access is negotiated versus coerced. Coercion is not
always intended, but in many cases the by-product of circumstance. In
our research, we brought food, toiletries, and various supplies into the
field. We did not make partaking in these supplies explicitly conditional
on participation in our research, but the implication certainly was that

these were to be exchanged for participation. On occasion, people took things and left without speaking to us. Others hung around and did not participate in conversation. Clearly they were not compelled. However, people most often stayed and talked. Since we were giving to people in great need, the question lingers about whether we unintentionally coerced, if not all, at least some of them. We continue to struggle with this question; our only reply has been our attempt to minimize the interpretation of our donations as exchange by trying to make it clear that we give with no strings attached.[39]

From another perspective, just being allowed to be present at the field site diminishes coercive concerns. As noted, in some very clear ways, those on the street held the power over us. We needed assistance in learning their language, and we wanted to be "allowed" to observe their activities. We needed guidance for navigating the streets. In part, bringing water, food, socks, and blankets allowed us to compensate, for their time, those who were homeless, but also allowed us access to the field whereby we could begin to build relationships. Murray Wax points out, "Over time modalities are developed so that assistance and information are exchanged for the goods and services that the ethnographers are able to distribute."[40] It got to a point that it seemed many enjoyed our visits, since it allowed them to talk about things, although any material help we had to offer was always appreciated.

There are a variety of ambiguities in our legal and ethical responsibilities related to the distinction and intersection of our roles as researchers, citizens, and fellow human beings. For example, it is clear that some of our participants were drug users. We knew who they were, who the dealers were, and could tell when they would buy and use drugs. They would disappear around a corner and come back sometimes incommunicably high on crack. Fifteen to twenty minutes later, their high would dissipate and they would reengage the conversation. Putting our role as researcher first, this would not be troublesome. It is just another observation. As fellow human beings, especially with the ultimate goal of helping, it is more troubling. We sometimes found ourselves encouraging them to be self-reflexive about their substance use and its underlying cause, but there is a fine line between concern and proselytizing, one that is all the more clear for "outsiders." As time wore on, we developed the type of relationships with some of them so that such conversations were seen as caring, rather than preaching, but our relationships with most made this a tenuous situation for us. Finally, as citizens, one might argue that we had an obligation to instantly call the police, since these activities were clearly illegal. This also would have ended our research, not to mention that, in our opinion, introducing the criminal justice system into the scene would have only made things worse for everyone.

Similarly, we occasionally gave money to those who asked. While not part of our official research protocol, at times one or another person would pull us aside and ask for a few dollars. We considered these moments to be effectively excused from our research protocol, as though we had instantaneously been transformed from researcher into some other, informal role. Giving money in these instances was in our view a matter of personal choice, not research protocol. Still, these instances raise ethical questions about knowledge and intention with which many people confronted by panhandlers struggle. For example, Wasserman once gave a participant two dollars so that he could pay for the bus to take him to a job in the morning. It was also clear that this person used drugs, and it was certainly possible that he spent the money Wasserman gave him on drugs. To what extent was Wasserman culpable? We remain concerned about such matters and, like most, unclear about the extent to which people are responsible for unintended but to some extent foreseeable consequences.[41]

Treating participants appropriately requires reflection; assumptions must be thought through. Early in the project, we went looking for one of our contacts who lived under a bridge, but no one was in the camp when we arrived. "You want to film this camp?" Clair asked. As soon as the question was posed, it hit us both. Why had we thought even for a moment that this would be okay? Of course, we were caught up in assumptions about what constituted public and private property. But those on the street redefine public spaces as their own. Although this is contested by most of the rest of society, we had to understand and respect it. Filming this public-made-private space would have been the equivalent of walking into someone's house unannounced and filming their home and possessions. People do not recognize this because social space is so neatly and officially categorized. At Catchout Corner, cars would slow down as people took pictures of the men gathered there, like animals in a zoo. The men are deeply offended by this but powerless to stop it. We had to make sure that our research did not objectify and intrude like those drive-by photographers.

These types of issues can be deeply personal. Ethical questions about doing ethnographic research are, to the researcher, ultimately questions about living a good life. Moral quandaries are not left in the field. The centrality of the ethnographer makes ethnographic research itself a moral experience.[42] While ethics has been wrangled by philosophy into an intellectual enterprise, one often devoid of feeling, for those in the crosshairs of ethical questions the emotional weight is quite real. Like most ethnographers, we are do-gooders walking an impossibly thin line between exposition and exploitation.

What ultimately needs to be conveyed is that some questions have no answers.[43] Are we just elitists meddling in the lives of oppressed people for our own self-interest? As homelessness researchers, do we by definition have a vested interest in the existence of homelessness? Have we enabled addictive behavior by donating money or even food? Should we try to uphold the letter of the law or our research when we cannot do both? These are not questions that can be thought through with only intellect but must be wrestled with at a deeper, more human level. For us, ethics is done in the field, and the only useful discussion of it consists of describing the struggle over these questions, not their answers. We struggle with these questions, we dream about them, we argue over them, and in the end we do the best we can. We look here to Clifford Geertz, who writes:

> The professional ethic rests on the personal and draws its strength from it; we force ourselves to see out of a conviction that blindness— or illusion—cripples virtue as it cripples people. Detachment comes not from a failure to care, but from a kind of caring resilient enough to withstand an enormous tension between moral reaction and scientific observation, a tension which only grows as moral perception deepens and scientific understanding advances. The flight into scientism, or, on the other side, into subjectivism, is but a sign that the tension cannot any longer be borne, that nerve has failed and a choice has been made to suppress either one's humanity or one's rationality. These are the pathologies of science, not its norm.[44]

Notes

1. Atkinson and Silverman, "Kundera's 'Immortality,'" p. 311.
2. Holstein and Gubrium, *The Active Interview*, p. 264.
3. Tewksbury and Gagne, "Assumed and Presumed Identities," p. 128.
4. We say that we cannot "fully experience" homelessness, because even when we stayed on the street, the circumstances that led us there and our options about staying were drastically different from those of our participants.
5. Harrington, "The Social Psychology of Access in Ethnographic Research," p. 599.
6. A small faculty development grant helped fund other areas of the project, but the things we brought as donations to our participants were paid for personally or donated by friends, family, and colleagues.

7. Ravindra Svarupa Dasa, with Shelter, audio recording, track 12, *Attaining the Supreme*, Equal Vision Records, 1993.

8. Harrington, "The Social Psychology of Access in Ethnographic Research."

9. Ibid.

10. See Szasz, *Cruel Compassion*, for a critique of forced commitment; see also Rowe, *Crossing the Border*, for a study of shelter outreach workers.

11. Horowitz, "Remaining an Outsider."

12. See Adler et al., "The Politics of Participation in Field Research."

13. If this surprises the reader, particularly since the 911 operators never told him to stop following the truck, all we can say is that it surprised us, too. We also wish to emphasize that he never attempted to apprehend the driver, only to let police know the hit-and-run driver's whereabouts.

14. See our discussion of "connectors" in Chapter 5.

15. Everyone seemed to agree that the jail in the county where Clair was arrested was the worst in the state.

16. See concluding discussion of the concept of friendship in Chapter 11.

17. Harrington, "The Social Psychology of Access in Ethnographic Research," p. 609.

18. Arnold, *Homelessness, Citizenship and Identity*.

19. See Anderson, *Code of the Street*.

20. Charmaz, *Constructing Grounded Theory*; Glaser and Strauss, *The Discovery of Grounded Theory*.

21. Coleman, "Relational Analysis"; this also has come to be known as a chain-referral sampling technique, or respondent-driven sampling; Salganik and Heckathorn, "Sampling and Estimation in Hidden Populations Using Respondent-Driven Sampling"; see also Wejnert and Heckathorn, "Web-Based Network Sampling."

22. This has been called saturation in Glaser and Strauss, *The Discovery of Grounded Theory*—a point where no new conceptual information is emerging from interviews, suggesting that the theoretical sampling process has exhausted the key issues on a topic; see also Charmaz, *Constructing Grounded Theory*.

23. Cohen and Crabtree, "Qualitative Research Guidelines Project."

24. This echoes Glaser and Strauss's original phenomenological justification of grounded theory in *The Discovery of Grounded Theory*.

25. Snow and Anderson, *Down on Their Luck*.

26. We provide tables on our website, www.athomeonthestreet.com, organized by chapter and theme to illustrate relevant parts of the coding process. While these excerpts do not exhaust the information we gathered on respective topics, they nonetheless provide the reader with a look into our data and analytic process.

27. See Charmaz, *Constructing Grounded Theory*; Clarke, *Situational Analysis*; Dey, *Grounding Grounded Theory*; Glaser and Strauss, *The Discovery of Grounded Theory*.

28. A more detailed discussion of our analytic methodology and, in particular, our innovations to grounded theory can be found in Wasserman, Clair, and Wilson, "Problematics of Grounded Theory." The brief description here should suffice for understanding the remainder of this book.

29. Fine, in "Ten Lies of Ethnography," gives a more thorough discussion of the "moral dilemmas of field research," generally where we draw decidedly on our own experience.

30. Geertz, *Available Light*.

31. Fine et al., "For Whom?"

32. Lofland et al., *Analyzing Social Settings*; see Arhem, "Millennium Among the Makuna," for a practical example; see Freire, *Pedagogy of the Oppressed*, for discussion of helping as oppression; see Gramsci, *Selections from a Prison Notebook*, for discussion of academics as hegemony-producing elites.

33. Erikson, "A Comment on Disguised Observation in Sociology"; Roth, "Comments on 'Secret Observation.'"

34. Fine et al., "For Whom?"

35. However, our conception of what this means is more aligned with notions of liberation and self-determination than more traditional notions of achievement of fixed ideals such as "home ownership," "gainful employment," and so on.

36. Thorne, "'You Still Takin' Notes?'" p. 288.

37. Fine et al., "For Whom?"; Lofland et al., *Analyzing Social Settings*.

38. Harrington, "The Social Psychology of Access in Ethnographic Research"; Lofland et al., *Analyzing Social Settings*.

39. Pippert, in *Road Dogs and Loners*, relatedly suggests that some type of giving back is incumbent on those who do research with those who are homeless.

40. Wax, "Paradoxes of 'Consent' to the Practice of Fieldwork," p. 275.

41. For an interesting discussion of this as an ethical question, see Frey, "Intending and Causing."

42. Geertz, *Available Light*.

43. Fine et al., "For Whom?"

44. Geertz, *Available Light*, p. 40.

3

Describing Those
Who Are Homeless

While it sounds like a rather simple undertaking, describing those who are homeless as a group is a difficult prospect, which becomes even more problematic for the subset of those who live on the streets. In this chapter we present some basic demographic information from the body of literature on homelessness and weave in our findings on some of these issues. We also briefly discuss previous findings about those who are street homeless, although, as we note, difficulties enumerating this population mean any distilled substantive assertions about their character ought to be considered with care. We found that, though well-intentioned, service providers understood those on the street to be additionally pathological relative to those enrolled in shelter programs, a disconnect not necessarily borne out by our ethnographic work or that of others.[1] We conclude by critically assessing this claim in light of evidence from our street participants and our own experiences, both in shelters and on the street. In the end, we dismiss the popular notion that living on the street is a particularly irrational choice. While we intentionally avoid a detailed discussion of mental illness and addiction as causes of homelessness (something we take up in the next chapter), we critically assess the pervasive assumption that the sociopsychological character of those who are street homeless is somehow inferior to those enrolled in service programs. Insofar as we developed our own preference for the streets, avoiding the shelters seems to us to be a quite rational decision.

Describing the Homeless Population

Though notoriously fraught with methodological problems, the demographic description we can give of those who are homeless is modestly successful. The 1950s and 1960s generated the classic image of home-less people as drunken ne'er-do-wells, and they were referred to even in academic literature as skid row bums.[2] While Howard M. Bahr empiri-cally found nationwide declines in skid row populations in the mid-1960s and attributed this partly to a prosperous national economy, reces-sions in the mid-1970s promoted sharp increases in the numbers of homeless and also notable changes in their demographic composition.[3]

Counting those who are homeless is itself a controversial endeavor.[4] Advocates for the homeless often have a vested financial interest in get-ting high numbers, especially of the most sympathetic homeless groups such as women and children.[5] Enmeshed in competition for funding with other metropolitan areas and other social programs targeting other populations, the financial viability of service institutions often is tied to perceived need.[6] Keeping homelessness in the public and political con-sciousness translates to real, desperately needed dollars. This is why Peter Rossi's substantially lower counts in Chicago in the 1980s pro-duced a great deal of controversy.[7] Counts are controversial because they determine the difference between defining whether "the homeless are an exceptional or anomalous population (small numbers) or a signif-icant group."[8] Lower numbers allow for the argument that those who are homeless are not a normal part of the population, making it harder to secure a portion of social welfare funds. Higher numbers convey that those who are homeless are not just the abnormal few, but a salient social group and therefore a more normative social problem needing to be addressed. Either way, enumerating the homeless population is a politically charged process with a lot of money on the line.

In the future it will be interesting to see if competing models of homeless services throw a twist into the "counting controversies."[9] New programs, such as Housing First (see Chapter 8) embody alternative philosophies of homeless service. Those working in the continuum-of-care model of service provision may in the near future have to compete with these and other types of programs. This could reverse the enumera-tion bias, making service providers more interested in lower counts that can be constructed as a reflection of the success of their respective serv-ice model.

Of course, the problems of counting those who are homeless entail describing the general composition of the population. Counts at shelters risk underestimating the street population, while counts that have attempted to include the street population have underestimated the avoidance factor of the individuals living on the street.[10] Additionally, studies adopting literal definitions of *homelessness* do not count those staying with relatives (what is known as doubling-up), and to our knowledge, no one has had any definite success directly counting that population, although some have offered statistically derived estimates.[11] For this reason, estimations of the number of those homeless have had such a large range that they are virtually meaningless unless specifically contextualized by their particular criteria. Shlay and Rossi note in a 1992 survey of sixty homeless studies that national estimates ranged from 250,000 to 3,000,000.[12]

Not surprisingly, 2008 national data collected by the Department of Housing and Urban Development tends toward the lower end of the spectrum, counting 672,000 people homeless on a single night in January, with 6 in 10 sleeping in shelters.[13] Of this total count, they suggest that 124,000 are chronically homeless and that two-thirds of those did not consistently use shelters. One of course should question whether January is an appropriate month to count those who are homeless and especially to make claims about those staying in shelters versus the street. While it might seem intuitive to think that a person always will avoid sleeping on the street if they can, the issue is not so black and white. Often those living on the street have some money from working odd jobs. Whether or not they pay for a hotel, or go to the shelter for that matter, is not just an issue of being able to afford to do so, but of balancing the costs and benefits of staying on the street.[14] If the weather is bad, as January often is, those living on the street may be willing to spend greater proportions of their money on a hotel than they would otherwise. Many times, three or four will pool their money to get the roughly thirty-five dollars needed for a private room on the coldest nights. This is not to suggest that those on the street can always go elsewhere. Staying in a hotel is usually not a sustainable way to live, and the money will eventually run out. But those living on the street often do have the ability to marshal resources for short periods of time. January weather might easily inspire someone to commit most or all of their money to a hotel or to call on friends for favors (keeping in mind that like money these, too, run out) and thus obscure the numbers of people who frequently otherwise live on the street.

The demographic makeup of the homeless population at the time of his writing also is difficult to encapsulate. Shlay and Rossi note that those who are homeless are homogenous for some variables and heterogeneous for others.[15] Additionally, data from a variety of sources are tenuous because measurement parameters are so varied. Still, some account of the projected demographic composition of the homeless population provides a good backdrop to our own study.

Single males constitute the majority of those who were homeless. Their mean age centered on 36.5 years when Shlay and Rossi conducted their meta-analysis.[16] Though their data are nearly 20 years old, later data from a variety of sources suggest this is still an accurate estimate, showing a preponderance of middle-aged, single males and disproportionately fewer older and younger people.[17] This seemingly contradicts the assertion that the family has become the new face of homelessness; however, there may still have been *more* women and children who were homeless at this writing than prior to the 1980s, even if they did not make up the majority.

Race and ethnic makeup of the population varies highly depending on region. In a recent Housing and Urban Development (HUD) study, 55 percent of the sheltered population (unsheltered data was limited to raw numbers and chronic status) was African American, compared with only 26 percent of the people living in poor families in the general population. This suggests that race carries a risk of becoming homeless above and beyond poverty itself. Hispanics and Native Americans also were overrepresented among the sheltered population, though at proportions equivalent to those of the poor population generally. However, regional variations with respect to race and ethnicity make interpreting this data somewhat difficult. In Shlay and Rossi's meta-analysis, the proportion of African Americans across all sixty studies was only 44 percent.[18] While this suggests they have disproportionately high representation relative to the general population, the large standard deviation (23, more than half of the total percentage) means statistically that 95 percent of all study populations ranged from 0 percent to 90 percent African American (two standard deviations on either side of the mean). Racial composition likely varies significantly according to region, since a disproportionately high number of African Americans live in the southeastern United States, for example. Regional governmental data from 2009 for the Birmingham metropolitan area suggest 69 percent of the homeless population is African American, while 30 percent is white and only 1 percent comes from all other groups.[19] This Birmingham data is also borne out in a study by Mark LaGory and his colleagues who found 68 percent of the population to be African American, 31 percent white and 1 percent other.[20]

There are a number of variables that are significantly higher among the homeless population relative to the general population, including mental illness, addiction, poor physical health, poor nutrition, incarceration, a lack of social ties, and being raised in foster care.[21] Of course, various measurement issues beyond the scope of this discussion need to be addressed to correctly interpret such data and the later governmental reports cited above do not contain such data on most of these. It also is important to note that the comparative prevalence of these conditions should not be confused with preponderance. For example, while the homeless population has significantly greater mental illness than the general population, most studies suggest that the majority of those who are homeless are not mentally ill.[22] Recent national estimates suggested 26 percent of the sheltered population experienced mental illness.[23] Additionally, we must consider what types of mental illnesses are being estimated by any given study. Serious mental illnesses such as schizophrenia are not preponderant, but depression seems to be.[24] This distinction is particularly important, since these respective illnesses are thought to be fundamentally different. Depression can be stimulated by environmental factors, whereas schizophrenia, although exacerbated by environment, has some biogenetic basis. Without clarifying such important distinctions, statewide Alabama data that attempts to include those living on the street suggested 27.7 percent of those who were homeless were mentally ill, while data from the Birmingham metro area found 39 percent in that category.[25] No explanation is given for this significant variation, and it is not clear whether measurements of mental illness were consistent across different regions of the state.

Substance use among those who are homeless is strikingly high, though as we detail in the next chapter, inferences about substance use as a *cause* of homelessness are suspect but still frequent. National data from 2008 suggested 39 percent of those in shelters are chronic substance users.[26] Statewide data for those who were homeless in Alabama also suggested 39 percent with a "chronic substance abuse disorder," but regional data for the Birmingham Metropolitan area were much higher, suggesting 53 percent of those who were homeless were "chronic substance abusers."[27] Exactly what is being measured and differences in measurements between the regional agencies and the aggregated statewide data are not specified. Still, causal inferences are made clear in the Alabama report by the supplementary quotes from individuals for whom addiction was the self-reported cause of their homelessness.

A 2005 homeless needs assessment conducted in Birmingham yields the most sophisticated, detailed, and reliable demographic data relevant to our study population.[28] Combining an actual count with statistical projection, LaGory and colleagues estimated 2,929 people homeless in the city of Birmingham.[29] It is worth noting that this is 39 percent higher than data from the state government published two years later, though it cannot be determined whether this reflects changes in the population or

biases resulting from the measurements utilized. Single individuals com-
posed 73.6 percent of the actual sample (n = 1,414), and males were the
majority with 69.9 percent. The mean age of all respondents was forty-
one years (standard deviation = eleven years).[30] While 27.3 percent of
women experiencing homelessness were accompanied by family members, this was far lower for men (2.7 percent). Similarly, 19.6 percent of
women who were homeless were accompanied by children, compared
with only 0.7 percent of men. An intensive survey on a representative
subsample (n = 161) showed that most of those individuals homeless in
Birmingham had at least completed high school (74.0 percent) and that
one in five had served in the military, with one-quarter of those having
seen active combat.[31]

In the end, what becomes clear from the variety of national, regional, and metropolitan data on homelessness, which as a whole lacks much
clarity, is that homelessness is a politically charged issue that intersects
diverse social problems. As such, understanding homelessness in general means becoming immersed in a complex web of social phenomena.
Complexity is not the strength of descriptive statistics. So when understandings of homelessness are formed from overly simplified information, and, moreover, when these are the conceptualizations used to fund
social programs, disconnects between the population and the problem
solvers risk creating more problems than are solved. This disconnect is
even more pronounced for those who are street homeless, since they are
even more difficult to enumerate and aggregate.

Difficulties Delineating
Those Who Are Street Homeless

It has been difficult for researchers to clearly distinguish and describe
those living on the street vis-à-vis those consistently using shelters. As
noted, 2008 HUD data does not even attempt to go beyond enumerating
the unsheltered population and estimating the length of their homelessness. This is important because, as noted in Chapter 1, those who live on
the street represent a significant portion of the homeless population that
services have failed to reach in a meaningful way. Those who are street
homeless are not only on the margins of society but also on margins of
homelessness itself.

To be sure, identifying those who are street homeless has been troubling to researchers. During the day, those using shelters and those living on the street may indistinguishably mingle in urban space.

Nighttime research attenuates this, but it has other problems, such as locating camps established so as to be intentionally difficult to find.[32] This creates a problem of selectivity for sampling those who are street homeless because those camps that are most hidden and difficult to access are, from our experience, also the most functional. Even more problematic in this regard were the several markers Rossi used in attempting to distinguish those on the street from those seeking shelter, including individuals whose appearance was relatively (1) "shabby, dirty, and unkempt"; (2) "incoherent, drunk, confused, or lacking lucidity"; and (3) "those who scored high on a scale measuring depression."[33] These, of course, make presuppositions about the nature of those who live on the street that are selective and may be unwarranted. Specifically, these markers assume that those who are street homeless are more dysfunctional relative to their sheltered counterparts, an assumption that we will later contest.[34] Rossi's criteria specify in advance nonfunctional characteristics of those on the street and thus risk creating a sample biased in highly problematic way.[35] His measurement construct inherently reflects existing stigmas placed on those who are street homeless, and so utilizing it in a sampling process naturally creates a biased sample, which can only confirm the prefabricated conceptualizations of those on the street.

Rossi and colleagues used a probability sampling design in an effort to capture those who are street homeless, but this method does not overcome a particular selectivity bias—what we might simply call the avoidance factor.[36] The homeless or a particular subset of them, which is even more statistically problematic, might avoid participating in surveys. Presumably the most suspicious and distrustful would be the least willing to be research subjects. Moreover, the police often accompany surveyors, particularly when doing counts at night, which would predictably heighten the avoidance factor.[37] Nearly by definition, those on the street resist institutions like shelters and certainly also the police, so it is not unreasonable to question how well various enumeration studies sample them. In fact, Rossi himself notes that those who are street homeless hold generally negative views of the shelters, but we might suspect that they are similarly distrustful of clipboard-wielding researchers, especially when they are accompanied by uniformed police officers.[38] Ultimately, if samples are selective—and, further, selective of particularly important characteristics such as whether one uses or avoids homeless services—assertions about the nature of the homeless population in general and especially those on the street have to be considered with care. We suspect, therefore, that characteristics particular to or exaggerated in those on the street are not well captured by traditional survey research, which of course supplies a warrant for in-depth ethnographic approaches such as ours.

Counting those on the street is also made problematic by the relative obscurity of their communities. While we all are familiar with those who remain in plain sight—sleeping on park benches, for example—a large proportion of those on the street tend to establish living areas that are hidden. This makes sense, since it minimizes their exposure to harassment from the authorities as well as keeps them safer from street crime. Thus, teams of researchers may have difficulty locating these more secluded areas. An excerpt from our field notes concerning a street count done by a coalition of service providers illuminates:

> The organizers of the homeless count seemed somewhat clueless about who the street homeless were and where they lived. For example, while James had told us about 80 people stay around Morris Ave., the organizer of the survey wasn't sure if they were even going down to that area. That seems like a no-brainer to anyone who knows anything about the street homeless in Birmingham.

In addition, those able to establish camps in hidden corners of the urban landscape may be more "functional" than those who randomly lie down on city streets. Excluding them therefore seems not only to risk underestimating the numbers of people living on the street overall, but also could predicate misinterpretations of the characteristics of the street homeless population in ways that exaggerate their dysfunction. This engenders a disconnect between the vision and goals of service providers and the needs of the street population. This also was the opinion of one of our participants, recorded in our field notes:

> I asked James what he thought of the survey. "It sucked," he said. "It was all about drugs and HIV." I recalled when James told us that what would help homelessness is more jobs in the area. "Do you think it will accomplish anything?" I asked him. "More money in their pocket," he said, "It won't do anything for me."

Our sample of those on the street fit many of the demographics described above. They were predominantly African American. Many of them had served in the military; most were middle aged, rather than decidedly young or old; and the vast majority of them had grown up relatively poor.

Several of the politicians and city officials we interviewed claimed that most of those who are homeless in the area were transients who had come to Alabama for the warm weather and were kind, charitable people. This rhetoric is eerily reminiscent of southern governments in the 1960s, which constructed the civil rights movement as the work of "outside agitators." But despite these political constructions that promote regional notions of "us" and "them," we found that the vast majority of our participants who were street homeless were from Alabama.

While changing demographics of homelessness, particularly growing numbers of women and families, may be extant in the general population,[39] from our experience this does not hold for those who are street homeless. That is, there seem to be relatively few women and children who live on the street. This is likely due to the greater availability of formal services for women and children and a greater willingness on the part of family and friends to help women and children.[40] Both of these seem tied to gender conceptions about the male-as-provider and women and children as those who need to be provided for. However, we must also note that because they live under greater threat, women and children living on the street may simply remain more hidden.

Many studies exclude, underrepresent, or obscure those who are street homeless, but David Snow and Leon Anderson's study is a notable exception.[41] Most generally, their ethnographic fieldwork illustrates that our initial research impetus had been correct: there are key differences between those who stay primarily on the streets and those who use shelters. They also found that the daily routines of those on the street revolve around getting work, despite popular conceptions that they are lazy. This is done by going to temporary labor services or by gathering at known spots, like Catchout Corner, where they informally arrange odd jobs. Selling blood plasma was a common way to make money as well.

Snow and Anderson note that those who are street homeless experience a disintegration of social ties and bear constant stigmas that erode their identity.[42] In response, they employ a variety of identity management techniques.[43] Despite these, many of those who are homeless begin to settle into street life as their social integration increasingly deteriorates. Snow and Anderson found also that most of those who are homeless are not mentally ill and that most alcohol and drug use is a means of self-medication.[44] These findings are important because they counter the pervasive assumption that those on the street are particularly deficient personalities. Rather, this study suggests a variety of rationales for supposedly irrational behavior—for example, that they use drugs and alcohol out of environmental stimuli in a way that mirrors social patterns of substance use generally. Ethnographies like that of Snow and Anderson are consistent with one of our earliest insights, that those living on the street predominantly are lucid and choose the streets for understandable if not justifiable reasons.[45]

Though street ethnographies make up a small portion of homeless research, they are nonetheless particularly important because they shed light into areas of the homeless phenomenon that statistical research is unable to attain owing to a distanced methodology.[46] We not only confirm many findings from previous ethnographic work but also add new dimensions. By staying overnight, for example, we had access to the homeless camps hidden away from public view. This allowed us to distinguish those who were primarily street homeless from those who used shelters at night and informal labor pools and blood plasma centers during the day. Studying the organization and regulation of these hidden communities adds to Snow and Anderson's inference that survival on the streets requires a creativity and will that counters the prevailing assumption that those on the street are the sine qua non of dysfunction.[47] Similarly, Michael Maharidge and Dale Williamson suggest that a "hobo reality" often is romanticized as one of innocent circumstance and structural causation.[48] They argue that one should realize that homelessness is potentially the ultimate outcome of rejecting "the system." Being "houseless" serves as punishment for a deviant identity, for being a "nonconformist." The streets become "a haven ... from the dominant world of regular jobs and nuclear family life."[49]

Still, the notion of those on the street as rational and conscious decisionmakers remains on the periphery. We turn now to evidence from our fieldwork to suggest that choosing the streets over the shelters does not represent pathology but is a legitimate and understandable decision.

Resistors or Rejects:
Exploring the "Choice" of the Streets

Ethnographic data does not produce the sorts of neat demographics and concise statements offered by statistics. Rather, ethnography intentionally hangs on to complexity because social life is so intensely complex. Our research ultimately blurred the lines of street homelessness more than it focused them. What follows then is an account of the difficulty of defining a person as homeless and specifically as "street homeless." Rather than producing for the reader a comfortable sense of clarity, as statistics tend to do, we hope that our struggle to pin down such notions accurately conveys their more realistic complexity.

"Who are the homeless?" This was our most routine interview question, a sliver of consistency in our unstructured interview protocol. Most often this would elicit a list of causes of homelessness, not a definition of who qualified for the label: "The homeless are substance abusers, the mentally ill, people who have lost their jobs, had a serious life crisis, have lost their families, victims of domestic violence." This betrays the pervasive way in which homelessness is constructed as a social problem, but it skips a more basic crucial step. That is, what is the definition of *homeless*? This more basic question should not be overlooked.

As we noted at the outset of this chapter, delineation of those who are homeless is ambiguous and contested. For example, sometimes people who "doubled-up" in apartments or who are staying in low-cost motels are considered to be homeless, while other times they are excluded as such. Some of the men who gathered at Catchout Corner had homes and came to the Corner solely for work. Moreover, some of them had homes and still occasionally slept under the bridge for any number of reasons—for example, if they had a fight with their spouse or had arranged an early job in the morning. But other men at Catchout were fixtures. This core group was our research focus, but many people less definitively homeless were nonetheless part of the subculture of the streets and therefore served as valuable informants. In the end, what mattered to us was getting authentic, firsthand knowledge, more than where one slept at night and how often. We leave definitions of that sort to those who do statistical counts. For our purposes, we loosely define those who are homeless as a group who routinely live on the streets even if they infrequently use temporary housing such as shelters. It should already be clear that a "loose" definition is the only sort that is possible anyway.

Although they sometimes stayed in low-cost hotels when they could afford to do so, and even sometimes cycled through the service programs at local shelters, for the purposes of this book those who were street homeless routinely stayed on the streets or in urban camps. This group often is tagged as, or conflated with, the "chronically homeless" by researchers and service providers, since they tend to stay homeless for longer periods, often measured in years, not days or weeks. While their dispositions toward services certainly fluctuate over such long stretches of time, we might say that those who are street homeless represent a subset of homeless people who resist staying at the shelters.

We initially were compelled to investigate the street when, during our initial interviews with homeless-service providers and experts, we became curious about and dissatisfied with their explanations of those who were street homeless. When we would pointedly ask whether those who were homeless generally were all mentally ill drug addicts, service providers would indignantly respond by noting that this was not the case. They would herald the normality of those who were homeless and list the myriad other causes for their plight. As one service provider told us:

> The homeless are basically just everyday people, just like you and myself. Some you see ... don't look to be homeless, but they are. They wear suits and ties, casual wear. They are down amongst the downtown crowd, they come out of the buildings down there, and they go in and out of those places. You wouldn't know they were homeless because of the availability of shelters where they can go in and they can clean up, but they are out there, so you never really know.

In the foreground of their consciousness, service providers resist the stigmas that people attach to those who are homeless.

This was not the case, however, when we asked them about those living on the streets in particular. While the service providers would mostly admit not having a good explanation for the choice of the streets over the shelters, most would venture suggestions. Specifically, they would assert that those who are street homeless are paranoid due to mental illness and therefore fear being around other people, or that they did not come in because they could not do drugs or drink in the shelters.[50] Our participants on the street found the latter explanation particularly insufficient. Lockett noted plainly, "I've smoked crack at the [shelter]." We asked the same service provider who above asserted the normality of those who are homeless generally about the conceptualization of those on the street as particularly pathological, posing the question: "Do you ultimately think that everybody out there is diseased in some way whether it be mental illness, alcohol, drugs?" He replied:

> I would think so because you do have those out there that suffers [*sic*] from mental illness, which has increased as a result of the disease of addiction. Initially ... people go out there with mental illnesses [and might] not really be into using drugs other than the one that is prescribed for them. But by being out there, and the addict ... sees them, and what he/she does is manipulate them.

Not only was this a pervasive conceptualization about those on the street among shelter providers who dealt predominantly with people inside their institutions, but also of outreach workers from those institutions whose job is to recruit those on the street into shelter programs.[51] The quotations above are in fact from one such outreach worker, whose primary job description involved working with those living on the street.

This is deeply ironic. While the service providers resisted the stigmatic notions of homelessness in general (or, more cynically, for those who were homeless who came directly under their care), they tended to repeat and reinforce those stigmas for those who were street homeless. According to them, those who were homeless were not all mentally ill or drug addicted, but those on the street (probably) were. However, right from the start, our impressions of those on the street did not fit assertions that they were particularly pathological. When asked why they did not want to go to the shelters, they would rattle off a standard list of quite rational explanations. As James put it:

> There's too many diseases and germs, and where you sleep at, there's no ventilation. And you don't know who's cooking the food with HIV, tuberculosis, AIDS, none of that. And you're in there, sleeping around a hundred guys, coughin', sneezin', fartin', all of that, all through the night. Uh uh; that ain't me. I'd rather sleep in a box where I know the only germ I'm going to catch is my own germ. But you got those that love [the shelter]. Me? It ain't nothing but a racket to me.

In addition, people commonly were concerned about their safety. Being around strangers, some who were unstable in various ways, in a stressful environment, simply made them feel unsafe. By contrast, on the street they could choose where they slept and who they were around. They could remain relatively hidden and in the proximity of friends. From these types of statements, it began to seem that those living on the street had a long list of lucid reasons for not using services and, in particular, for not staying in the shelters at night.[52]

As noted, most of those who are street homeless would intermittently stay in cheap motels, particularly if they had worked enough to afford them. We learned early on that the number of people at Catchout Corner at night varied directly with the time of the month and the past week's weather. Government checks issued on the first of the month meant that many people could afford temporary refuge in low-cost motels. Similarly, if the weather was favorable during the week, work tended to be more plentiful, causing some reduction in numbers of people sleeping on the street. This tendency suggests that those who are street homeless do not particularly favor the streets as much as they resist service institutions.[53]

Though the service providers were stymied by the idea that someone would choose the streets over the shelters, we began to sympathize with it. It occurred to us that we ourselves would rather stay on the street than the shelter. We had spent nights on the street, and it was uncomfortable compared with our normal lives, but not scary or threatening. As do most of those who are street homeless, we isolated ourselves in homeless camps and communities that are relatively hidden. Our stays on the street not only felt relatively safe, they were downright exciting. Indeed, a sense of freedom was palpable. While we certainly longed for the comfort of our homes, there also was a calm and peaceful feeling in these camps, particularly at night, similar to what one would feel when camping in the woods. It was not difficult to understand why someone would prefer to stay in an urban camp over a crowded shelter. We found ourselves looking forward to these moments, coming to feel that as much as we were doing research, we also were getting away from the stressors of our busy daily lives.

When we suggested all of this to a shelter director, Steve, he rightly challenged our assumption that we would prefer the streets. "Well, you can't say that until you've stayed in the shelter." He was right. We had jumped the gun.

We got permission from him to stay in his shelter. So that we did not take a bed from someone in need, Steve declared an inclement weather day, which meant that the shelter would take in people even after all of the beds are full. He promised not to tell the staff, and when we overheard their confusion about why he had declared inclement weather procedures on such a beautiful spring day, it was clear that he had kept his word. He was particularly interested in our report, anyway, and we agreed to give him a full account.

Despite Steve's implicit hope, our own preferences for the streets only increased as a result of our stay at the shelter, and the accounts from those on the street were solidified as accurate. In an effort to cover more ground and avoid attention, we did not interact with each other. Waiting outside, we both saw a guy stash what appeared to be drugs (the cellophane wrapper is a giveaway) between his legs. Moments later a car pulled up front, and the driver leaned down and mimicked the motions of lighting a crack pipe to Wasserman, an offer of sale. Just after that, a man clutching a paper bag full of sample prescription medicines was forcibly escorted out of the building and three police cars instantly swarmed in. Wasserman later found out that he had threatened an eighteen-year-old man waiting to check in, saying to him, "I'll gnaw your fuckin' face off." He tripped on the sidewalk and was loaded into an ambulance to be taken for a mental evaluation. Our stress levels already were high, and we had not even checked in.

About an hour later, at dinner, Clair overheard several men at his table sizing up someone as an undercover cop. "Look at his eyes; he's too clean, never done any real drugs." They asked Clair, "Hey Bigman, you think that guy is a undercover cop?" To Clair's surprise, they were talking about Wasserman.[54] They proceeded to claim that if he was a cop, they were going to stab him in the neck. When everyone went upstairs to bed, one of the men pointed Wasserman's bunk out to Clair. And so obviously the concern about safety that had regularly been listed by those on the street as a reason not to go to the shelter became very real to us.

As the threats against Wasserman stilled after bedtime, other complaints about the general discomfort of the shelter were unmasked.[55] After pacing around the bathroom and smoking some cigarettes with a few of the other residents, even though it was technically against the rules, Clair returned to his bunk hoping to be tired enough to fall asleep. He slept little however, disturbed in turn by dirty underwear that fell from the top bunk, two men talking in the bunk to his right, and the incessant chorus of coughing from the room, including the man on his left who was in the end stages of lung cancer.

The next morning, intimidation against Wasserman for supposedly being a cop resumed with candid shouts of "5-0" when he would walk by and "oink-oink" calls when his name was called out for the morning chore list. We left separately as we had arrived, heading back to Catchout where we got a round of "I-told-you-so's." We indeed felt safer, cleaner, and freer under Interstate 65 on a cold, rainy night, or sleeping in a parking lot on Morris Ave.

Our regular participants who lived on the street spent the next several weeks discussing our shelter experience. They were pleased that we tried the shelters and seemed validated by our now solid preference for staying in their camps. We were believers. Despite the fact that where we stayed was considered one of the best shelters in town, if we became homeless tomorrow, we would ourselves much rather find some space on the street than stay in the shelter.

Progressive-minded service providers, who generally resisted stigmatic conceptions of homelessness, had very stigmatizing views of those living on the street. For them, to choose to stay on the street rather than in the shelter was not rational and could be explained only by mental illness or addiction, both of which cause people to act irrationally. What we found on the street were people with quite rational explanations for their resistance to the shelters. With our stay in the shelter, we ironically found our own preferences decidedly aligned with the supposedly irrational group.

Kim Hopper suggests that "inhuman" conditions at the shelters kept people on the street in New York City during the 1980s, and Arline Mathieu notes the decrepit physical conditions of service institutions.[56] The shelter we stayed in was not inhuman in terms of the facilities or the staff. In fact, it was fairly well run by these standards. But even this well-run facility with good-hearted staff reflected Kathleen R. Arnold's observation that "many shelters and agencies ... are disorganized and pathological. Of course, these terms are often reserved for those who are homeless, not 'us.'"[57]

This all contradicts the notion that those who are street homeless, more so than the service-using population, are especially dysfunctional or sick. Those value judgments simply did not reflect the street population we encountered, at least not in ways that signified any real difference between those on the streets and those in the shelter. Rather, those who are street homeless seem far more rational than they are given credit for, particularly when it comes to their choice of the street. The implication from service providers had been that two populations would be easy to delineate, because they were markedly different in their individual character. We discovered, however, that the choice of the streets did not itself betray a deficient personality. Defining those who are homeless as a group is a difficult proposition, and the influence of stigmas surrounding those who live on the street make delineating that subpopulation even more problematic. So while it may seem tautological to say that those who are street homeless simply are those who tend to live on the street, the statement contains significant and hard-fought negative space. That is to say, the important realization here is not who the street homeless are but who they are not.

In the next chapter, we examine the purported causes of homelessness, specifically those of mental illness and addiction. These are very frequently used to define those who are homeless and those on the street in particular, but we hope in this chapter to have disaggregated them in favor of more fundamental considerations. Doing so will help support the critical approach of the next chapter.

Notes

1. Hopper, *Reckoning with the Homeless*; Snow and Anderson, *Down on Their Luck*.

2. See Bahr, "The Gradual Disappearance of Skid Row."

3. Arnold, *Homelessness, Citizenship and Identity*; Bahr, "The Gradual Disappearance of Skid Row"; Mathieu, "The Medicalization of Homelessness and the Theater of Repression"; Mossman, "Deinstitutionalization, Homelessness, and the Myth of Psychiatric Abandonment"; Rossi, *Down and Out in America*; Shlay and Rossi, "Social Science Research and Contemporary Studies of Homelessness"; Snow and Anderson, *Down on Their Luck*.

4. See Rossi's own specific remarks in "Half Truths with Real Consequences."

5. See Passaro, *The Unequal Homeless*, for an excellent explanation of the hegemonic problems with this construction.

6. Rossi, *Down and Out in America*; Rossi et al., "The Urban Homeless"; Shlay and Rossi, "Social Science Research and Contemporary Studies of Homelessness"; Guard, in "Programs That Focus on Chronic Homelessness Will Hurt Homeless Families," ties together need and sympathetic demographics in arguing that funding for programs focusing on the chronic homeless will hurt programs for homeless families.

7. Rossi, *Down and Out in America*; see Rossi's own specific remarks in "Half Truths with Real Consequences."

8. Arnold, *Homelessness, Citizenship and Identity*, p. 104.

9. Hopper and Baumohl note, in "Held in Abeyance," that service agencies compete with each other for funding.

10. Rossi, *Down and Out in America*; Rossi, "Half Truths with Real Consequences"; see Wagner, *Checkerboard Square*, for discussion of problems of collecting cross-sectional data primarily at service agencies; see also Rosen's ("The Problem of Homelessness Is Exaggerated") more extreme position that methodological problems so dramatically inflate the numbers of those who are homeless that he concludes the problem itself is exaggerated.

11. See Rossi et al., "The Urban Homeless"; LaGory et al., "Depression Among the Homeless"; LaGory et al., *A Needs Assessment of the Homeless of Birmingham and Jefferson County*.

12. Shlay and Rossi, "Social Science Research and Contemporary Studies of Homelessness."

13. Department of Housing and Urban Development, *The Third Annual Homeless Assessment Report to Congress*.

14. Shelters often require "copays" for staying there and also entail other less quantifiable costs discussed in detail later (see Chapter 9 especially).

15. Shlay and Rossi, "Social Science Research and Contemporary Studies of Homelessness."

16. Ibid.

17. See Department of Housing and Urban Development, *The Third Annual Homeless Assessment Report to Congress*; Alabama Governor's Statewide Interagency Council on Homelessness, *Homelessness in Alabama*; LaGory et al., *A Needs Assessment of the Homeless of Birmingham and Jefferson County*.

18. Shlay and Rossi, "Social Science Research and Contemporary Studies of Homelessness."

19. Alabama Governor's Statewide Interagency Council on Homelessness, *Homelessness in Alabama*.

20. LaGory et al., *A Needs Assessment of the Homeless of Birmingham and Jefferson County*.

21. Shlay and Rossi, "Social Science Research and Contemporary Studies of Homelessness"; Pippert, in *Road Dogs and Loners*, and Rowe, in *Crossing the Border*, both discuss the salience of loss of social ties.

22. Shlay and Rossi, "Social Science Research and Contemporary Studies of Homelessness"; Snow et al., "The Myth of Pervasive Mental Illness Among the Homeless"; see also Failer, *Who Qualifies for Rights?*

23. Department of Housing and Urban Development, *The Third Annual Homeless Assessment Report to Congress*.

24. LaGory et al., in "Depression Among the Homeless," report 75 percent with depressive symptoms in their study.

25. Alabama Governor's Statewide Interagency Council on Homelessness, *Homelessness in Alabama*.

26. Department of Housing and Urban Development, *The Third Annual Homeless Assessment Report to Congress*.

27. Alabama Governor's Statewide Interagency Council on Homelessness, *Homelessness in Alabama*.

28. LaGory et al., *A Needs Assessment of the Homeless of Birmingham and Jefferson County*.

29. Ibid.

30. Ibid.

31. Ibid.

32. LaGory et al., "Depression Among the Homeless"; Rossi, *Down and Out in America*.

33. Rossi, *Down and Out in America*, p. 103.

34. See also discussions of functionality and rationality of those who are street homeless in Mathieu, "The Medicalization of Homelessness and the Theater of Repression"; Hopper, "Homeless Choose Streets over Inhuman 'Shelters'"; Hopper, *Reckoning with the Homeless*; Snow and Anderson, *Down on Their Luck*.

35. Rossi, *Down and Out in America*.

36. Rossi et al., "The Urban Homeless."

37. See for example Rossi et al., "The Urban Homeless"; this also was the case for a local homeless count conducted by a coalition of service providers in our city.

38. Rossi, *Down and Out in America*, p. 104.

39. See for example Nunez and Fox, "A Snapshot of Family Homelessness Across America"; this also is contested, see Shlay and Rossi, "Social Science Research and Contemporary Studies of Homelessness."

40. See Passaro, *The Unequal Homeless*, for a discussion of how this tends to reproduce gendered concepts of female dependency; Pippert, in *Road Dogs and Loners*, similarly draws on gender theory to explain a lower level of support for programs that target men who are homeless.

41. Snow and Anderson, *Down on Their Luck*.

42. Ibid.; also, Arnold, *Homelessness, Citizenship and Identity*.

43. Snow and Anderson, "Identity Work Among the Homeless."

44. Snow and Anderson, *Down on Their Luck*; Snow et al., "The Myth of Pervasive Mental Illness Among the Homeless."

45. Snow and Anderson, *Down on Their Luck*; see also Dordick, *Something Left to Lose*; Hoffman and Coffey, "Dignity and Indignation"; Hopper, "Homeless Choose Streets over Inhuman 'Shelters'"; Hopper, *Reckoning with the Homeless*.

46. Wagner, *Checkerboard Square*.

47. Snow and Anderson, *Down on Their Luck*; see also Hopper, *Reckoning with the Homeless*; see also Jencks, *The Homeless*, for a disturbing account of presumed dysfunction of those who are homeless in general.

48. Maharidge and Williamson, *The Last Great American Hobo*, p. 31.

49. Depastino, *Citizen Hobo*, p. 268.

50. Hopper, *Reckoning with the Homeless*.

51. See Rowe, *Crossing the Border*, for an excellent study focused specifically on outreach workers.

52. See also Dordick, *Something Left to Lose*, especially concerning safety in the shelters.

53. Wagner, in *Checkerboard Square*, also characterizes those on the street as resistors, not only to service programs but also to a variety of social norms.

54. It is interesting to note that while they mistakenly thought Wasserman was a cop, they were correct that he was not homeless and was an outsider with an ulterior motive. This echoes Rosenhan's experience reported in "On Being Sane in Insane Places," where the mental patients recognized that the researchers did not belong, whereas the hospital staff was oblivious.

55. See also Hoffman and Coffey, "Dignity and Indignation."

56. Hopper, "Homeless Choose Streets over Inhuman 'Shelters'"; Mathieu, "The Medicalization of Homelessness and the Theater of Repression."

57. Arnold, Homelessness, *Citizenship and Identity*, p. 2.

4

Causes of Homelessness

In the last chapter we dealt with fundamental issues of describing characteristics of those who are homeless in general and those on the street in particular. We therefore intentionally sidestepped questions about whether things such as mental illness and addiction *cause* homelessness, but these are so conflated with the condition of being homeless that we could accurately say that in the estimations of most people, they are its definitive features. Still, questions about causality raise issues beyond whether or not there are high rates of mental illness and substance use found among those who are homeless, and so we more fully take up discussion of them here.[1] In opposition to those individualized explanations, we also examine social structural factors purported to cause homelessness, such as political and economic circumstances.

As noted, when we posed a pointed question about the prevalence of addiction and mental illness among the homeless population, service providers mostly would try to soften the sharp edges of their rigid interpretations. They would tell us all the other things about the homeless population that make them appear less detestable and make themselves appear less judgmental. Those who are homeless are not just crazy drug addicts, but simply are poor people who have encountered acute hardships. They would lament a social structure in which individuals were on their own in such an extreme and consequential way. This all was pleasant to hear, but as we became more familiar with the service institutions, their organization and practices betrayed limitations to these structuralist admissions. This is not to say that they were disingenuous in their discussions of social structural factors, but rather that despite their broader, more complex understandings of homelessness as a social phenomenon, their institutions were more narrowly focused on dealing with homelessness at the individual level. The counseling services most commonly offered at the shelters are for addiction and mental illness. Some services that speak a little more directly to economic obstacles faced by those who are homeless were offered too, but mostly they supplemented the treatment programs. Job training and placement, getting government benefits, legal assistance, and the like commonly were available only to those first enrolled in treatment for addiction and mental illness. In the end, beliefs and rhetoric to the contrary, service institutions were modeled on popular conceptions about pathologies of homelessness. This led us to critically examine the role of mental illness and addiction, and the way those understandings were to a significant extent driven by negative stigmas of homelessness.

Since the demographic composition and even the raw size of the homeless population is hotly contested, it should be no surprise that consensus about what causes homelessness also is elusive. Addiction and mental illness clearly are by far the two most popular. Sometimes these are asserted explicitly as causes of homelessness and other times more vaguely conceptualized as inextricably intertwined with the condition of being homeless.[2] Either way, they are mainstays of understandings about why people are homeless. While some research has attempted to shift focus toward structural conditions, which predicate homelessness, individual pathology concepts such as mental illness and addiction have been resilient.[3]

In this chapter we begin by assessing the mental illness and addiction explanations of homelessness first by examining critiques in the literature and then by utilizing our field experiences to contest their overly simplistic nature. That is, while mental illness and substance use do seem to be more prevalent among those who are homeless than the general population, it is not at all clear that they commonly *cause* homelessness. That is, input from social structural factors seems necessary in most if not all cases. Moreover, insofar as mental illness and addiction typically reflect character assessments of those who are homeless—as deviant, for example—it is not at all clear that the types and stimuli of their mental illness or their motivations for substance use are much different from the norm. This is a particularly problematic misconception because statistical observations of prevalence rarely remain properly situated as aggregated descriptive data, but instead are the foundations on which we form understandings about the causes of homelessness and in turn influence how we treat those who are homeless. This is known as the reductionist fallacy, but inferences of this sort are common practice among not only the lay public but also the social service sector and social scientists. If nothing else, this is an error we hope to correct in this chapter.

Mental Illness and Addiction:
Oppositions in the Literature

Assertions that mental illness causes homelessness typically are grounded in the belief that the closing of state mental hospitals has cast significant numbers of those who are mentally ill into the streets. This logic is buttressed by casual observation where the most obviously mentally ill people are the most visible public figures. Mental illness as a cause of homelessness also is appealing because much research shows significantly higher rates of it among the homeless population.[4] One study conducted in Birmingham, Alabama, showed a mean Center for Epidemiology Studies Depression (CES-D) score for the sample of 23.5, suggesting significantly high levels of clinical depression among the population.[5] Research suggests that over one-third of those who are homeless self-report a mental illness, and estimates of actual prevalence often are as high as two-thirds.[6] These figures hold for later government data, of the early 2000s, however reliable the actual numbers.[7]

The deinstitutionalization hypothesis is suspect in a number of ways. The process of deinstitutionalization of state mental hospitals began in the late 1950s, but massive increases in the number of those who are homeless did not begin until the early 1970s.[8] Critiques of the deinstitutionalization hypothesis assert that if large numbers of individuals were forced into homelessness by the closing of state mental hospitals, the increase in numbers of people who are homeless would have begun much earlier.[9] Defenders point out, however, that a third wave of deinstitutionalization saw the worst-off released during the same period when homelessness began to increase. Still, the continued fluctuation in the numbers of people who are homeless since that time, rather than just a short period of dramatic inflation, suggests other factors are operating.

Arline Mathieu points out that the deinstitutionalization explanation is at least partly politically motivated, in that it allows city governments to blame state governments for their residents who are homeless.[10] Kathleen Arnold notes that even if the deinstitutionalization of those who were mentally ill was a factor, it could not have operated in a vacuum, but rather required social structural underpinnings in order to cause homelessness.[11] Specifically, those deinstitutionalized who did become homeless

became so because (1) outpatient mental health services never materialized, (2) Medicare and Medicaid cuts meant less services for the poor, and
(3) certain populations could not be targeted for care (ex-inmates, run-
aways, and so forth).[12]

Moreover, the mental illness explanation partly is one of visibility.[13]
The image of people who are mentally ill and homeless talking to themselves or imaginary others is salient because those people are particularly visible.[14] Their behaviors draw attention, whereas the person who is
homeless but does not exhibit these behaviors is more likely to go unno-
ticed. Still, while logical assessment contradicts the stigmatic conceptions held about those who are homeless, when prevalence rates match
one's day-to-day experiences around the city, inferences about the relationship of mental illness and homelessness are easy to make, even
when methodologically invalid. These stigmas are therefore difficult to
uproot, since they are firmly lodged in the minds of so many people and
then continually confirmed by daily interactions.

While it is often implied that mental illness causes homelessness, it
clearly could be the other way around.[15] Data from Birmingham in 1995
by Ferris J. Ritchey and colleagues shows that homelessness is a condition associated with increased daily hassles, decreased social support,
decreased health status, and increased adverse life events, all of which
ultimately are related to amplified depressive symptoms.[16] In short, the
homeless condition is a stressful and depressing one. We might intuitively conclude then, that higher rates of mental illness among this population are the natural result of the condition, not the cause of it.
Furthermore, the types of psychosocial measures mostly used to assess
mental illness cannot differentiate causal types.[17] The CES-D is the
most common measure of depression, but it cannot distinguish those
whose depression is the result of brain chemistry from those who are
depressed because of circumstantial factors (e.g., because they recently
have become homeless), nor can it discern whether a chemical imbal-
ance is genetic or is itself environmentally stimulated.[18]

Despite the precarious position of the mental illness explanation, it
remains convincing to both the general public and service providers, at
least insofar as the latter tends to focus resources on treating it.
Moreover, this is not simply a matter of problematic thinking about
homelessness, but these understandings form the basis of practice where
homelessness is engaged as a social problem. As we will discuss in
Chapters 8 and 9, this has engendered particularly problematic types of
responses from policymakers and service providers.

Another equally prominent and individualistic explanation for homelessness is addiction to drugs or alcohol. Over the last several decades, addiction has been increasingly approached from a disease perspective. While this has produced an institutionalized treatment model, it does not seem to have tempered the stigmatization of addiction among those who are homeless or other disfranchised groups. The general public continues to count addiction among the variety of bad choices made by the individual who is homeless, even in an era where the growing medicalization of addiction expectedly would reduce stigma. Instead, addiction seems to be held as a disease of celebrities and the upper classes and a bad choice of the poor, a reflection of their character. Alcohol and drug use clearly is prevalent among the homeless population.[19] Ritchey and colleagues found that over 50 percent of the individuals in their Birmingham sample reported that alcohol had "caused a problem in their life."[20] Further, nearly 30 percent of the respondents in their sample reported using drugs other than alcohol at least once in the previous month. National data from 2008 suggested 39 percent of those who were homeless in the shelters were "chronic substance users," whereas 59 percent were counted as such in the Birmingham metro area.[21] But accurately capturing rates of substance use is difficult. Self-reported measures of addiction, as with the case of mental illness, would expectedly tend to underestimate the real rates of substance use. Moreover, raw usage of substances is not the same as having a substance abuse problem; however, there is an implicit assumption lurking in questions about substance use in homeless research that seems to take for granted that any use by a person who is homeless is problematic.[22]

Stigmas attached to those who are homeless also might cause overestimation of addiction in more directly empirical measurements (e.g., behavioral observation), since those who are homeless and drinking will more readily be labeled addicts, regardless of whether they truly possess addictive symptoms. Addiction itself lacks definitional consensus; what differentiates use and addiction is contested and far from objective. Judgments of character about those who are homeless or the types of substances they use certainly color perceptions and ultimately the labeling process.[23] A person of high socioeconomic status who "unwinds" with a cocktail before dinner, wine with dinner, and a nightcap (not an uncommon drinking pattern) is not likely to be stigmatized, whereas a person who is homeless who drinks cheaper varieties of alcohol also to reduce stress likely will be labeled an addict. While addiction helps construct perceptions of those who are homeless, homelessness also helps construct perceptions of addiction.

Clearly addiction can be an obstacle to keeping or obtaining housing. The obvious logic is that money that could be used to house oneself is instead spent on drugs and alcohol. But we again are confronted with causal ambiguities. Dalton Conley notes that 82 percent of the respondents in his study reported increasing their substance use after becoming homeless.[24] While addiction is certainly an obstacle, particularly to one's getting off the streets once there, we cannot conclude that it causes homelessness, since it may often be the case that homelessness causes or at least exacerbates addiction.

A substantial portion of the general population uses illicit substances, but most do not become homeless.[25] This suggests that other factors are at work (e.g., poverty and the lack of affordable housing), or at least that these other factors must converge with addiction in order to cause homelessness. Furthermore, the patterns and nature of substance use among those who are homeless may not be significantly different from patterns of use in the general population, in that use seems largely related to self-medicating in both cases.[26] A substantial portion of the general population also uses legal substances, even prescribed narcotics to medicate themselves for reasons such as stress and depression. It would stand to reason, then, that there would be increased substance use among those who are homeless, since there is increased stress and depression among them.[27]

It is clear that mental illness and addiction are two popular conceptions that are conflated with homelessness. While these statistically are prevalent, research design and measurement problems cloud the issue, statistical limitations cannot specify causality, and it often is unclear what types of mental illness and substance use are being measured. But while staples in contemporary images of homelessness, the salience of mental illness and addiction as viewed from the perspective of those on the street are often overlooked. This is important, not only because it constitutes firsthand knowledge about homelessness, but also because even those focused on solving homelessness by addressing those pathologies suggest that "the first step is to admit you have a problem." But if those who are homeless generally and those on the street in particular reject those conceptions of homelessness, then it would seem we are at an impasse and moving past it first requires coming to an understanding of how those on the street see the world.[28]

Mental Illness and Addiction:
The Perspective of People on the Street

Although the qualitative nature of our research cannot resolve the varied methodological issues related to evaluating addiction and mental illness in the homeless population, our participants shed light on various problematic ways in which the pathologies of mental illness and addiction have become inextricably intertwined with the concept of homelessness. Generally, those on the street were not in outright denial of their particular pathologies but resisted those as total explanations, refusing to minimize structural factors.

Our interviews and observations produced a clear difference between those living on the street and those using the shelters with respect to the construction of homelessness as a pathology. Those who are street homeless resist the conceptualization of their situation as being defined by addiction or mental illness, whereas those in treatment programs overwhelmingly concede to it.[29] This is not to say that those on the street are in denial about their individual problems. Where appropriate, most readily admit having substance abuse problems and struggling with anger or depression. However, when it was suggested to them, for example, that addiction was the cause of their homelessness, or that addiction treatment was the solution, the typical response involved making concessions to addiction as a problem while still retaining the importance of structural issues in the discourse. That is, even when they would admit having a substance abuse problem, those on the street typically resisted or offset the causal implications of this with a structural consideration, most often related to work and economic opportunity. Potato Water was an admitted alcoholic but claimed to be a "functional alcoholic" largely on the grounds that he worked hard and as often as he could. He expanded this character defense to the rest of the men at Catchout:

> But still, this right here, sure there is a lot of cutting up and this and that, that goes on down here, but also this is a work block. This is where people … they don't come down here just to bum around. … I'll tell you one thing, let somebody be … standing down here holding up a sign or something like that. They're getting' run off, right quick. This is a work block; we work here. No, we don't have regular jobs, but all of us will go out and work.

Moreover, our data illustrate a focus on notions of retaining autonomy.[30] Hammer clearly expressed resistance to "their way" and concedes willingness only to work *with* the service providers and then only after he has some power and control in his own life, in the form of employment.

> I don't need nobody to tell me I got a alcohol problem or I got a drug problem. I know this. [But] your way might not be a solution for my problem. What is making me drink and get out here might be totally different circumstances than from what made you do it. Everybody can't see what I see. I can't see what you see. We are all different people. Different solution to different problems. They want to do something, then they should survey and find out how many people want to work. Start right now. How about: "Can I take you down here and get you a job?" [I would say,] "Yeah! Let's do that."

Autonomy and work were frequently connected. Like many others, Jeff expressed the sentiment that it was through his willingness to work that he felt entitled to retain autonomy, even the autonomy to stay on the street:

> I don't want all [those services]—I just want to work. You want to come around and work me like a Hebrew slave, I'll do the work, but just give me my money. You get my back, give me my money and leave me alone. Give me what I earn, and I'll worry about how I spend it. That's how I see it.

The primary concern with work and wages even when those on the street were willing to admit substance use reflects a disconnect between those on the street and the service providers' treatment programs, not to mention the widespread notion of homelessness as an addiction problem. Most important, this runs counter to the embedded logic of addiction treatment programs that steadfastly hold that anything less than a full admission of addiction as the root of one's problems constitutes denial and prohibits "getting well." Our experience was that few would deny that addiction was problematic for them and sometimes even a significant contributor to keeping them on the streets. But those on the street typically would refuse to allow this to be the sole issue. They just as steadfastly held to the idea that economic circumstances were primary. Catchout Corner, they would remind us, is a work block. "We come here to work, and what we need are jobs."

This was not the case among those people we interviewed who were staying in shelters. Certainly there is some selectivity operating. It is legitimate to assume that addiction is more likely to be a core problem for those people who are enrolled in addiction programs. Ideally, that is why they are there. Nonetheless, the attitudinal difference between those homeless who are sheltered and those on the street is notable.

The men in the shelters readily committed to the idea that addiction is the root cause of both their own homelessness and homelessness in general. In a test of sorts, we tried to steer conversations toward structural economic conditions. While there was sympathy for those explanations, it was interesting that, without fail, those in the shelter would return to the idea that their own choices and specifically their addiction were the cause of their homelessness. Statements on the subject typically would echo what one man said:

> Yeah, it's hard. You can't get a job that pays anything; you owe a lot of money. It's real easy to fall through the cracks. [pause] But I have to take responsibility for my own situation and actions. I made those choices [to drink or do drugs].

Several times during one interview in particular, if someone in the group spent too long talking about structural economic circumstances, another member would remind them to "take ownership."

While selectivity certainly is at work, whereby addiction programs recruit those with addiction problems, there seems also to be a socialization process. The typical Alcoholics Anonymous model of addiction treatment employed by the shelters requires the initial step of "admitting that you have a problem." Treatment cannot proceed without this admission. Structural explanations of homelessness threaten this notion, and so being in the shelters requires letting go of those standpoints. Vincent Lyon-Callo illustrates this from his work within a homeless shelter.[31] Our research confirms his from the other side. Those on the street, more often than not, tend to be people unwilling to let go of structural explanations for their situation.

Moreover, our participants directly call into question the issue of causality for both mental illness and addiction. Echoing Conley's study, our participants tended to report that their addictions had worsened or that they had developed addiction to new, harder drugs since becoming homeless.[32] Hard drugs, especially crack, are prevalent on the street, and drug dealers often sell off the same corners where those who are homeless congregate to catch work. Exposure to drugs is a condition of being homeless and seems to significantly contribute to the level and type of addiction.

As with addiction, some types of mental illness also are a likely outcome of living on the street, rather than a cause of it. Here, distinctions need to be made among types of mental illness. We can easily see how depression can result from being homeless. If any of us found ourselves suddenly living under a bridge, having lost our possessions, jobs, homes, cars, and in all likelihood most of our family and social ties, we likely would become depressed, probably even seriously so. But while homelessness cannot cause in a physiological sense more severe conditions than depression, such as schizophrenia, it certainly can exacerbate them. The symptoms of schizophrenia—delusions, paranoia, and so on—can be triggered by stressful situations, and few circumstances are as pervasively and continuously stressful as being homeless.

The delivery of services also is particularly problematic for people who are homeless with these sorts of debilitating mental conditions. For many, the effects of mental illness can be mitigated with medication, but those who are homeless encounter structural barriers to getting that medication and getting it consistently. In the first place, most cannot afford medication. But, additionally, access to services that might provide such medication require a person to think linearly. For many, being unable to think linearly is part and parcel of having a mental illness. To get services, one must consciously aim at the end of getting medication and then put in order the several steps needed to get it. Often this requires going to government agencies or other institutions such as shelters, which might assist, but for a person experiencing paranoia, and particularly that of the sort directed at institutions (such as, in this case, the university hospital), this is easier said than done. Even if one can successfully negotiate the institutional bureaucracy, taking the medication consistently and getting more medication when one's supply runs out thrusts the mentally ill person repeatedly into that linear system they might find difficult to negotiate.

The point here is twofold. The condition of being homeless can, in fact, trigger mental illness. For environmentally stimulated conditions, such as many cases of depression, this is self-evident. But for physiological conditions it also is true, as for example, the stressful nature of homelessness can exacerbate psychosis in those predisposed to it. Moreover, management of mental illness is structured such that it can be nearly impossible for a person who is mentally ill and homeless to get aid. Not only does the model of service provision require the person who is homeless to go to the services, but also it requires a series of ordered steps, forms, interviews, and so forth, which might be difficult for a person with mental illness to execute.[33] For the person who is mentally ill, getting off the streets is analogous to getting out of a straitjacket. A sane person is able to get out of a straitjacket; it simply requires that certain moves be done in a certain order. However, mentally ill people most often cannot order their thoughts and actions, and so the jacket can effectively restrain them. The environment of the streets and the nature of service institutions form a structural straitjacket for those who are homeless and mentally ill. In the end, the streets both can make you crazy and keep you that way:

> You got to be strong out here, mentally. I see people over time just going crazy. They're normal at first, and then after a while they just lose it. Like they're not there anymore. —*Motown*

> I feel bad for Marvin. There's a dozen of us real people right here for him to talk to, but he's got a dozen people talking in his head. I'm surprised he's staying around, since you guys are from [the university]. He hates [the university]. One time, he walked by here with an arm full of bricks and went over to one of those [university] buildings and started breaking their windows out. He said they were hitting a button in there that was making his arm hurt. —*Potato Water*

Since addiction and mental illness are not particular to the homeless population, they are insufficient explanations for the problem. While clearly these problems contribute, they are individual pathologies constrained by a variety of structural conditions, such as poverty.[34] Kathleen Arnold suggests that rates of mental illness and alcoholism have not increased (if one attenuates for changes in measurement), but rather that more of the mentally ill and the alcoholic are not housed.[35] At the very least, this speaks to the significance of the opportunity structure in which the variety of individual behaviors are carried out.

Social Structural Influences

Research into social structural factors influencing homelessness has been illuminating, although social responses tend to disregard or prove impotent in dealing with structural conditions such as pervasive economic inequality.

Although it sounds simplistic, homelessness is, in large part, a housing issue.[36] Todd Depastino writes, "For however it is imagined, the

American home remains an essential means for gaining access, belonging, inclusion, and power."[37] We have witnessed a decrease in available low-income housing since the early 1970s.[38] During the 1980s the Reagan administration cut the budget of the federal agency HUD (Housing and Urban Development) by 80 percent, and in 1985 there were only half as many low-income houses as there were low-income families.[39] Conley notes that the process of obtaining available housing aid is plagued with bureaucratic complexity, often insurmountable for those homeless individuals who might lack government identification and, we would add, the skills to negotiate complex bureaucracies.[40]

Because increases in homelessness coincide with economic downturns, it is reasonable to conclude that lack of employment opportunities is an important consideration.[41] Since the early 1970s, corporations in the United States have been outsourcing manufacturing jobs to other countries. In earlier time periods the manufacturing industry propelled many unskilled, uneducated workers into the middle-class, but, at this writing, there is a deficit of such jobs. Furthermore, the wages in the United States are not keeping pace with inflation, meaning that workers have been earning less in real dollars.[42]

Homelessness often is precipitated by costs associated with the health-care and criminal justice institutions.[43] For example, people without health insurance who suffer an injury or illness may incur costs that they cannot afford; these costs may push them into an economic crisis in which they lose their home, transportation, and job. Likewise, even minor encounters with the legal system often carry fines, or time in jail, and can have similar consequences.[44]

The health-care and criminal justice systems become increasingly problematic obstacles once an individual becomes homeless, since contact with them becomes more frequent.[45] Individuals who are homeless are more likely to become sick as a result of their living conditions or injured because of the type of work they perform. Exacerbating the latter, the informal nature of their employment leaves those who are homeless little recourse for work-related injuries. They are also more likely to be arrested for misdemeanor crimes such as vagrancy, because they are forced to do private things in public spaces.[46] Since they are often unable to pay the fines for these, arrests they accumulate debt in the court system.

Lack of basic facilities presents another obstacle to overcome. Those who are homeless often mention that the inability to bathe and have clean clothes is in large part what prevents them from getting a job or housing. As Potato Water said in his first interview with us, "Look at me, man. ... I'm scruffy as hell. But I worked a couple days last week [implying he did not get a chance to clean up]. But I got my razor, and I'm going over to the library today, hopefully [where he intended to shave and wash up]." Similarly, Conley writes, "One knowledgeable and articulate respondent waved his hand over himself and proclaimed, 'No one will rent to someone looking like this.'"[47]

Even when focused primarily on mental illness and addiction, most research pays at least some attention to structural conditions that predicate homelessness. But public sentiment, government policy, and service provision alike have continued to operate on the premise of homelessness as an individual pathology.[48] Moreover, the individual pathology approach is not exclusive to public and political circles. A glaring academic example is Christopher Jencks's book *The Homeless*. Explaining his use of census data, Jencks writes, "Living with the homeless is both disagreeable and dangerous, so only the adventurous want to do it."[49] Apparently lacking a sufficient sense of adventure, Jencks uses distanced, secondary data analysis as his evidence and therefore largely ignores political and economic structure. He writes, "If no one drank, took drugs, lost contact with reality, or messed up at work, homelessness would be rare."[50] Later, he gives a nod to political-economic structure, but clearly downplays its importance: "Stable housing and daily work might reduce alcohol and drug consumption a little and might make some mentally ill a little saner, but they will not work miracles."[51]

Jencks and others employing the social-deviant explanation of homelessness—in addition to typically employing research methods that keep them distant from actual people who are homeless—also miss a crucial overarching fallacy that destabilizes such a position. If homelessness is the result of individual moral bankruptcy and the numbers of those who are homeless have increased drastically, we would have to conclude that there simply are more bad people in the world.[52] This makes precious little sense, even if we are willing to put out of our minds the nagging correlation between increasing structural inequality and rising homelessness.

Jobs, Justice, Family, and Health: Structured Life Chances of People on the Street

The microlevel observational framework of ethnographic data like ours still produces structural insights, though these need to be qualified as the experience of individuals within particular structures rather than observations of macrostructure itself (something that requires data collected at a different level of scale). Nonetheless, insofar as individuals live in reciprocity with social structures, the experiences of our participants yielded insights into the structural conditions of homelessness.

Work and Economy

The 1970s saw rises in homelessness, at about the same time as the manufacturing sector began to shrink and wages in real dollars began to decline. These trends continued into the 2000s, and for many of the poor employment is forever a tenuous prospect. This was clear for many of our participants who lived on the street. James's story was particularly representative:

> I had two jobs. One a warehouse ... and the other I was working at [a fast food restaurant]. ... I was [within] walking distance from both jobs, couldn't beat that with a stick. [One] folded, [the other] couldn't handle my bills, so I came downtown, and I got another good job doing construction work. I'm a certified cement finisher. So I'm working for a cement company over on Southside. I get me a hotel room, trying to save up some money again to get me another place, [and then] they fold. I went to [the shelter]; that wasn't going to get it. So I heard about some of the guys talking about living on the street.

One of the most broadly popular concepts of homelessness among the lay public is that they are lazy people who do not want to work. Statistics disprove this, and in the course of our research, we came to find it utterly laughable. In an interview with two homelessness researchers in Birmingham, they noted that, in a 1995 survey, the average person who was homeless worked thirty hours a week.[53] "[High rates of depression] make that statistic even more startling," one added. Many people find getting up for work everyday difficult enough. To work at the kinds of jobs that those on the street do, while living in those conditions, is nearly inconceivable to most of "us." When work trucks pulled up to Catchout Corner, there was a startling rush to get the job. Before we would even know what was happening, a stampede of men would literally be running toward a potential employer. The laziness concept was overturned early.

On hearing that those who are homeless actually work, most people inevitably ask, "Then why are they still homeless." The answer partly lies in the nature of the work and the two unsatisfactory ways they can get it: through a temp service, or off the corner on their own. The typical process for the temporary labor services is as follows: Show up at five-thirty in the morning to enter your name in the lottery. *If* your name is drawn at seven-thirty, then you get to work that day (it is not uncommon that there are more workers than jobs). You are taken by van to the job site and only then are you "on the clock." This means that you have three hours invested in the day before you have even made a dime. Moreover, you often are charged five dollars for transportation and a sack lunch. So by the time you begin to get paid, you actually are five dollars in the hole. Because of the demand, jobs typically pay minimum wage. Without a bank account, checks are cashed for an additional fee. Most reports are that if you get work three out of five days, you have had a good week. Estimates suggest an average net pay of thirty dollars a day at best, not quite enough for a single night at the cheapest single-occupancy hotel, which cost thirty-five dollars (at the time of this writing).

To avoid this exploitation—and most of those on the street consciously see it as exploitation and avoid it at all costs—independent work blocks like Catchout have emerged. While illegal immigrants have recently brought this method of employment back into the national spotlight, those who are poor and homeless have been working this way for decades, most famously in the labor camps of the Great Depression.

Though they claim to make more money by working independently, we were not sure if this was the case. In the end, while their hourly pay was greater, the jobs were often shorter. They retain more control over the process in some ways but also face additional risks. Many had stories about being physically assaulted by people who had picked them up for work.

Almost all of those who regularly caught work at the Corner got shorted on their pay at the end of the day and sometimes got stiffed altogether:

> A guy will pick you up on Monday and say he's got five days of work and that he'll pay you on Friday. So you work all week and then on Friday, he never shows to pick you up. I stopped doing that. You gotta pay me everyday. —*Potato Water*

Those who caught work off the Corner would talk often about being left in other parts of town at the end of the day and not taken back to Catchout Corner after the job was done.

The point is that those who are homeless are victimized in their attempts to work, whether legally exploited by temporary labor services or stolen from and physically assaulted when they gain jobs on their own. Moreover, those who are homeless have little recourse when they are victimized, since the police and public generally repudiate them, often quite openly. This was true not only when victimized by the strangers who picked them up for odd jobs, but also when they worked for the temp services. They had little ability to ensure fair treatment in disputes about pay, hours, job safety, and the like. We heard stories, for example, about people not getting their checks from the temp service and then being banned from the premises and sometimes escorted out by police for arguing with the staff. This of course meant they likely would never get any money they were owed.

Perhaps the most common legal way to earn extra money is to sell blood plasma.[54] At this writing, donations could be made twice a week for a total of forty dollars (fifteen for the first donation and twenty-five for the second). Almost all of those on the street "donate" twice a week, every week, something that eventually will have ramifications for their health, particularly in light of the fact that their diets nutritionally cannot sustain this taxing practice. Lawton (one of our participants) drew out the irony, "These hospitals around here couldn't operate without a blood supply. The homeless have no health care, but they supply the blood for these hospitals. Birmingham is *literally* living on the blood of the homeless."

Hustling is another way that those who are homeless work. Most people do not consider it a job, but it has all the essential characteristics. It takes time, energy, talent, and produces a profit. By and large those on the street did not engage in serious criminal activity. They sometimes escorted customers to drug dealers or ran drugs from the dealers to customer's cars, but most did not, and the dealers themselves were not homeless. More often, those on the street scavenged and sold things they found or engaged in minor cons. For example, when the Olympics were in Atlanta in 1996, some soccer games were played in Birmingham. As is typical of local governments around the country, the city of Birmingham issued one-way bus tickets to any of those on the street who would take them. While this predated our study, we asked them about it. "Yeah, most of us just took them down to the bus station and sold them. Got about forty dollars," Potato Water recounted.

Another time, a local music festival staged in a lot adjacent to Catchout Corner provided opportunity to make some money. Part of the field was designated as free parking for the concertgoers, so some of the men from Catchout decided to charge five dollars to all the entering cars. The police eventually responded to complaints from concertgoers who figured out the scam. Some of the men from the Corner got away, while others had to return the money to complainants.

Whether formal or informal, legal or illegal, those who are street homeless engage in various forms of work. But the type of work that they do exposes them to various risks. The physical nature of the work exacerbates poor dietary practices, and leads often to injuries, which are inadequately treated. The exploitative nature of the labor services mean many are unwilling to use them and therefore face being victimized physically or financially by strangers offering jobs. Important here is that work is the experience of our participants in the economy. In other words, the disadvantages that they face as they try to earn a living are structured disadvantages related to their disfranchised social position.

Crime and Polity

Entrance into homelessness is predicated largely by the collusion of structural conditions and acute events. For example, someone who has always been poor encounters some sort of life crisis with which they cannot cope given their environment and social position. Encounters with the criminal justice system account for a significant portion of these acute events. Getting put in jail, even for relatively minor offenses is expensive in a variety of ways. Even when attorneys are provided, court costs and fines can be difficult to pay, and when unresolved, they eventually result in more jail time and collateral damage to one's life. Spending time in jail usually means losing your job.

One of our radical advocates, Ralph, was a director for a drug-testing program that served as an alternative to incarceration. Ralph was particularly critical of the criminal justice system and the way it was structured. He noted that the criminal justice system was a fractionalized, "Cartesian" system, which was extraordinarily difficult for poor people without resources or institutional savvy to negotiate:[55]

> By Cartesian I mean it is based on rules, it's based on timetables, and it's based on a supposedly logical way of dispensing this concept called justice. And it worked to some extent a long time ago, they tell me. Right now all I see is a broken, broken, desperately broken attempt at managing a whole variety of very needy, poor folks. It's not a system, let's get that straight from the word *go*. It's not a criminal justice *system*. It's a whole variety of about five, six, seven different players and offices, some elected and some not, with separate budgets. The only person that really sees it as a system is the poor person that is trapped in it.

Another radical homeless advocate would make the connections between the criminal justice system and homelessness even more explicit. "Another thing that keeps people homeless is the police, the criminal justice system, [or rather] the criminal injustice system."

For many of our participants, encounters with the criminal justice system represented an acute event that had a negative impact on their ability to work, and in some cases precipitated their entrance into homelessness itself. Jeff was the driver of a car when his friends stole a case of beer. They were arrested, and since he was poor, even before he was homeless, he could not pay the fines and as a result spent sixty days in jail. During his short incarceration he lost his job, his apartment, and his car. In a city without reliable public transportation, all of these must be maintained at the same time. Like juggling three balls, if one loses their home, job, *or* car, they risk losing all of them.

Jeff had been on the streets for seven years since his short incarceration; one might say that his sixty-day punishment turned into an indeterminably long sentence of homelessness in light of the structural disadvantages he faced when he was arrested. A hard worker, after his release he managed to get steady, informal jobs, sometimes for consecutive months, and by the time of this writing, had worked his way into living in a shabby, single-room occupancy hotel. For him, the criminal justice system represents an acute event that, when combined with a structural position such as poverty, causes homelessness. As one local researcher noted in an interview, "[If you're poor] and something bad happens to you, the choices that you have to deal with it are likely to be fewer in number [compared with a wealthier individual]."

Once someone becomes homeless, breaking the law is nearly impossible to avoid. In Chapter 1 we discussed the historical emergence of vagrancy laws and the effective criminalization of being homeless. Lessons from our fieldwork confirm that being homeless is basically equivalent to being vagrant and naturally entails the violation of all sorts of "quality of life" ordinances.[56] For a person who is homeless to stay on private property is trespassing, while for them to stay on public property is vagrancy. They literally cannot be homeless without breaking one law or another. Additionally, since most cities do not have public restrooms, those who are homeless are forced to urinate and defecate in public places. Citations for this carry fines that they cannot pay. In turn, these unpaid fines escalate and eventually result in warrants and more jail time. Those who are homeless also are at greater risk for arrest for public intoxication. Whereas the general public is able to confine their substance use to private homes and appropriate businesses, those who are homeless are exposed when carrying out these same behaviors.[57] Public intoxication perhaps was the most frequent offense among our participants. Even when not committing a crime, those on the street reported that they were detained and questioned by the police on a fairly regular basis. Ed complained:

> I don't have no problem out here with any of the homeless guys or anyone else but the police. The police will come down to your camp and harass you, shine their light in your eyes and ask you, "What are you doing?" [I feel like saying,] "What do you think I'm doing—it's two in the morning. I'm sleeping." You're just trying to sleep so you can get up and go to work in the morning.

While we have already talked about how those who are homeless are put at risk in the process of getting work, they frequently are also the victims of street crime. When we first met Potato Water, he had recently been mugged. "I was over by the park, and two guys came up to me. No words were spoken. One hit me in the head with a bottle. The other was in my pocket before I hit the ground. They got three dollars." Getting one's possessions stolen was common, since their storage spaces, often in urban camps, cannot be very well secured. James noted that his car washing supplies are frequently stolen, directly affecting the main type of work that he does. But even when they are victims of crime, those who are homeless get little assistance from the police, and most would not bother trying. More than that, the city routinely cleans out urban camps, often trashing the possessions that are stored there.

Often by virtue of being homeless, those on the street have broken the law, and their inability to afford the penalties results in the escalation of originally minor offenses. Complicating this cycle is the fact that having open warrants keeps many people who are homeless from seeking legitimate jobs, homes, and even enrollment in treatment programs. Among our participants, several refused to be on camera for the explicit reason that they had open warrants and did not want to be found. For these people, staying out of jail basically means staying on the streets.

In addition to his scathing critique about the current system, Ralph suggested an alternative approach focused on building community relationships in contrast to the punitive process that he believed only exacerbated poverty and crime:

> There needs to be that dialogue. Some of the community courts are starting to develop that in some of the areas of the country where you have folks that can get services right there at court. Not let's go

to court to go to prison, [but] let's go to court for help. Imagine that! What a concept! Let's go to court for help where they are given lots of services, where they are getting medication, getting referrals, treatment, and also the folks that are pressing charges [are] able to sit down and mediate some solutions. And those are the kind of things that need to be looked at in terms of different ways of doing business. We have to redefine this old stuff.

The notion of community and dialogue was explicitly addressed by all of our radical participants. Their criticism was directed at power structures, including the government and service providers. Community for radicals like Ralph and Lawton is measured by one's relationships with the most marginalized, not by the extent to which one is assimilated into the dominant social structure. That is, for them, relationships with those who are homeless was not conditioned by the extent to which those on the street were willing to conform or reassimilate, but based on notions of their humanity in and of itself (see also Chapters 8 and 9).

Many individuals, including those who are homeless, face immense disadvantage exacerbated by both the complexity and the formalized, callous nature of the immensely bureaucratic criminal justice system. Ultimately what Ralph and others are calling for is a more humane system capable of interactions beyond the routine execution of rules and procedures. The diversity of problems and needs in society is not well matched with a system that cannot fluidly adapt to meet those challenges (see also Chapter 11).

Family and Culture

Most of our participants had a great deal of family strain in their biographies.[58] While some of those on the street maintained contact with their families, the majority of them had tumultuous childhood experiences. Many felt abandoned by their families, though they usually would simultaneously blame themselves for the discord.

Earnest was a dignified elder at Catchout Corner. One day he appeared agitated and insisted on doing a filmed interview, and so he and Wasserman went away from the group to do it.[59] It seemed that something family-related precipitated his state. Our field notes recorded the emotion that surrounded his near-weeping interview:

At the end of the interview, I asked Earnest what else he wanted to say. He thought for a second and he said, "Tell 'em, if I had a family member like this or that lived out here, I would help them out, you tell him that. If I had a house, I would help them out. You tell him that." Tears were coming down his face; it was a pretty powerful experience because a lot of the time, these guys have a lot of emotions inside of them, but they can't let them out because you have to act tough on the street.

Other difficult childhood experiences were couched in stories intended to be humorous. Consistent with Timothy Pippert's study, we found that while some of our participants maintained contact with their families of origin, most had extremely strained, and often nonexistent, relationships with them, clearly feeling more at home with their street family.[60] Matty talked about how tough his father was growing up, but the details of the story betray more than just a strict upbringing. He never expounded on the effects of his childhood, tending to be more private and stoic, but stories such as this were common, though, as with Matty, they were not usually psychoanalyzed by the people themselves:

> Matty told a story about how his Dad, whom he referred to as his "sperm donor," had once challenged his brother and him to see who could drink the most shots of tequila and make it to the mailbox and back. Matty lost, and his brother subsequently took him into the garage and tattooed Matty's name onto his shoulder. To add insult to injury, his own brother spelled his name wrong (his name has been changed here, but the spelling of his homemade tattoo indeed did not match the way he spells his real name).—*Field notes*

Many of our participants were estranged from their families in some way. A man nicknamed Waffle House described at length that his family did not want him around, alluding to the fact that his addiction had caused a rift. Even when they maintained some contact with their families, and even when they had decidedly amicable relationships, there usually were stories of past conflict. Potato Water described how the pastor kicked him out of the local church, and, in turn, his religious father kicked him out of the house. When he was fourteen, his parents dropped him off at the YMCA (Young Men's Christian Association). This did not launch his extended stay on the street because an aunt picked him up about a week later, and he lived with her until he joined the military at age seventeen. Nonetheless, this type of family strain was common. He still talked to his family on holidays and had visited them a few times, but as he explained, "We just don't see eye-to-eye on things.

They're real religious, their church is kind of like a cult, and that's fine for them, but it's not me."

In addition to pervasive, general family strain and dysfunction, one very prominent kind of acute stress was the death of a loved one. As noted in Chapter 1, Matty was a highly functional person, having built an impressive urban camp with a variety of amenities. He also had a bachelor's degree in agriculture. These sorts of facts naturally beg questions about how he became homeless. While he never talked about it, others told us that his wife and infant daughter had been killed in a car accident and that it had basically sent him over the edge. As far as we could tell, he had no contact with other family members.

Wayne, who lived in the same camp as Matty, had a similar story. He said he had become homeless after his father and mother died within a few months of each other. He noted with some rare emotion in his voice that he had been particularly close to his father. "I just kind of couldn't deal with it anymore. I started coming out here and eventually just stayed." He admitted that he drank, referring to it as an "elbow problem," and that he had used drugs in his adolescence, but had largely stopped except for marijuana. These were habits at the very least exacerbated by the death of his loved ones. Similarly, Ed lived under a bridge not far away from Matty and Wayne. "My wife died, and I just started drinking, trying to grieve it all out," he explained.

These same types of stories were repeated over and over.[61] Lawton put these stories in a broader cultural context and placed structure as a pervasive shared condition of the individual stories of family background:

> Most American males do not know how to do anything in crisis except get drunk or get high. And so some kind of death, tragedy, or difficulty, then they get drunk or start using drugs. Then they are caught, and they never deal with the root problem. And the root problem is usually some sort of major injustice.

Often, family strains were embedded in poverty. Nearly all of our participants on the street grew up poor.[62] A large proportion of them lived in government housing, others in extremely indigent neighborhoods. This environment can add to family strain and break down of social support, particularly in light of the fact that regulations exist about who and how many can live in each unit of government housing. For some, even if their families would have been willing to house them, doing so meant risking losing their subsidized home altogether. Hammer angrily noted the disadvantages of his childhood in light of the idea that homelessness was the result of bad choices:

Just 'cause they got a good job, wear all suits and shit, and smell all Frenchey like a whore and shit, you looking good and got your family taken care of, your parents brought you up right, and you was able to go to school and get an education. Lot of us didn't have that opportunity. I was on the street when I was nine years old and shit and trying to survive. Didn't have nothin'. Damn, give a man something to try to fight for. Everybody wasn't fortunate enough to have good parents. You know, all of us didn't make bad decisions.

A discussion of childhood with a man named J. K., who had established a well-organized camp under an interstate viaduct, yielded for us some very personal insights. J. K. grew up in a rural area in a house with dirt floors and no running water. It occurred to us that the trials of living on the street are relative. For those of us who grew up in middle-class homes, living under a bridge is a radical departure from daily life, an existence deprived of countless comforts that we take for granted. For J. K., the distance between that bridge and normal life was a lot shorter.

Health and the Body

It will come as no surprise that those who are homeless experience disproportionately more health problems than the average person. Nutrition, lack of access to health care, exposure to the elements, and problematic health behaviors all contribute to this. Of course, these are endemic to poverty in general, but those on the street face quite extreme health disadvantages. As noted, most of those who are homeless work, but the types of work that they do are physically taxing, something compounded by inadequate nutrition. Most of them get injured on jobs with some degree of regularity, but have no recourse since they work under the table.

Russ told me that his homelessness resulted from an injury sustained on the job. He worked at a tree-cutting place and fell three stories off a ladder. He is working toward a settlement and workers comp. In the meantime he stays at a house with a man whose church pays him a couple hundred dollars a month to house someone. —*Field notes*

The temporary labor services are no solution, since the work is equally difficult and the sack lunch provided (for a fee) is calorically deficient for the types of work being performed. Moreover, there is some speculation that these agencies actually give preference to people who have been drinking or who they know will test positive for substances so that in the event of an injury, the company will not have any liability. Of course, we have no way to substantiate this.

Chronic illnesses also are prevalent and can complicate injuries. For example, many of those on the street reported having diabetes, and injured diabetics do not heal well. A man named Lockett once showed us his cut-up knee, saying that he had been injured on a job.

They wanted to take me to the hospital, but I was like no-o-o-o. Just give me my money. I'm diabetic so it's hard for it to heal, but it's doing okay. The doctor told me that if I was going to drink, then I should just not take my medicine so that's what I do. I guess I'm lucky to be alive, but God is good.

Acute illnesses are common as well. Exposure during the winter means almost everyone on the street nearly always has flulike symptoms during the colder months. It became our habit during the colder months to bring over-the-counter cold medicines, and it was always a popular donation. Injuries and illness are also problematic because they interfere with one's ability to work. Motown badly hurt his foot once and was out of work for several weeks. While the others on the Corner helped him to some extent, his circumstances became fairly dire, and his mood reflected it.

Other indicators suggest ongoing problems, particularly nutritional ones. When the men would take off their shoes, their feet would betray their hard lives: yellowed toenails that sat up on their toes like they were about to fall off, calluses, and blisters. Their feet were the most obvious casualties of hard work and poor diets. While housing-first programs (see Chapter 9) are contested on a variety of grounds, one area where they seem to have demonstrably positive outcomes is related to physical health; homeless individuals who have been discharged from hospitals directly into supported housing had a fairly dramatic reduction in hospital visits.[63]

To Conclude with a Warning

The structure/agency debate is fundamental to the social sciences. Most admit that social life is made up in some part of each one, but just how much potency individual choices have amid clearly powerful structural forces remains contested. For the purposes of this chapter, we have confined our discussion to this dichotomy, exploring individualist notions of disease in the form of mental illness and addiction, on the one hand, and, on the other, structural conditions in the form of economy (work), polity (criminal justice), and culture (family), along with a discussion of how the physical bodies of those who are homeless are contextualized by structural health disadvantages. While social structural conditions cause or exacerbate disadvantages for those who are poor and homeless, it is crucial not to automatically propose social structural fixes such as the remediation of economic inequalities as though that is deductively entailed by recognition of the significance of structure. The social sciences tend to do so. That is, they remain trapped in the traditional confines of the structure/ agency dichotomy, where prioritizing agency leads to blaming the victim and conversely entails social structural repairs. But these only replace the preeminence of institutional authority from local governments or service programs (see Chapters 8 and 9) with the structural authority of broader social programs and do not therefore speak to liberation of the oppressed, only to a more comfortable life of oppression.

We later will propose a way out of this dichotomy (see Chapters 7 and 11). For now, suffice it to say that structural conditions clearly predicate homelessness, but, without attention to ways of working with those who are oppressed as creative individuals, social structural fixes can also be problematic.

Notes

1. Rowe, in *Crossing the Border*, also gives a clear discussion of this issue.

2. See Mahoney, "Substance Abuse Contributes to Homelessness."

3. Arnold, *Homelessness, Citizenship and Identity*; Depastino, *Citizen Hobo*; Gibson, *Securing the Spectacular City*; Hopper, *Reckoning with the Homeless*; Lyon-Callo, "Medicalizing Homelessness"; Lyon-Callo, *Inequality, Poverty, and Neoliberal Governance*; Snow and Anderson, *Down on Their Luck*.

4. Conley, "Getting It Together"; Jencks, *The Homeless*; LaGory et al., "Depression Among the Homeless"; Rossi et al., *The Condition of the Homeless in Chicago*; Shlay and Rossi, "Social Science Research and Contemporary Studies of Homelessness"; Snow et al., "The Myth of Pervasive Mental Illness Among the Homeless."

5. Derived from Ritchey et al., Raw Homeless Data Set from a Population in Birmingham, AL; on the CES-D, a score of sixteen or greater indicates clinical depression.

6. That is, it is widely asserted that about a third of those who are homeless have a mental illness but do not report it; estimates for Birmingham reflecting the roughly one-third reporting mental illness were derived from Ritchey et al., Raw Homeless Data Set from a Population in Birmingham, AL.

7. Department of Housing and Urban Development, *The Third Annual Homeless Assessment Report to Congress*; Alabama Governor's Statewide Interagency Council on Homelessness, *Homelessness in Alabama*.

8. Arnold, *Homelessness, Citizenship and Identity*; see also Failer, *Who Qualifies for Rights?*

9. Baer et al., *Medical Anthropology and the World System*, 2nd ed; Mathieu, "The Medicalization of Homelessness and the Theater of Repression"; Mossman, "Deinstitutionalization, Homelessness, and the Myth of Psychiatric Abandonment."

10. Mathieu, "The Medicalization of Homelessness and the Theater of Repression."

11. Arnold, *Homelessness, Citizenship and Identity*.

12. Ibid., p. 92.

13. Mathieu, "The Medicalization of Homelessness and the Theater of Repression"; Snow and Anderson, "Identity Work Among the Homeless"; Rowe, *Crossing the Border.*

14. Liebow, *Tell Them Who I Am*; Mathieu, "The Medicalization of Homelessness and the Theater of Repression"; Snow and Anderson, "Identity Work Among the Homeless."

15. LaGory et al., "Depression Among the Homeless"; Mathieu, "The Medicalization of Homelessness and the Theater of Repression"; Mossman, "Deinstitutionalization, Homelessness, and the Myth of Psychiatric Abandonment"; Snow et al., "The Myth of Pervasive Mental Illness Among the Homeless."

16. Derived from Ritchey et al., Raw Homeless Data Set from a Population in Birmingham, AL.

17. Horwitz, *Creating Mental Illness.*

18. While discussions of causes of mental illness often neatly categorize them as either biogenetic or environmentally caused (even when diagnostic criteria cannot distinguish the two because symptoms are utilized to make diagnoses), these can be related. in that our bodies have a biological reaction to environment; see also Horwitz, *Creating Mental Illness.*

19. Conley, "Getting It Together"; Rossi, *Down and Out in America*; Shlay and Rossi, "Social Science Research and Contemporary Studies of Homelessness."

20. Derived from Ritchey et al., Raw Homeless Data Set from a Population in Birmingham, AL.

21. See Department of Housing and Urban Development, *The Third Annual Homeless Assessment Report to Congress*; Alabama Governor's Statewide Interagency Council on Homelessness, *Homelessness in Alabama*; see also Burt's suggestion, in *Over the Edge*, that hard drugs, especially crack, were an underlying cause of increases during the 1980s.

22. The question by Ritchey et al. concerning whether alcohol had caused a problem in one's life is a step toward differentiating problematic versus "ordinary" alcohol use, but its success turns on what constitutes a problem in the eyes of the respondent (serious or minor) and whether having had problems caused by alcohol use necessarily constitutes addiction (versus isolated problems caused by alcohol). Still, their measure will capture those who are genuinely addicted and for whom homelessness is caused by alcohol use, though it likely will capture some for whom this is not the case, which should therefore inform future research.

23. Baer et al., *Medical Anthropology and the World System*, 2nd ed.

24. Conley, "Getting It Together"; see also Arnold, *Homelessness, Citizenship and Identity*.

25. The nationwide estimates from the National Survey on Drug Use and Health (NSDUH) show that over 8 percent of the nationwide population twelve and over "admit" to using some form of an illicit drug. The average for prescription drugs is 11.3 prescriptions per individual each year nationwide.

26. Baer et al., *Medical Anthropology and the World System*, 2nd ed.; Rowe, *Crossing the Border*; Snow and Anderson, *Down on Their Luck*.

27. LaGory et al., "Depression Among the Homeless"; Rossi, *Down and Out in America*.

28. This echoes approaches emerging in the early 2000s to addiction generally and homelessness in particular called motivational engagement, whereby one first figures out how a person sees the world and his or her addiction, what motivates him or her, and so on, and then works from there. We are concerned that some versions of motivational engagement do not reflect a sincere attempt to work dialogically with the "client" (see discussion of Paulo Freire in Chapter 11), but rather just more sophisticated approaches at persuasion and manipulation whereby a person is more slowly and kindly coerced into ultimately accepting the paradigm of the treatment model (see Chapter 9).

29. Lyon-Callo, "Medicalizing Homelessness"; Lyon-Callo, *Inequality, Poverty, and Neoliberal Governance*.

30. See also Dordick, *Something Left to Lose*; see Hoffman and Coffey, "Dignity and Indignation," for a discussion of the perceptions of those who are homeless of problematic power differentials in the shelter.

31. Lyon-Callo, "Medicalizing Homelessness."

32. Conley, "Getting It Together."

33. See Rowe, *Crossing the Border*, for a discussion of outreach workers and their encounters with the street homeless; also, Failer, in *Who Qualifies for Rights?*, does a good job covering the depth of mental illness issues.

34. Hopper and Baumohl note, in "Held in Abeyance," that social structural discussions need not oppose the existence of individual pathologies.

35. Arnold, *Homelessness, Citizenship and Identity*.

36. Ibid.; also, Feldman, *Citizens Without Shelter*; Hopper, *Reckoning with the Homeless*; Mathieu, "The Medicalization of Homelessness and the Theater of Repression"; Moore et al., "The Politics of Homelessness"; Rossi, *Down and Out in America*; Shlay and Rossi, "Social Science Research and Contemporary Studies of Homelessness."

37. Depastino, *Citizen Hobo*, p. 271.

38. Arnold, *Homelessness, Citizenship and Identity*; Axelson and Dail, "The Changing Character of Homelessness in the United States"; Burt, *Over the Edge*; Rossi, *Down and Out in America*; Shlay and Rossi, "Social Science Research and Contemporary Studies of Homelessness."

39. Axelson and Dail, "The Changing Character of Homelessness in the United States"; Mathieu, "The Medicalization of Homelessness and the Theater of Repression"; Moore et al., "The Politics of Homelessness."

40. Conley, "Getting It Together"; see also Gibson, *Securing the Spectacular City*.

41. Arnold, *Homelessness, Citizenship and Identity*; Mathieu, "The Medicalization of Homelessness and the Theater of Repression."

42. Bernstein, "Wages Picture."

43. Arnold, *Homelessness, Citizenship and Identity*; Hopper, *Reckoning with the Homeless*.

44. Ibid.

45. Arnold, *Homelessness, Citizenship and Identity*.

46. Ibid.; also Gibson, *Securing the Spectacular City*; Waldron, "Homelessness and Community."

47. Conley, "Getting It Together," p. 32; see also Gibson's discussion, in *Securing the Spectacular City*, of the need for cities to provide public hygiene centers.

48. Arnold, *Homelessness, Citizenship and Identity*; Hopper, *Reckoning with the Homeless*; Marcus, *Where Have All the Homeless Gone?*; Lyon-Callo, "Medicalizing Homelessness"; Lyon-Callo, *Inequality, Poverty, and Neoliberal Governance*; Rossi, *Down and Out in America*; Snow and Anderson, *Down on Their Luck*.

49. Jencks, *The Homeless*, p. 44.

50. Ibid., p. 47.

51. Ibid., p. 121.

52. Arnold also makes this point in *Homelessness, Citizenship and Identity*.

53. Data from Ritchey et al., Raw Homeless Data Set from a Population in Birmingham, AL.

54. Snow and Anderson discuss this as well, in *Down on Their Luck*.

55. See Chapter 8 for more discussion of the criminal justice system.

56. See also Kusmer, *Down and Out on the Road*; Schweik, *The Ugly Laws*.

57. See Waldron, "Homelessness and Community," for a discussion of homelessness as private life forced into the public sphere.

58. See also Pippert, *Road Dogs and Loners*.

59. As noted, the camera often served as a welcomed outlet for our participants to vocalize their experiences and frustrations.

60. Pippert, *Road Dogs and Loners*.

61. See also ibid.

62. See Burt, *Over the Edge*, for poverty rates predicting homelessness in the 1980s.

63. Sadowski et al., "Effect of a Housing and Case Management Program on Emergency Department Visits and Hospitalizations Among Chronically Ill Homeless Adults"; see also Kertesz and Weiner, "Housing the Chronically Homeless."

5

Urban Space and Relations on the Street

Our first research insight was that people experiencing homeless are everywhere (see Chapter 1). Of course, we all see the eccentric people who yell at phantoms and who look decidedly like the homeless image we have in our minds. These people force themselves into our sight, but are ultimately a very small proportion of those who are homeless. Such "tragic caricatures of homelessness" are not representative of the hundreds or even thousands of people who are homeless living invisibly within our midst.[1] How can we not be noticing? The answer has to do with the way that environments are engineered physically and socially to prevent such recognition.[2]

Concrete Islands: Homelessness and New Urbanism

In the novel *Concrete Island* by J. G. Ballard, an ordinary businessman is driving along a busy road, having explicitly ordinary thoughts, when he crashes through a retaining wall and finds himself marooned in a large drainage ditch between three busy city streets, a concrete island.[3] Due to injury and the inability of other drivers to see him—they ironically are as oblivious as he was before this crisis—he descends into madness while trapped in his "new" environment, a place that he used to drive by everyday without taking notice. Ballard's intention is to illuminate the ways in which urban ecology frames what we can see, our familiar environment, and by contrast obscures all sorts of residual spaces. The busy drivers are physically able to see into the ditch, but they have been conditioned not to notice. The crisis of the main character opens up worlds unseen to the rest of us caught up the humdrum of everyday life.

The connection to street homelessness is not difficult to see. Wasserman read Ballard's book around 1999, but it did not resonate until around 2003, when we were taking James from his camp on the north side of the city to a gas station on the south side so he could get carwash supplies. During our interview earlier that day, James had estimated there were between sixty and eighty people living around the tracks. We thought he surely had to be exaggerating. But as we crossed the bridge over the train tracks that delineate the north and south sides of the city, he began to point out the various camps we could see from the elevated vantage point. It was remarkable. We had driven and even walked over that bridge for years, but for some reason had never seen all of the tarps and tents of those people who lived on the banks of that locomotive river. It was as if they materialized right in front of us as James pointed them out.

In some ways, that those who are homeless remain relatively hidden is a mutually beneficial relationship. Society does not want to see people who are homeless, and most often people living on the street do not want to be seen. But the limits of the urban landscape and economic patterns of gentrification increasingly violate the symbiosis that emerged from postwar urban flight. As wealthier people repopulate urban areas, those who are homeless ever more often have their environments assaulted.

In this chapter we describe the environments in which those on the street live. The spaces that those who are street homeless claim for themselves reflect their strong sense of autonomy, a rugged individualism not unlike that of American icons in the old West. The environments they create for themselves also illuminate their relationships to one another and their sense of community.[4] But when it comes to their relationships with those who are not homeless—those returning from the suburbs to redeveloped city centers—the urban environment becomes a field of conflict on which those who are homeless nearly always lose.

Ironies of Urban Ecology

Sometimes insight is not the product of long reflection or intense thought but, rather, strikes like lightning if one is simply willing to allow their environment to work on their mind. Our first day in the field was one such experience. We have described those initial meetings with people who were homeless, but our initial immersion into the environment of the street was no less educational. In hindsight, it was a mistake to bring the camera on that first visit; it was presumptuous and additionally intrusive when our surprise arrival already was an intrusion. Since it clearly made the men nervous, Wasserman waited for the introductory conversations to wane and made himself and the camera scarce. He went up onto the train tracks that run just north of Catchout, intending to kill time and hopefully lessen the tension for Clair and the men from the Corner on whom we had just made the research equivalent of a cold call.

Wasserman began to take stock shots of the skyline, the empty field, the train tracks, graffiti-covered buildings, and so forth. By definition, stock shots lack significant meaning, and we had not anticipated finding much. But shooting film forces a person to directly engage what is in front of them, to reflect on what one sees in ways not explored by casual observation. Though it is something not often considered research in an academic sense, reflexively allowing the environment to work on one's thoughts can yield insight.

Wasserman set the camera directly on the rail of the train line and pulled the zoom back and then pushed it forward. As he watched through the viewfinder, a switch—a place where the tracks diverge— was coming in and out of the frame. This stimulated thoughts about the limited vision society tends to have of people, and particularly of those who are homeless. We like to look just at the switch, not the whole track. But the prehomeless identities and life stories of our participants are no less real than the fact that they presently are homeless. Identity in our culture is a rather static concept. Who someone is, or at least is recognized to be, becomes fixed by a presentist mentality. Our sense of reality is dictated by our cultural disposition toward the empirical, that is, what we can see in front of us. The past therefore is quasi-real at best because we have to remember or imagine it. So in addition to the way in which it is intensively stigmatized, one's identity as homeless eclipses all other biographical features because it is at the time the most visible feature of one's life course. While we talk about "life course" in the social sciences, our sense of identity tends to be very materialistic, that is, something that must be manifest in the present as a role. If as a culture we find our way to a genuinely life-course-driven perspective of the person, this might go far in moving away from the rigid and often devastating effects of stigmatizing those who are homeless specifically, but also for all sorts of disfranchised groups.

Trains have always provided a backdrop to homelessness. Train-riding hobo adventurers, "bums on the rod,"[5] have been replaced with people for whom homelessness is lived in a static location and results from economic disfranchisement, but the train is still there. The practical reason is that the train company owns the property around the tracks, but it is too large an area to be policed by them—although they make sporadic attempts. This gives tentative cover to those on the street. But there is a symbolic aspect as well. The train comes to have a much deeper meaning. Our participants nearly all spoke romantically of the train. "I love those trains, man," Wasserman once told Matty while we were staying in his camp. He understood, "I do, too. There's something about them. I can't hardly sleep anymore if I'm away from 'em." People who hop freight trains talk about the excitement of limitless possibility, of giving oneself over to the power of the moving steel. After ending up heading in the opposite direction than he had intended, one train hopper chastised himself, "Don't ever call it 'the wrong train.' There is no wrong train."[6] Perhaps, in a way, the reverence of those who are homeless for trains echoes that of their hobo ancestors. It is clear that many see their lives fading into the horizon somewhere far away from where they now live. When asked if they ever saw themselves getting off the streets, nearly all of our participants said yes. They see their lives on a course: one switch sent them into homelessness and another in the future will take them out of it.

The second ecological revelation that occurred that first day was by no means novel. It is obvious that urban centers bring the wealthiest people in proximity to the poorest people.[7] Towering skyscrapers with powerful corporate logos loom ever visible over homeless camps. Some of our stock shots started with close-ups of these buildings, and as we pulled the shot back, more and more poverty and desolation entered the frame. People are fond of saying that urban flight and the decline of the manufacturing sector left little job opportunity in city centers. But they should be more specific. There still are jobs there, predominantly of two kinds. There are high-paying professional jobs and low-paying jobs in fast-food restaurants, which serve the highly paid professionals who do not have time to go home for lunch. After five o'clock, when the professional workday is done, all of the restaurants are closed because there is no one to serve. While it is quickly redeveloping, our city still is eerily quiet at night. There are no second and third shifts in the city center, just the highly stratified nine-to-five. For those who are homeless, decent economic opportunity in the downtown areas is all but a ghost of the past, but the collateral benefit is that this provides those who are homeless with desired solitude. At night they can claim city spaces for themselves, but even this meager compensation is eroding.

Gentrification is a problem that major cities like New York have been dealing with for many decades. For smaller cities, slower on the change curve and with populations that are only in the early twenty-first century making suburban sprawl problematic for commuters, the redevelopment of city centers is a more recent phenomenon. As with other cities, the redevelopment of downtown Birmingham has entailed the remodeling of old downtown buildings into trendy postmodern lofts, replete with exposed ductwork and concrete floors.[8] Like a lot of people, we have been torn in our general approval. For someone disapproving of suburban sprawl, the redevelopment of these ghost-town city centers is a welcomed change. But the collateral effect on the poor is unacceptable.

While postwar suburban life afforded more freedom and privacy, people also tended to become more isolated.[9] As legal desegregation stimulated the white flight, the resulting suburbs not surprisingly represented resegregated spaces, particularly along class lines, but also very clearly by race.[10] In the suburbs, people could be around others who mostly were like themselves. But this is not achievable in more compact and diverse urban spaces.[11] Part and parcel to city civic life is that we do not always get to select the members of our society but have to play the hand we are dealt, to find ways to come together under a common sense of who we are despite our differences.

The suburbs mitigated differences and therefore made civic life comparatively simple.[12] In Birmingham, suburban development has included the secession of wealthier suburbs, which form their own cities and school districts in efforts to secure the revenue from their own wealthier tax base. While this was devastating to the downtown area, city center redevelopment has brought wealthier people back to Birmingham.[13] Though this has promise for generating a new sense of collectivity across the diverse races and classes in the city, it has generated significant assault on the poor and especially on those who are homeless. It appears that new urban settlers returning to downtown are retaining suburban expectations of privacy and homogeneity.

In Birmingham entire housing projects and at least one homeless shelter at the time of this writing had been swept under the glacier of urban renovation. More directly relevant here is that those who are homeless are becoming more visible, and while this would ideally invigorate activism on their behalf, it has instead produced class conflict. Down-town lofts now overlook the train tracks and the homeless encampments that pepper the area. Complaints about people who are homeless have skyrocketed, and the propertied residents readily admit that they simply do not like to see people who are homeless when they look out their windows.[14]

As more lofts are developed and upscale bars and restaurants open in repopulated areas, those who are homeless are under increasing scrutiny. Complaints continue to file into the police and city council, whose response has been to randomly do "sweeps" of areas with high concentrations of those who are homeless.[15] On more than a few occasions, we would show up to find a camp or work block that had been completely cleared of all furniture and any other indicators of human life. We would begin to drive around looking for our participants living on the street, and nearly always would happen on, or be flagged down by, someone we knew who would fill us in. "Everyone's at the camp. We can't be at Catchout after six o'clock anymore." "Why?" "That's just what [the police officer] said. I don't know; I don't mess with 'em." Prohibitions on being in this or that spot would last several weeks and then fade. Those on the street had learned not to question them. They would simply "move along" and wait it out.[16]

Getting shuffled around the city was not the worst possible fate. At other times, city workers would show up accompanied by police to take all of the possessions of homeless residents. In the more favorable of these occurrences, residents of street communities would be given some time to gather things they did not want to get taken to the city dump. After salvaging what they could, a city worker would collect their mattresses, tents, boxes, blankets, and anything else they could not carry with them. These incidents were spawned by complaints, but also by city events such as local festivals. We showed up at Catchout once, a day after a local marathon, to find that Corner occupants had been totally cleaned out. This was our first encounter with a sweep, and we were noticeably angry about it. The men at the Corner took it mostly in stride, a testament to the pervasiveness of their fatalism. "It's alright, we'll get more stuff," one would say. "Someone will come by here with some mattresses and some pallets to burn. We'll be alright." Compared with us, they were calm to a man. Across town, after James was cleaned out by the city, he betrayed a similar intersection of mild annoyance and fatalistic acceptance and belief that he would get more stuff soon enough:

> I had a box spring, queen-size bed, mattress, and all that, furniture, till a man … called the city to come and take my stuff away 'cause he said it ain't right for a homeless guy to have a loft under a bridge. [said with a sarcastic tone:] Picture that! A loft under a bridge!
>
> [*How often does that happen?*]
>
> A lot, [but] everybody on [the] avenue give me more stuff.

Aside from the immediate injustice of taking away the few simple possessions of those who are homeless in order to sanitize the image of a city,[17] there is a deeper effect of the gentrification-driven assault on homeless communities. Completely powerless against the forces of the police, business, and wealthy loft residents, those who are homeless have only the defense of a fatalistic attitude (see Chapter 6). In the same collective breath, society will sweep away homeless camps and wonder why those who are homeless do not take more initiative to get off the street. But the fatalism produced by such sweeps is the diametric opposite of such initiative.

Shifts in urban ecology that bring together those who are wealthy and those who are homeless yield more than a symbolic representation of the growing economic gap in the United States. Gentrification contributes directly to the problems that those who are homeless encounter, in both a physical and psychological sense. They lose what little they have and are left with no option but to throw up their hands and accept life as it comes. Politicians and the public feel put-upon by those who are homeless, but indeed reap what they sow in the form of people who, in defense of their own sanity, have to stop caring. *Que sera sera.*

Homeless Camps and "High-Class Tramps"

Homeless camps are segregated in various ways, including by race and class. Some camps are nearly all white, others nearly all black. There is some mingling during the day and little overt antipathy, but the divisions were clear. Moreover, some camps are much nicer than others, and the nicer ones, not by coincidence, tended to attract less attention from the authorities. This has made them more stable and long lasting. At least partly because they are left relatively undisturbed, the camps that are largely white are able to become more established and comfortable. By contrast, Catchout Corner was populated nearly entirely by African Americans and was routinely "swept up" by the city.

While some people stayed at Catchout full time, most retired to more private places to sleep. Despite frequent raids by the city, Catchout was able to maintain a modicum of organization—a fire pit and barbeque rack, boxes with blankets off to the side, and chairs organized around a wooden-spool table. But none of this prepared us for the level of organization we found on our arrival at the Second Avenue Camp. Located under the interstate, it was bordered by train tracks to the north and a stone company to the east.[18] It was surrounded on all sides by a fence, and entering it required climbing onto a shopping cart and stepping over the fence onto stacks of rubber composite rolls used in construction of some sort. This was difficult by design. Strangers did not casually wander into this camp, and its residents wanted it this way.

Regulating membership and visitors was a common practice, illustrated keenly when a stranger would approach. Even after Matty left the Second Avenue Camp and moved east of downtown, when a man walked into Matty's new camp claiming that he knew Potato Water, Matty was visibly irritated at the intrusion, obviously protective of the boundaries of the camp. Potato Water knew this and flatly rejected the stranger. "Man, I don't know you. ... I mean, I've seen you around, but I don't *know* you." "See you later," Matty said, firmly indicating that the guy needed to leave immediately, and he did.

Despite its forbidding exterior, the Second Avenue Camp was an amazing sight on the inside. We were struck by the normality. Aside from the lack of walls and a roof, the camp was an organized and decorated home.[19] The owner of the stone company had run an extension cord out to them. It was a mutually beneficial exchange; the men at the camp got power, the owner got built-in security. They even had her phone number in case of emergency. She also left an exterior bathroom door unlocked and allowed them to use it at night.

The camp was organized around a fire pit, surrounded by a living room with chairs, a couch, a TV stand, and a TV. In the "kitchen" on the far west side of the camp was a microwave, crock pot, and barbeque grill, along with a prep table, dishes, pots, and pans. Individual "bedrooms" were located off to the sides. Matty had a dresser with folded clothes and a laundry bag hanging off to the side; that night we watched as he put away his clean clothes. At the other end of the camp, the oldest, but not the most senior resident, Roger, had his possessions stored in a shopping cart at the end of his couch-bed. The other men had tents or tarps converted into tents. Jeff had made four walls out of crates and fixed a tarp over them as a ceiling. He had all of his supplies and possessions organized in his room. Later that night we remarked to Potato Water how impressed we were with the camp. "Shit yeah. We may be tramps, but we're high-class tramps!" he exclaimed with an air of pride.

Shortly after we arrived, J. K. returned from his job doing maintenance at a nearby park. He was friendly toward us and told us to go ahead and set up our tent, pointing out, as we began, that we had picked a bad spot, directly under drainage holes in the highway where water would poor in when it rained (which it later did). He motioned for us to set up closer to Jeff's hut. When we expressed hesitance to crowd Jeff, J. K. replied, "Well I say its okay, and that's all that matters. I've been here the longest. I brought in Potato Water, and he brought in Jeff and Matty." This was more than chronology; it was a description of their political arrangement.

Seniority in the camp makes for a very real hierarchy among the residents. Overall, things work in a communal fashion, but in any dispute, seniority garners influence. This was the case in all the camps and gathering spots. Having been there the longest, and especially having invited others into the community, elevated one's status. Matty's situation clearly illustrated the process. Although on the bottom rung at the Second Avenue Camp, after he left and established his own camp, he became the clear leader. Whereas Potato Water had invited Matty into the Second Avenue Camp and so was "over" him in that environment, the opposite was true when Matty invited Potato Water into his new camp.

It is important to keep in mind that this hierarchy remained informal and without much real power. Tribal cultures often are organized around a similar hierarchy, whereby the elders have symbolic power, but not such that they wield a great deal of ostensible control over the lives of the others. The latter kind of power dynamic is not needed in small societies with agreed-upon codes, and it is likewise not needed in homeless camps. Enforcing the rules becomes unnecessary when everyone largely agrees to and obeys them without coercion.

Camps and work corners had explicit rules that were not often violated. Women were not allowed at the Second Avenue Camp or at Catchout. There were exceptions when females would pass by and stop in, but the residents were not terribly friendly or welcoming. They gave various explanations. Lockett noted, "Most of the women that come around here are working [like us], but they're doing a different kind of work, if you know what I mean. We don't need that kind of heat around here." Others would say more generally, "Women just cause conflicts. People will get to fighting. [Women] take stuff but don't give nothing [to the camp community]."

While drugs were plentiful and only thinly disguised at Catchout, hard drugs were banned at the Second Avenue Camp. Crack especially was forbidden, again on the idea that it brought unneeded attention from the authorities and caused conflict within the camp. Rules such as this were possible to establish and maintain, since the population of the camp was relatively controlled both physically and socially. The boundaries of Catchout were more permeable, and it was more difficult to regulate who came in and what they did.

Ultimately, the Second Avenue Camp was reduced to shambles after the police forbade people to sleep at Catchout Corner at night. In the midst of this emergency, refugees from Catchout were allowed into the Second Avenue Camp, and its organization and order dissipated within months. Except for Jeff, all of the residents left the camp in short order. Roger began to draw Social Security and pay room and board at some hostel-like establishment. Matty moved across town and established another highly organized camp, and Potato Water eventually followed him. The area under the bridge became the nighttime sleeping spot for the men from Catchout Corner, and later, in two separate but likely connected incidents, both the stone company and the entire contents of the camp were burned to ashes.

These overall patterns of movement among homeless communities run parallel to those of ordinary neighborhoods. As lower-class minorities begin to move into certain areas, upper- and middle-class white people tend to move out. Likewise, as nicer homeless neighborhoods experience the influx of certain people, the original residents will go elsewhere. It is difficult to sense any consciously racist motivations among those on the street, just as it is for most of those who move to the suburbs when their neighborhood "goes to hell," but the pattern is unmistakable.

Homelessness is defined, in part, by environment. The structure of the urban environment creates conflicts between those who are homeless and local governments, authorities, and wealthier people who are repopulating the formerly abandoned refuge of the urban landscape. From this conflict comes instability for those on the street as they see their homes and possessions routinely swept away. This is mitigated by the organization and stability that those on the street create for themselves (see also Chapter 7) as they develop and maintain urban campsites, which often resemble normal homes in their organization, structure, rules, and sometimes even amenities. However, despite their many successes, pressures from authorities typically win out, and stable camp environments eventually are thrown back into disarray. In the end, the ecology of homelessness is a search for stability in the midst of encroaching storms of chaos.

Relationships Among Those on the Street

In the previous section we discussed the way in which urban environments relate to homelessness and contribute to phenomena connected with it, such as fatalism. Here we address the relationships among those who are homeless to one another. In a conversation with a homelessness researcher, the researcher suggested one benefit of the shelters by contending, "There's no community on the streets." We found this to be wholly incorrect.[20] There was a rich community with normative patterns, folklore, a lexicon, and with structured relationships, all of which promoted community.

Competitive Cooperation:
Sharing, Hoarding, and Regulating

As we noted, we always arrived at homeless camps and gathering spots with armloads of donations. We regularly would bring food, socks, cigarettes, and toiletries. When we came across them, or when friends, family, and colleagues donated to us, we also brought batteries, clothes, shoes, sleeping bags, tents, mattresses, chairs, radios, televisions, or whatever else we could get our hands on that our participants would want or need. We noticed early on that our donations were not a free-for-all, but distributed rationally, based on negotiation and need. By and large, there was an ethic of sharing and taking only what one could use.

The process was interesting. People would begin to sift through the donations and as they selected an item, typically would issue a justifying statement with a partly rhetorical quality, but which seemed at the same time directed at the entire group. Someone would take socks and say, "Yeah, I need these—mine got holes in them." They were also aware of the needs of others. Someone would say something like, "I don't need a blanket, but Mike does. Mike! Come get this blanket." Other times we entrusted people to deliver our donations to others who needed them. "Give this to Milton; he needed it." With one exception, people later confirmed receiving these items. If more people arrived after donations were divided up, people generally would redistribute their take. For example, if someone had taken two pairs of socks, they would give one to the person just arriving.

People generally did not take things they did not need. The consumption ideology of Western culture might suggest that people with nothing are willing to take anything. That this was not the case suggests a parallel to nomadic cultures with preinstitutional economies, where material desires were attenuated, perhaps because excessive possessions were seen as burdensome.[21] Those who are homeless face difficulty storing possessions safely. Residents of camps can to some extent, but even they get robbed and cleaned out by the city. Others must carry what they own on their back, and as with other nomadic people, they simply do not want to carry anything they do not need.

As always, however, social life is full of contradiction. While the ethic of sharing was palpable, hoarding regularly took place as well. On our early visits, we remained oblivious to the practice. On the surface, everyone professed to share and attempted to keep up the appearance. As time progressed, however, we began to notice that some people would use sleight of hand to take more than their "fair share." Whether or not one hoarded depended both on personality and current conditions. Certain people were known for hoarding, and those new to the communities sometimes did so. Other times, hoarding seemed to occur when work was slow and times desperate.

Jeff was the quintessential hoarder. After we became more aware, we would watch as he subtly slipped things into his pockets, often making off with an impressive haul. He was quite skilled in the sleight-of-hand technique. Someone would ask Jeff to pass a granola bar and in a swift motion he would pick up two, sliding one into his pocket and passing the other. Through multiple iterations he would fill all his pockets. When it was dark, he would walk over to the stash of donations and visibly take a reasonable amount while slyly tossing other things into the wooded area, later picking them up. Other people were less adept and therefore less successful at hoarding. A pile of donations we brought to a camp once were carried in and set down by some of our regular participants. When they came back to the car to help with the rest, some unfamiliar people began grabbing armfuls of donations and running off. Some stopped and returned them after the more senior residents instructed them to do so, though a few people made away with a good bit.

We thought a lot about our obligations regarding the distribution of our donations and talked at length about it ourselves and with some of our participants. We certainly did not like to see some people taking more than their share, while others who, by virtue of their meekness or commitment to the sharing ethic, came up short. But in the end, we decided that the distribution of goods was a community function and something they needed to work out for themselves. We encouraged those with a dedication to fairness to take more initiative in the distribution. To this end, we began passively putting people in charge of distribution by handing them our donations when we arrived and casually saying, "Here, pass these around to everyone." This successfully mitigated the hoarding, although it did not eliminate it.

Openly trying to take control of distribution was a rather serious offense called "regulating." True to the notion of freedom and autonomy, those who tried to put themselves in control of how goods were distributed were deeply resented. This was not always unwarranted. Early on, Jeff sometimes would place himself in charge of distribution and this was certainly a self-serving move on his part. Other times, someone would do so in a sincere effort to prevent hoarding. Motown and Big E were particularly good at this. Both made every effort at fairness and kept open records of who took what. Big E in particular was sensitive to the hesitations of the others about having him in charge of the distribution. He would acknowledge this: "I'm not trying to be a regulator, but we've got to make sure everybody gets some." But underlying motivation and even outright disclaimers did little to buffer one against the criticism. Being a regulator meant that one was subverting equality and autonomy on the Corner, trying to be in charge not only of the donated objects, but of the other people. As those on the street tend to resist the control of institutions, it should not be surprising that they typically resisted any semblance of control asserted by others on the street. Someone with seniority could get away with doing it to newer people, but other veterans would not stand for it.

The dual practice of sharing and hoarding speaks to a broader ethos. Life on the streets is at once cooperative and competitive. This is certainly related to environmental conditions. When there is a lot of work, people are willing to pass on a job so that someone else can have it. When work is scarce, they race for the stopped trucks and push and shove to win out even against their friends. This is not really surprising. Most of us would likely act this way, giving when we can, taking when we need. The point again is to retain the complexity of vision when seeing the social phenomenon of street homelessness. It is not as cutthroat as most would envision, the group retaining a definite communal ethic. But those on the street are not transcendent personalities wholly given over to cooperation and community.[22] Rather, they act like the rest of us, out of what we might call a qualified self-interest. Most people share among their friends and communities (defined in social but certainly not geographic terms), but they do not do so when they perceive that their own needs are not met. In the latter circumstance, nearly all of us look out for "number one."

Protectors and Connectors

Community relationships, of course, extend beyond the exchange and distribution of goods—that is, economy. Depending on personality, those on the street played various political roles in their communities. We have already touched on how one's status was related to seniority, but these were not the only political roles and not necessarily even primary ones. Individual people tended to fill various needed roles that served the maintenance of the community.

A key political function of any community is the security of its members. This notion can be traced back as far as political philosophy itself. From the ancient Greeks through enlightenment thinkers such as Hobbes, Locke, and Rousseau, the formation of community has been considered fundamental to human existence, at least of any length or value. Contrary to the perception that those on the street have become lost in an urban "state of nature," communal relationships engender security for members, albeit a more tentative version than most of us experience. Essential to this security are "protectors," who are adept at managing threat and conflict.

Protectors, as the name implies, interject themselves on behalf of others. Within communities on the street, the strong often take care of the weak. As noted, James lived under a bridge but in close proximity to expensive lofts. James was something of a character and knew nearly everyone in the area by name. He cheerily called out "hello" to people walking by, and typically they smiled and politely responded. During our first interview with him, we quickly noticed how people would walk by, see us filming him, and smile or chuckle as though to say, "That James is always into something." It was his strong personality that allowed him frequently to fill the protector role. When we asked him if he had any contact with the other people who were homeless in the area, he replied, "I go and check on 'em a lot. They get hassled all the time. I go see if they need anything." Because of his personality, James seemed able to garner resources and supplies more so than the average person on the street, and he professed to help others in this regard.

We benefited personally from those who filled protector roles. The day after our altercation with the drug dealers (see Chapter 2), we returned to Catchout Corner in passive defiance of them. Hammer, as noted, a former boxer who had spent significant time in prison, had heard of the previous night's events and came and sat with us. This was no small gesture, since sides clearly had formed when the drug dealers moved under the bridge. As we mentioned, everything worked out in the end with all of this, but Hammer's reaction—and more than that—his ability to react, is worth comment. When one of the dealers went over to get a bottle of water from the community stash, Hammer confronted him about his right to take it.

James's power mostly is charismatic, whereas Hammer's is primarily physical. However, both use their respective personal resources to defend the community in various ways. While Hammer and James are clear protector personalities, nearly everyone would, at one time or another, play a protector role. Men in the camps and on the Corner would mediate conflicts among others simply by interjecting rhetorically. Sometimes we would be the fulcrum for the mediator who would settle down simmering conflict by saying something like, "Ya'll knock it off. We've got company." What was important about these interjections was that it allowed the arguing parties to disengage from the conflict without losing face. They could end their altercation on the premise that it was for our benefit rather than because they were intimidated. Looking weak on the street is dangerous and getting out of an argument takes tact.

The physical authority or rhetorical persuasion of protectors maintained social ties *within* the community, but ties *among* various communities in different locations around the city also were important.[23] These ties were maintained by people we might call connectors, a term we take from Malcolm Gladwell's popular book *The Tipping Point*.[24]

As in all urban cities, various neighborhood pockets have a different character and attract different types of people. One area will be known as trendy, another a working-class neighborhood, another a high-class residential area. Street homeless communities reflect the similar patterns. Catchout Corner was decidedly a place to get labor, whereas the camps farther east along the train tracks were nicer and more secluded, having an almost suburban quality. Five Points South was an area of the city known for nightlife and dining. True to this, those living on the street in that area have more often been younger. It was in Five Points that one would tend to find squatters, punk-rock train hoppers, and nouveaux hippies.

It seemed that those on the street always knew what was going on outside their circles. Information was passed around by those people with the ability to move between groups. For example, we could show up at Catchout and someone would say, "Yeah, I hear you went to Matty's camp a couple of days ago." These locations were several miles apart, and residents of one rarely were present at another. In fact, as we noted earlier, most residents of one community were not welcome at other communities. Still, there were certain personalities who were able to move among communities.

Potato Water was a clear example of a connector. We first met him at Catchout Corner, where he immediately stuck out as the only white man. He confirmed this as an anomaly: "It took me three years to get fully accepted out here as a white man." This was perhaps what enabled him to connect communities. When we first began spending time there, mostly white men populated the Second Avenue Camp. But even though Catchout was only a few blocks away, Potato Water was the only one of them who went there to get work. Because of him, the men from Catchout began to visit the camp. As we have discussed, this led ultimately to its demise, but from another perspective, it also gave refuge to the men from Catchout during a period when they were banned from sleeping at the Corner.

Matty was another connector. During a stay at his camp, Wasserman walked with him to a park about ten blocks away where a church was hosting a street meal. The path took them by one mission and through the east end of the downtown area where the sidewalks were peppered with dozens of people who were homeless. Matty knew nearly all of them by name. As we walked, he would talk to people, not only saying "hello," but also asking something specific, as, "Did you get that job the other day?" Or he might tease them: "Look at this guy, he's causing trouble. I'm going to call the cops to come pick you up again." He shook more than half a dozen hands as they passed the mission. When they arrived at the park, Matty had to make rounds before they settled into a card game. Matty made introductions, and Wasserman immediately was accepted as legitimate. When unconnected, as in our early days on the street or during our shelter stay, we were the objects of suspicion, possible cops. But this was not the case when Wasserman was with Matty. It was not only that Matty knew a lot of people, it was that he knew about them as well, and, in turn, they liked and respected him.

It is worth mention that the notion of connectors amounts to more than a taxonomic classification. As Gladwell points out, those distributing information could benefit from recognizing and targeting these types of people.[25] Gladwell focuses on advertising, but this would hold true for public health initiatives and other campaigns designed to target groups difficult to penetrate. The hypothesis is that spreading any message is more effective when targeted at a smaller group of the right kind of people, rather than diffused across a mass audience. Connectors who are homeless represent a good strategic target group for disseminating information, in particular, but more generally are possible focal points for building community relationships between those who are homeless and the new urban settlers repopulating downtown.

* * *

There is most definitely a community on the streets. Relationships are guided by behavioral codes and actively maintained in diverse ways and by people serving different roles. Not only are those living on the street engaged in a network of relationships within their own small groups, but different groups maintain relationships with one another through connectors. Perhaps the general failure to recognize the sophistication of street homeless communities stems from a conceptual linkage between community and institution. After all, to talk of the somewhat nebulous roles that those who are street homeless fill as political positions likely has a hint of (intended) contradiction for the average reader. Certainly, there are not elected leaders and formalized structures within or among homeless communities on the street.[26] But the lack of institutional formality on the street should not cloud the issue. There are clear and observable community relationships among those who are street homeless; moreover, they can be quite sophisticated.

All of us are members of noninstitutionalized communities. When we go to dinner with friends, usually there is no one in charge, no real penalty for being late, no mandate about what to order, and no requirement for showing up at all.[27] But we all are nonetheless able to maintain these sorts of groups, often across significant periods of our lives. Further, within these groups, people fill various roles as needed. The connector of the group might be the person who calls everyone; the protector will complain to the management about bad service or will mediate a heated discussion. Street homeless communities can best be understood as similar informal groups. However, the maintenance of these types of friendship-communities becomes more consequential because the homeless members depend on the friendship-community more than the rest of us, since we are able to draw on other resources (e.g., financial, institutional, familial, and so on).

The notion of street homeless communities as consequential friendship networks is further supported by the way in which relationships are maintained between those who are able to get off the street and those still on it. While we lost personal contact with him, reports were that Lockett eventually left the streets, got married, and acquired a relatively stable job. The men at Catchout Corner told us that he still comes down and spends time with them. Motown noted, "He comes by and hangs with the fellas, helps us out when he can, you know. He knows this is where he came from. The Corner helped him out, and now he helps out the Corner."

Out-Ties: Relationships with Society

Those who are street homeless develop relationships with one another that have implications for their survival.[28] But they also are enmeshed in a variety of relationships with institutions, despite their implicit or explicit attempts to disengage from them. In this section we characterize the strained relationships between society and our participants on the street, including service providers and those who are homeless and using shelters, local government and business, and the general public. While later chapters will deal in more detail with service providers, governments, and businesses, here we focus on delineating the perspective held by those on the street of these institutions.

As mentioned earlier, "street homeless" is an unavoidably nebulous category (see Chapter 3). Nearly all of our participants had been to various shelter programs, and some of them cycled on and off the streets on their own. Rather than a definitive life condition, "street homeless" is more indicative of attitude. Nonetheless, it is important to note that several of our participants tried various programs during our study. Big E has been the most successful. After getting sick and going to the hospital, he went to the shelter. He told us that his hospital stay gave him a chance to reflect on his life, and when he got back on the streets, he decided he "couldn't do it anymore."

We followed Big E through the various stages of his recovery. Having been on the streets for seven years, he adapted to the structured treatment programs surprisingly well. It seems to us that the most successful in the shelters are those who had been homeless for only a brief period of time, but never adjusted to the lifestyle or became thoroughly fatalistic. Big E was something of an exception in this regard, perhaps an archetype for the value of hitting rock bottom. Those on the street sometimes refer to the treatment programs as "going through the steps," which rather accurately characterizes the linearity of that system. Big E spent about four weeks in the shelter, attending meetings and counseling there until he was admitted to a twenty-eight-day intensive drug-treatment facility. True to form, the treatment facility was located in a poor neighborhood with a fairly substantial drug problem. Despite these environmental challenges, Big E excelled and was eventually elected leader of his wing. From there he went back to the shelter for a period and then into transitional housing. He eventually began volunteering at the shelter one day a week and at our last contact was working to get disability assistance for his lupus. Remaining in good spirits through all the shifting around, Big E met the challenges at every stage. His trajectory afforded a look into the highly ordered process involved in the continuum-of-care model that most shelters, as of this writing, employ to varying degrees.

When we interviewed Big E during treatment, he repeatedly conceptualized homelessness as an addiction problem. Our experience suggests a socialization process within the shelter treatment programs that at least in part leads to this perspective. Grunberg and Eagle describe the implications of this process as "shelterization, ... a process of acculturation endemic to shelter living. ... The adaptation to shelter life includes the development of a shelter vocabulary, the assimilation of shelter themes, the acceptance of shelter ideals and beliefs, *and an eroding will*."[29] But looking back through our earlier interviews and two years' worth of field notes with Big E before he went through "the steps" suggests an additional consideration, though one that does not negate the idea of "shelterization." Unlike most of the others on the street, Big E had always conceptualized homelessness as an addiction problem, even before he went to the shelter. This was true to his personal experience, a connection driven by his own biography. That this perspective was congruent with treatment program mandates surely aided his decision to go to treatment and his ultimate success. He fit into the system unlike those whose are, or believe themselves to be, homeless because of political economy.

Big E also noted how frustrating it could be to live in such crowded conditions and under so many restrictions. One had to be humble and passive to go to treatment. "You have to give in to it," he said. This stands in conflict with the notion of autonomy that is so palpable on the streets.[30] Clearly Big E had to let go of that notion, but in many ways it was never as central for him as it was for others.

Those who are street homeless generally have an extremely negative opinion of the shelters. Despite this, when someone from the community decided to go to a treatment program, the others were generally supportive. The shelter where Big E began "the steps" is located only about four blocks from Catchout Corner, and after he entered treatment, he still visited the Corner to see his friends during free time. Like Lockett, his ties to the community did not end when he got off the streets. And while this seemed like flirting with temptation, Big E told us that he figured he was always going to be around drugs and so he might as well learn how to live sober in that environment. Moreover, the men at Catchout, rather than being resentful and predatorily tempting, encouraged him in his efforts. When Big E visited Catchout, nearly everyone there would give him at least a dollar, which they called a "lookout." This was a normative practice intended to help the person going through treatment, since they could not go through the program and work at the same time.

The day we watched all of the men "look out" for Big E, Carnell was uncharacteristically rough with him. As mentioned in Chapter 1, Carnell and Big E are cousins and had been close friends on the street. So we were quite surprised when Carnell was rude and even openly aggressive toward Big E that day. "Get the fuck out of here, man." Carnell would push him a little and play-fight, but he seemed only to be half-joking. A few days later during an interview at the shelter, we asked Big E about it. "Let me explain what Carnell was doing for me. Carnell's like a brother to me; he knows that I'm still weak. He was telling me to get the fuck out of there because he cares about me and he knows all the temptation that's out there." Later in the interview, Carnell walked up. His manner now was totally different toward Big E, and he confirmed that he did not think Big E should be going down to the Corner.

We have already discussed that those on the street get "cleaned out" by the city and that most often this is the direct result of complaints lodged by businesses and wealthy loft-residents returning to the city center after a five-decade absence. Those who are street homeless generally deal with their direct losses by adopting a fatalistic attitude. What choice do they have? Opinions about local government and businesses are diverse. We might expect that oppressed, disfranchised people who routinely have their possessions taken away would uniformly resent the culpable powers. To be sure, many do. But it was also common for fatalism to bleed over into a live-and-let-live attitude, even toward those with whom they were frequently in conflict.

Sometimes we would encounter someone in a near rage over an incident. A cop once detained a man named Tim, and by Tim's account treated him poorly because he had earlier been walking with a man who later caused some disturbance. Tim was livid about it and implored Wasserman to film him telling the story. The camera often was an outlet for anger. Tim also noted distinct ironies about the way those on the street were treated by the city. "They got parks over there where they give you bags and a little trash can so you can let your dog take a shit. Why don't they have any public bathrooms for us to use? They don't care about us as much as they care about dogs."

But just as often we heard a more understanding perspective. "They're people, too—just have a different way of looking at things," they would say, in various formulations, about a police officer who had hassled them, the city councilman who was pushing vagrancy legislation, or the gas station attendant who banned someone for taking too long to select a snack. These estimations contained a hint of fatalism, but also a logic that suggested that if they wished to have their way of life on the street validated, to be left alone and not hassled, then they could not deem another's way of life and opinions invalid, even if they did not agree with them.

Just as our participants were quite aware of how the city and businesses felt about them, they were keenly aware of how they were seen by the general public. A common question we asked during formal interview sessions was, "What do you think that the people in the suburbs think about you guys?" It was not something they had to ponder—bums, dangerous, filthy, rats, no good, and so on. It also was common for them to note that most of those who would judge them were only a few paychecks away from being homeless themselves. This was a statistic that we heard from researchers and service providers as well, but for those on the street, it did not reflect the tentative security afforded by political and economic structures as much as it was an assertion of normality, of the fact that they were not corrupt, but just average people in not-so-average circumstances.

Perhaps the most interesting indication of the ways in which the public sees those who are street homeless was the "rubbernecking" of those driving by Catchout Corner. Cars would approach and see a group of men who were homeless sitting in a circle, sometimes around a fire. The occupants of the car would come to a near stop sometimes, as they stared in awe. Sometimes cars would go by and then turn around and make another pass in order to take it all in, passengers often taking photographs from their car windows. Potato Water said of this:

> I don't like it when people come by and look [he demonstrated with a craned neck and bug-wide eyes] and take pictures. You feel like an animal at the zoo. And then sometimes a car will slow down to look and the guys will run out to it and the people will get scared and speed off. Man, those guys are just looking for work. They think they're comin' to pick somebody up for a job.

Most of us would likely feel intruded upon if a stranger took our picture in public, much less if it happened routinely. At least when people intrude on celebrities in this way, it is mostly because they revere them. Imagine if people continually took photographs of us because they thought we were pitiful and pathetic.[31] The psychological effect would have to be damaging, especially over a matter of weeks, months, years, and sometimes decades.

While there are numerous panhandlers in certain areas of the city, many panhandlers are not homeless and most of those who are homeless do not panhandle.[32] The public mostly fails to make this distinction and lumps the two together as they complain about the inconvenience.[33] The morning after our first night staying on the streets, Clair was sitting on the sidewalk resting, and a woman came by, handed him a dollar, and walked away. He naturally was a bit shocked. His initial reaction was to clarify for the person that he was not homeless. While he later realized that this was the natural impression he was giving off, having not bathed, sitting on the street with his backpack, the shame he felt in that first moment is important. Even when thoroughly conscious of the structural causes of homelessness and sympathetic to the idea that those who are homeless are victims, the stigma of homelessness is pervasive and it infects all of us at a subconscious level.[34] Waffle House talked of similar feelings: "People come up and hand me a dollar. That's embarrassing. That doesn't make me feel like a man."

From our experience, most of those who are homeless do not beg. Early on, we were occasionally asked for various things when we approached a spot, like Catchout Corner. But we never saw them approach strangers on the street, so even when we did get asked for things, it was qualitatively different than panhandling; we had approached them, not the other way around. Many of those who are homeless openly refused to beg. A shelter resident made an interesting observation, "If I was a beggar, I wouldn't be homeless. Part of my problem is that I can't ask for help." A man living on the street named Tim further pointed out, "I can't stand being told no, so I don't beg. I just get what I can for myself."

Those who are homeless are keenly aware of the way that the general public sees them. Not only do they clearly know the general negative stigmas, but also they know specific misconceptions that the public holds, such as the idea that they are all beggars who refuse to work. These are not benign recognitions; they cause real feelings in those who are homeless, real damage to their self-concept and their relationships to the rest of society. Society wants those who are homeless to "pull it together," to get off the streets and reintegrate into the mainstream. However, like punching someone in the face and asking the victim to be your friend at the same time, we stigmatize and ostracize those on the street and then chastise them for withdrawing.

Notes

1. Liebow, *Tell Them Who I Am*, p. 2; see also Dordick, *Something Left to Lose*.
2. See also Bickford, "Constructing Inequality," on the "architecture of citizenship."

3. Ballard, *Concrete Island*.

4. See Toth, *The Mole People*, about such communities in the subway tunnels of New York City.

5. "Bum on the Rod" is a song by Utah Phillips.

6. Anonymous, *Evasion*.

7. See for example Bickford, "Constructing Inequality"; Gibson, *Securing the Spectacular City*; Kyle, *Contextualizing Homelessness*.

8. Ellin, *Postmodern Urbanism*; Podmore, "(Re)Reading the 'Loft Living' Habitus in Montreal's Inner City"; Zukin, *Loft Living*.

9. See Bellah et al., *Habits of the Heart*, and Putnam, *Bowling Alone*, for discussion of the negative consequences for those leaving the city; see Wacquant and Wilson, "The Cost of Racial and Class Exclusion in the Inner City," on the negative consequences for those left behind. More generally, a variety of organizations and civil-society programs have utilized the term *social inclusion* to counter this problematic concept of community.

10. See classic expositions of postwar residential patterns in Jacobs, *The Death and Life of Great American Cities*; Wilson, *The Truly Disadvantaged*; Whyte, Jr., *Man and the Modern City*.

11. See especially Peterson, *The New Urban Reality*; see also Whyte, Jr., *Man and the Modern City*, for a discussion of suburbia as "anti-city."

12. See Scribner, *Renewing Birmingham*, for a description of these processes specifically in Birmingham.

13. For discussions of "new urbanism," see Duany et al., *The Rise of Sprawl and the Decline of Nation*; Hall, *Cities of Tomorrow*; Morris, *It's a Sprawl World After All*.

14. See Chapter 8 for more discussion; see also Kyle, *Contextualizing Homelessness*; Phelan et al., "The Stigma of Homelessness"; Waldron, "Homelessness and Community."

15. Wagner notes, in *Checkerboard Square*, that these only move the homeless from one place to another and therefore are merely symbols of social control rather than genuine solutions.

16. For coded data related to this see our website, www.athomeonthestreet.com.

17. Arnold, *Homelessness, Citizenship and Identity*.

18. It is gone now, and so we feel comfortable that this description does not endanger anyone.

19. See also Toth's observations in *The Mole People*; Marc Singer's documentary film *Dark Days*, released in 2000. Tent cities became famous during the Great Depression (then called "Hoovervilles"), and their visibility reemerged in the wake of the economic recession beginning in 2008, when the mainstream media covered them to some extent, making comparisons with those of the 1930s. We emphasize here that this way of life is not exclusive to times when the stock market dips, but rather persists during economic booms as well as busts.

20. See also Pippert, *Road Dogs and Loners*, where the "road dogs" reflect the ability to form relationships on the street. While Pippert focuses on dyads, the qualities, motivations, and processes of their relationships are informative for the notion of homeless communities more generally.

21. Sahlins, *Stone Age Economics*.

22. Wacquant, "Scrutinizing the Street."

23. See also Wagner, *Checkerboard Square*, for an excellent study on street communities.

24. Gladwell, *The Tipping Point*.

25. Ibid.

26. There are these structures within various treatment programs for those who are homeless, where senior members are given official leadership positions.

27. See Chapter 11 for more extensive implications of the concept of friendship for understanding and working with homelessness.

28. See also Pippert's discussion of "fictive kin" in *Road Dogs and Loners*.

29. Grunberg and Eagle, "Shelterization," p. 522, italics added; see also Lyon-Callo, "Medicalizing Homelessness"; Hopper and Baumohl, in "Held in Abeyance," attribute the term *shelterization* to Sutherland and Locke, *Twenty Thousand Homeless Men*, who describe flophouses of the 1920s and 1930s as places of enforced idleness and isolation to which one had to adapt mentally.

30. See also the discussion of characters in Chapter 7.

31. Snow and Anderson, in *Down on Their Luck*, make a similar observation.

32. The small population of those who are homeless and travel routinely seems more likely to do so, particularly by "flying signs" asking for donations as described in Pippert, *Road Dogs and Loners*.

33. For example, two opposing-viewpoint essays on panhandling itself are included in a book titled *The Homeless*, edited by Louise I. Gerdes.

34. See Goffman's *Stigma* for a classic statement on the phenomenon.

6

The Complex Dispositions of People on the Street

Social life is a web of contradicting thoughts and feelings. We felt safer on the streets than in the shelter, but we saw drugs, guns, and fighting there, too. Those who are street homeless speak of a peace of mind on the streets, but nearly all of them would prefer to leave. And then when they do, they talk about missing it. Society tells the homeless to "get some initiative," but then renders them all the more powerless as they sweep away their possessions, leaving utter fatalism as the only alternative to insanity. People who are homeless speak of a multitude of hardships on the streets but also of laughter and joy. As Ed put it, "You've gotta laugh to keep from cryin'."

In this chapter we discuss the values, feelings, and dispositions of life on the street. This entails understanding the coexistence of things that seem in polar opposition. Feelings of danger and security, boredom and excitement, emotional pain and psychological peace—all of these permeate life on the streets. Additionally, we will discuss our own feelings as we attempted to experience living on the street. While we cannot fully approximate things such as the overwhelming feeling of being trapped there, other aspects, such as the physical exhaustion and boredom, became perceptible in robust ways.

"He'll Be Sorry About It Tomorrow, But Tonight He'll Shoot You"

There is a palpable mood on the streets. It appeared to us to be related to environmental circumstances. After the stone company that supplied their electricity burned down, the Second Avenue Camp residents were left without power, and the camp became overcrowded because of the prohibition on sleeping at Catchout. Work had been scarce because of the rainy weather, and when we arrived with food, socks, and toiletries, we could sense tension and desperation. While our participants always were appreciative, normally our donations were met with comparatively casual interest. Those on the street typically are not starving or without clothes. On this particular night they clamored for the food and ate as though they had not eaten in a long time. Though not unfriendly, they were agitated and spoke about how things were "getting tough." The streets were in a bad mood.

Volatility is endemic to street homelessness. Tension ebbs and flows with things like work, weather, and police repression. When the mood on the streets is bad, things are more strained and tempers quicker to flare. This was not simply the characteristic of particular people, but rather any given person encountered at the wrong time. This is not difficult to understand; not many of us are totally immune to stress. We each have a breaking point, and the stressful nature of living on the street likely would get the better of any of us from time to time. "All of us are good people," Potato Water put it, "but any one of us … you catch the wrong person at the wrong time, it can be bad."

Physical altercations actually were rare. Most squabbles often were brotherly in nature and quickly resolved with friendships intact. Fights rarely erupted, even from the most heated arguments, because no one really wanted to fight. All seemed to recognize that life on the streets is dangerous enough without fighting one another. Conflicts would reach a pinnacle where a fight seemed imminent, but rather than boil over, the parties usually would begin carefully working their way out of the conflict. This took skill because reputation is an important protective veneer on the street.

However, we did hear about conflicts taken to that next level and in a handful of cases saw this happen. Jeff once slapped Potato Water for touching his wine, knocking him back onto a couch. Another time a man nicknamed L.A. got into an altercation with a man nicknamed Jesus. L.A. left the Corner claiming he was going to go get a gun, but never returned. Though we do not know why he never returned, because we did not follow him, the threat was likely one made to save face while leaving the altercation. In the most sensational story, Jeff once shot at Motown, but the two had made up by the time we next saw them.

In the most remarkable incident, Jeff got into an altercation with Carnell, Motown, and the others who accused him of trying to be "a regulator." As things got heated, he left to get his gun. He returned and brandished the weapon at Carnell, whose only response was to calmly sit in his chair and say, "Go ahead and shoot then, motherfucker." As noted in Chapter 1, Carnell is something of a legend for these sorts of displays. Another man, Junior, maintained a tough posture, directing comments to the group but clearly for Jeff's benefit, "I'm getting tired of whippin' that boy's ass." Jeff ultimately pocketed the pistol and rode away on his bike. After he left, Motown commented to everyone, somewhat sympathetically, "Don't you think he's tired of getting he ass whipped? Don't you think that's why he got a gun?" Later, Clair remarked to Carnell that he really did not get the feeling that Jeff was going to shoot anyone. After all, we knew Jeff well at that point, and he had been very kind and open toward us. Carnell corrected him, "You should be worried. Jeff doesn't want to shoot anyone, and he'll be sorry about it tomorrow, but tonight he'll shoot you." The point was clear: Anyone in the wrong circumstances and the wrong frame of mind is dangerous.

Again, such incidents were few and far between. Still there seemed to be several predictors of actual physical violence. While volatility and intense arguing were possible from any of our participants on the street under the right conditions, most regulars avoided physical violence. People new to the Corner were far more aggressive, often acting like they had something to prove. For example, there was a large gathering around the fire at Catchout one night that included several newcomers. As we mingled, a relatively short man whom we had never met began talking to Clair, who, as a former college football offensive lineman, is rather formidable in size. "I wanna fight you, Big Man," he kept saying. He seemed to be just half-joking, and, being new, we could only take him seriously. "Why?" Clair asked. "The way I figure it, as big as you are, if I can whip you, I'll get some respect out here," he said. As this same exchange repeated itself a few times, we became increasingly suspicious that this was not a joke. Eventually, senior members Hammer and Carnell let the man know that fighting Clair was not an option, and he abandoned the issue. Reputation on the street garners respect and security, but, ironically, those without it can be the most aggressive because they are trying to get it. Carnell noted later that he was going to have "to regulate" some of the new guys.

While new people tend to be overly aggressive, they either calm down and settle in or they are not around very long. James described the volatility of the street:

> It sounds like it's rough, … but it's only rough how you make it.
> You want to be Joe Gun, you will get what you are looking for. You
> want to be a nice guy, that's how they will treat you, like you are a
> nice guy. You want to be a big bully, … you'll get what you are
> looking for 'cause there is always somebody out there waiting on a
> bully. And they love that. This is like being in a jungle.

And while some of those on the street do act aggressively and generate violence and conflict, more often than not, those on the street are victims of violence. Not only was this consistently noted by a variety of service providers, but also nearly all of our participants who lived on the street had stories about being attacked. Those who slept at Catchout Corner invited us to stay on the street with them, but also warned that we would be better off going to someone's camp that was more secluded. They claimed that, particularly on Friday and Saturday nights, intoxicated people would drive by and throw things from their cars, sometimes even firing guns into the field and under the bridge where they slept. Less dangerous but certainly disturbing, some people would honk their horns as they drove under the viaduct, and one could count on being awakened multiple times a night. Similar reports came from Southside, where harassment and outright assault of those living on the street came from intoxicated bar hoppers and increased especially during festivals and city events.

Volatility is something that permeates life on the streets. A feeling of total safety is never warranted, and such a constant stress surely wears on the psyche of those on the street. When convicted felons are first incarcerated, they describe a process of having to become tough and even violent in order to defend themselves, both from direct attacks and to minimize the extent to which they are targeted. Many note that it is a difficult mindset to let go of once released. Living on the street seems to be a similar experience in this regard. All people bend under stress, and most of us can break under sufficient amounts of it. The volatility on the streets is directly related to waxing and waning of stressful conditions such as a lack of work or accelerated pressure from authorities, especially when this means the sweeping away of community camps. Within their own groups, violence is mostly managed through a variety of interpersonal strategies, either in argumentative discourse or through the intervention of others. But these strategies do nothing to ward off threats from outside the community, from the attacks of random criminals or those generated by businesses and local governments in the form of warrant sweeps and camp "cleanups."

Stealing Time: Coping with Boredom

In the movie *Office Space* the main character dreams of quitting his job and literally doing nothing. After being hypnotized into complete apathy, he skips work the next day, telling his friend with confirmed enthusiasm, "I did nothing. I did nothing, and it was everything that I thought it could be." But as the adage goes, be careful what you wish for. Those on the street are confronted with hours upon hours of idle time, and the human psyche was not built for such deprivation. Boredom is a problematic condition that often is absent from research and discourse on homelessness, but it should not be underestimated in its significance, especially for those who are street homeless. For those who enroll in shelter programs, daily activities, workshops, and various therapeutic groups fill days and mitigate the effect of boredom. The organization and maintenance of camps helps give some structure and routine, but these remain limited. For those on the street, passing time becomes something of an art.

If any of us made a list of the things that we do to pass the time that do not cost any money, we likely would have short lists. Much of life consists of working to make money and filling the rest of the time spending that money in various ways. Without these two things, time becomes a difficult obstacle. Some of us may occasionally go sit in a park and enjoy a quiet moment, but these are brief periods of respite from what we normally do, and few of us, if honest, would trade our daily activities for a total absence of them. We may say we hate school or the daily grind of our jobs, but we mean we want other things to do; no one wants to do nothing.

As mentioned, work for those living on the street is sporadic. This yields a great deal of unoccupied time. Passing the idle time takes various forms, some of which, like drinking, routinely are attached to the concept of homelessness, although without any conscious recognition of the role of boredom. Here we draw out two implications of boredom, its connection to the supposedly missing initiative of those on the street and its connection to substance use and the way it might exacerbate addiction. These insights were generated by our ongoing experiences on the street, where we experienced a good deal of idle time ourselves, as much as direct mention from participants.

A popular sociological concept is that of habitus.[1] This is the notion that our actions largely are motivated by subconscious attitudes that we have learned throughout our social lives. We move through our lives mostly without conscious direction. For example, most people will wake up on a weekday morning, brush their teeth, bathe, and go to work. They probably will not wake up, ponder all of their options, the costs and benefits of not brushing their teeth or skipping work, and rationally decide whether to do those things. We do not rationally think through most of the things that we do. Rather, our daily lives come to have a basic routine, and we mostly go about that routine without a great deal of reflection. These habit-forming processes are an essential part of life that serves the useful purpose of freeing people from many aspects of life that would be overwhelming were we always required to be aware of them. It would be mentally exhausting, for example, if we had to consciously remember all the individual finger and hand motions required to type out a sentence on a keyboard. Nor in a broader sense would we want to wake each day with no structure, having to figure out each and every activity. So these habit-forming processes are as essential to social life as is sleeping to physical and psychological life. During sleep our bodies, freed from the daily cares we inflict on them, are able to refresh. Similarly, habitualizing processes free our social energies from some areas of social life so we can consciously work on others.

However, people often fail to gain an understanding of the meanings and purposes behind habitual patterns, and therefore ignore their ability to be reflexive about their habitualized existence in ways that might enable them to improve their lives. They effectively "sleep through" social life. Both the effects of the absence of routine and also the ability to creatively respond to it were palpable on the street.

Part of becoming homeless is the obliteration of routine. The things that motivate in a subconscious way most of what we do are no longer in place and no longer compel us through our daily motions. While most of us represent the daily structure of our lives as something of a "grind," the effect of the absence of this on one's psyche is significant. Emile Durkheim used the term *anomie* to indicate a breaking of social ties. We might easily include here ties to one's various routines, which keep us from becoming disconnected from the structures of our own lives. Those on the street often experience a disintegration of ties to people, but nearly all of them also experience the breakdown of daily structure.

Not coincidentally, it was an interview with a psychologist that first illustrated the role of boredom. In hindsight it seems obvious, but in the face of the many sensational problems endemic to homelessness—crack, violence, sleeping under bridges and in bushes—boredom does not immediately rank as significant. The psychologist put it plainly:

I don't think you realize how boring homelessness can be if you don't have a job to go to, if you don't have a home to maintain. [W]hat do you do with those big chunks of time? ... And what do you do when you do come back from work and you don't have a big screen TV, a DVD player, a computer, an Internet, the options are pretty limited. ... People don't realize how exhausting that is.

The absence of things to do appears to manifest in several behaviors. Those who are street homeless spend a great deal of time sitting and talking with each other, something that also contributes to the development of community. Most become quite skilled storytellers, who have what might almost be considered performance routines. Having spent considerable time sitting and talking with them, we heard many stories repeated. Interestingly, these changed very little, but seemed to be codified and have rehearsed punch lines. It did not seem that they were intentionally doing an act; they had just spent so much time sitting around talking and telling stories that they had unconsciously developed these various bits.

In a cyclical way, camps mitigated the boredom of the streets by offering an organizational center for activities, but these were the products of those most adept at staving off the boredom. As noted, people have the capacity to step outside of habitualized lifestyles, though they often do not. Those who are homeless are essentially forced to do so. Some respond to this boredom in unhealthy ways to reenter a mind-numbed state, often using drugs or alcohol to achieve it. Others however, employ quite healthy creative practices to fill their unstructured time. As a highly organized and creative personality, Matty included among his daily activities searching for recyclable copper along the train tracks, dumpster diving for materials and working on the infrastructure of the camp, playing horseshoes, and hitting golf balls into the train yard. Many of these activities were made possible by the organization of his camp, which provided a stable center for storing the copper, golf clubs, and so on. The other members of his camp partook in some of these as well, but for them and many others on the street, a primary coping mechanism included drinking.

In prison, taking long naps is a coping strategy referred to as "stealing time." In sleep, one's consciousness is freed from the prison environment. We never heard this term on the street, but it fits in several ways. For many of those on the street, drinking or drug use, rather than sleeping, was a way to steal time. They did not offer this explanation themselves, but it was indicated in several ways. During our stay on the streets, Potato Water tried to catch work one morning. Unsuccessful, he noted that he might as well get drunk, and he did. This was a common practice. Substance use would be delayed in hopes of getting work, but in the absence of work, it became a way to steal time. In contrast to the perception that substance use directly is a factor preventing those who are homeless from "gainful employment," for most of those on the street, drinking and drugs were readily set aside for the opportunity to work.

Regardless of whether substance use was directly or consciously used as a tool to pass the time, boredom clearly is the enemy of sobriety. Anyone who has quit smoking or even eating sweets knows that the most dangerous times for relapse are those when you have nothing to keep you busy. When Wasserman quit smoking, he began to write and exercise, not because those were especially beneficial, but simply because they passed the time and kept his mind occupied. But sobriety for those living on the street might be a difficult accomplishment, in part because of the sheer number of unoccupied hours they have to contend with.

Laughter and Joy

A researcher we interviewed remarked on an irony among those who are homeless, "They are in the midst of a depressing situation, but they are not depressing people." Indeed, those on the street often are colorful storytellers and jokesters who pass the time by talking about sports and women and teasing each other good-heartedly. James put it succinctly, "Don't get me wrong—there's a lot of good times on the streets, a lot of laughin'." Nothing exemplifies this somewhat surprising feature of life on the street more than when they would throw parties. Those in established camps would host get-togethers for particular events such as birthdays. Before they lost power at the Second Avenue Camp, everyone would get together to watch the Super Bowl or the other major sporting events.

Joking with and teasing one another was a constant source of entertainment, and most of the guys were very funny people, probably in part from practice (the same reason they are mainly good storytellers). They teased us, too. Wasserman is a vegetarian and has a lot of tattoos. These were fodder for much good-natured ribbing. Clair was teased about his size, his trials and tribulations raising three sons, his feminine cigarettes, and his run-in with the law. Carnell was fond of teasing us. He would make fake phone calls on his cell phone, pretending to narrate events to the imaginary person on the line, but for the benefit of the group. After Jeff left on the night he had brandished his pistol, Carnell spent a long time on a fake phone call saying things such as, "Yeah, the Professor and Jason started all of this—bring free stuff down here. … No, they're good people, but they came down here and started a bunch of shit [referring to our donations and Jeff's alleged regulating]." As with all jokes, there was an air of truth, since it was in fact our donations that initiated the dispute, but everyone laughed hysterically as Carnell ribbed us thoroughly throughout this imaginary conversation.

Often times the laughter went side-by-side with the pain. In a particularly honest moment, a conversation about *Crime and Punishment* interested a man who began to ask questions about whether we thought guilt would always inevitably overcome people. As the discussion wore on, the personal resonance of Dostoevsky's theme was evident on the man's face. He eventually explained that years before, he, his wife, and a friend had been in a hotel room shooting-up drugs. His friend was not capable of doing it himself and had asked the man to do it for him. When he did, his friend died. He was racked with guilt, and of course, the suggestion that he had not in fact murdered his friend did little to make him feel better. As horrible as the story was and how deeply it afflicted the man, it was not off-limits for jokes. Carnell again led the way with a refrain uttered to no one in particular and in the same manner as one might narrate a story, "We have a killer among us." He also made several of his famous fake cell phone calls to the "police."

Since we often filmed interviews and other moments in the field, the camera could become the focal point of joviality. People would walk up and say, for example, "Get out the camera, Jason. I wanna get off these streets and go straight to Hollywood."

The Values of Those Living on the Street

Street homelessness may not produce any particular value orientations. At best, it builds on those already instilled, but there are some interesting and observable tendencies. The thrust of this section, therefore, is not to discuss values that are the domain of those on the street, but rather to describe particular value-oriented themes that they hold in common with society. This should not imply any uniformity, but rather ought to counter the expectations of liberal academics, like ourselves, who sometimes expect an oncoming class-consciousness to produce liberation ideologies.

The southeastern United States is predominantly conservative religiously, politically, and socially. While stigmatized and ostracized from society, those on the street in the region still tend to reflect these same ideals. It is somewhat difficult to reconcile the way that the conservative ideologies of the American South seem directly antithetical to the destitute circumstances and freedom-infused ethos of the street. But this historically has been the case with oppressed peoples. Paulo Freire notes that the parameters of the world are defined by the privileged often leading the oppressed to work within the very framework that oppresses them.[2] History, especially in the South, is punctuated by examples. In Alabama, wealthy politicians representing the privileged sectors of society once used race to keep poor whites and poor blacks from voting together in an undefeatable political block. In the twenty-first century, religion is used in much the same way to subdue the recognition of economic needs with the result that the poor continue to vote against their economic interests in astounding numbers. While they mostly do not vote, having difficulty registering or being prohibited because of criminal records, those who are street homeless reflect this same pattern, holding ideologies, which ostensibly counter their own interests.

Politics Make Strange Bedfellows, Even for Those Without Beds

At a dinner once, the historian Alan Kraut reminded us that class consciousness has always been a widespread liberal dream and much less of a social reality. Those on the street are no different than many of the poor who hold socially and politically conservative ideologies. Their position in favor the US war in Iraq was a good indicator. There certainly were some who railed against the war. For example, Junior once commented, "We need money here—we got starving people here. You're gonna go blow up a country and then spend billions of dollars to rebuild it. Then whad'ya blow it up for?" But these sorts of protests were in the minority. By and large, those on the street were deeply offended by the 9/11 tragedy and thought that war was a just response. Tim, who was particularly critical of the local government, nonetheless once said, "We had to go over there and show them who's boss or they would think they could come over here and do whatever they want." Those who were veterans living on the street especially supported the war, just as veterans in general tend to do.

Those who are street homeless tended to be very patriotic as well. Their estimation was not unlike that of most Americans: "We've got problems, but this is still the greatest country on earth." After the Abu Ghraib prison scandal, we were in Matty and Potato Water's camp, and one of us said that those events were an embarrassment to the United

States. Matty responded quickly, "I'm not embarrassed to be an American … no matter what. I'm proud."

While those on the street were more likely than their sheltered counterparts to talk about structural economic problems as the cause of their homelessness, this did not seem to infect their opinion of the social structure of United States. With very capitalist ideologies, most did not seem to feel like they were owed anything. At Potato Water's camp one day, a train rolled by carrying what we estimated to be more than one hundred military tanks—millions of dollars of military equipment. We asked Potato Water if we could film him standing in front of it, since he had been in the army. "Marines!" he corrected us with the typical *semper fi* pride. He stood there, homeless in his military jacket, with the military industrial complex literally right behind him. We asked how he felt about it all, noting that we found it ironic. He did not. "I don't feel like they owe me anything or nothin'. I mean I've gotten some benefits from it; I can go to the VA [Veterans Administration] for medical stuff, so that's nice, but I don't think I'm owed."

The fatalism we have discussed as emerging from particular hardships on the street certainly bleeds over into the assessment of political structures by those on the street. Political cynicism was not in opposition to the opinion that the United States is the greatest country on earth. They loved their country but hated their government, as the cliché goes. Those on the street typically see no hope for using political structures for solving social problems. Big E once said about the prospect, "Only thing that will work is for Jesus to come down and change some hearts." The opinion was widely shared that politics is ineffective because it is hopelessly corrupt. Hammer half-jokingly said on one occasion: "I like George Bush, man. He's a straight-up crook. He does it right in the open. The rest of them hide about it." Not everyone was always so calm about political oppression. Tim and L.A. could become very angry, particularly in rants about local politics. But mostly, those on the street were thoroughly fatalistic about the corrupt nature of government and the limited prospects for political solutions to the problems of the street.

From a class perspective, the patriotism and procapitalist ideology of those on the street are perplexing. But because academic social scientists find the issue of class so important, we are prone to forget that most people do not, even when they are poor. The view is always good from the cheap seats. However, since freedom and autonomy are central to those who are street homeless, the notion of American individualism, which culturally is tied to democracy and capitalism, make the irrelevance of class among those on the street more understandable. People who are street homeless eschew shelters and other social services and thereby more closely resemble those postagrarian homeless hoboes of the past than do their sheltered counterparts. Likewise, they are intensely individualistic. This plays out quite clearly in their political opinions—many having no hope or aspirations for help from government—and in the ways that they reflect classic US ideals and patriotism.

Moreover, individualist values are inherent in their views of homelessness, especially of other people who are homeless. While they often tended to recognize their own homelessness as the result of political-economic structure, the idea of choice remained prevalent. Many of those on the street held that they had chosen to be on the street, that their homelessness was their own fault. It seems appropriate to point out again that the notion of structural displacement would seem to preclude the notion of homelessness as a choice. But not only is social life punctuated by these sorts of contradictions, social scientists as renowned as Weber and Bourdieu have pointed out that choice and chance simultaneously are critical.

Carnell was the most ardent supporter of the choice perspective, to the extent that he had a hard time coming to terms with our presence as researchers. He clearly liked us as people, but when it came to our research, he would continually ask, "What do you want to know?" with a tone insinuating that there was, in fact, nothing much to discover. Carnell would tell us, "There's nothing special about it out here." Once, after listening to a group of people talk about not being able to find jobs or make a living wage, he said to us, "That's all bullshit. We put ourselves out here." While Carnell tolerated us, it took a couple of years before we ultimately came to terms, when after one discussion we found common ground in the notion that even if social structures were not ultimately responsible for homelessness, at the very least they could make it easier or more difficult to get off the streets.

We also encountered a lot of discursive separating of oneself from "them."[3] Potato Water and his camp mate Wayne were a clear example. In an interview they noted that, unlike themselves, a lot of people who are homeless are lazy and do not want to work. "We try to go out and work everyday, but there's a lot of 'em that don't do nothing all day." They indeed both were hard workers, yet our experience had been that this was true of nearly all of those on the street.

While sometimes the judgmental perspective seemed deeply embedded in one's consciousness, other times it appeared to be more of a surface strategy. On one occasion we were driving a man back to his camp from Catchout Corner. Though we had all been sitting around in a friendly conversation before we left, once alone with us, the man began employing a distancing rhetoric, saying things like, "Yeah, I don't go hang out down there that much. I'm not like those guys." We responded, "There's a lot of good dudes down there, man." With this the man seemed to relax, either in recognition that we were not going to judge him for having been at the Corner, or because he did not want to say anything about any of the other men that might offend us.

There are no clear lines between strategy and consciousness, but the stigmatic concepts of those on the street toward others on the street seemed to be varying mixtures of genuine sentiment and concern about not being stigmatized by outsiders. Either way, Freire's notion of taking on the oppressor mentality seems clearly to fit.[4] Rather than the recognition of their common interest, those on the street often replicated the stigmatic, judgmental views held by the general public.

Racist Victims of Racism

As with the tendency of those on the street toward conservatism despite being stigmatized by socially conservative ideologies, racism also ironically is manifest. As a condition intertwined with poverty, a disproportionately high number of those who are homeless are, at this writing, African American, especially those on the street, and most especially those in the American South.[5] Race and poverty are related in infinite complexity, but there is widespread agreement that racism, both historical and contemporary, contributes to the disproportionately high representation of African Americans in the lower socioeconomic strata.[6] Data also bear witness to an African American disadvantage related specifically to homelessness. As noted in Chapter 3, African Americans enter homelessness at a rate more than twice that of their representation among the poor, comprising 56 percent of those in shelters but only 26 percent of those in poor families.[7] Logically then, one would expect that those on the street would oppose racism. However, as with class, race-based disadvantage historically has not been a strong buffer against racism.

In the late 1960s black-power activists like Stokely Carmichael began to frame US racism in radically different terms than previous civil rights leaders had. Whereas Martin Luther King, Jr., and the Southern Christian Leadership Conference (SCLC), along with early incarnations of SNCC, focused on the notion of racial difference as the foundation of racism, Carmichael and others drew on Marxist philosophy to suggest an economic impetus for racism. Disfranchised African Americans, they suggested, provided a surplus labor source, which helped keep wages for white laborers low, because white workers could easily be replaced.

Similarly, economic conflict seems to drive the racism of those on the street, especially directed at Mexican immigrants.

In 2009, illegal immigration was still a heated issue on the US political landscape. Conservatives railed against illegal immigrants, often arguing that they were taking jobs away from Americans. A common and convincing response to this assertion has been that the types of jobs that illegal immigrants are performing are those that most Americans will not do. This argument holds for the average US worker, but it breaks down for those on the street. Their means of employment and the types of jobs that they typically perform are the same as those of illegal immigrants, who form their own "catchout corners" around urban areas. Thus, although most of the complaining about immigrants stealing jobs appears to have little merit, those workers on the street represent an exception.

Even though they certainly betray racist views of Mexican immigrants, those living on the street also make explicit economic arguments. They quite consciously argue that immigrant labor undermines both their ability to get work and the earning power they command. James put it clearly, "Catchout Corner used to be a jumpin' spot, 'til all the Mexicans got here. Now there ain't no jobs 'cause the Mexicans work cheaper." Others were upset by the idea that illegal immigrants are given preference to native-born Americans, such as themselves. Motown put it passionately, "We was born and raised here, and they're gonna go hire someone that just got here?" They blamed employers and also the government for not effectively stopping illegal immigration. Anti-immigrant rhetoric could reach fever pitch. A rant by Tim once captured not only the language but the emotion widely shared on the issue as well: "Instead of blamin' everything on the fellas at the corner, they need to be doin' something about the Mexicans, man! I was born here, but they gonna go hire them fuckin' Mexicans, and we can't get no work." The cumulative racial disadvantage, rooted in legalized segregation and its lingering social and economic consequences, plays a significant role in the disproportionately high numbers of African Americans who are poor and homeless in the twenty-first century. But this does not necessarily inspire unifying attitudes among them. In short, those on the street often are racist victims of racism.

Religion and the Apocalyptic Cosmology of the Deep South

As in southern society generally, much discourse on the street was infused with religious ideology. We have discussed previously how religion contributes to fatalism—for example, Big E's comment that the only thing that will improve the situation for the homeless is for "God to come down and touch some hearts." Here we discuss the broader role of religion in coloring the life and language of those living on the street.

As it is for poor people in general, and especially for those in the South, religion is a personally and socially significant component of life and a lens for understanding the world in which we live. Those on the street find validation in their religious ideals, frequently citing popular tenets, like the idea that "one's reward lies in heaven," that "the meek will inherit the earth," and biblical references to Jesus' ministry to the poor and undesirable. It is notable that institutionalized religious groups reinforce these, including those who volunteer at shelters and come to the streets to preach (see Chapter 10). For worldly bystanders, this seems counterproductive. The religious ideals of those who are street homeless tend to justify, or at least trivialize, their poverty. But for those on the street, it also seems to have a soothing quality. Social activists all feel the maddening effect of injustice. That same injustice is so pervasively a part of the street homeless condition that perhaps the pacifying religious ideologies that they hold serve as respite, as a psychological buffer for inexplicable forces of unimaginable unfairness.

Religious imagery pervaded discourse among homeless individuals, even for nonreligious subjects. An angels-and-demons framework often defined discussions of provocative issues. Crack was referred to in these terms. Even hardcore addicts would talk about it as a demon, noting that the "devil got a hold" of them. L.A. described it: "It's like inhaling demons into your lungs." These types of fantastic themes could become quite exaggerated. While high, Hammer was especially prone to espousing the idea of life as a war with demons and that to survive, one had to be a "spiritually pure warrior." He also spoke of seeing demons. One might attribute this to schizophrenia, or drug-induced paranoid psychosis, but it never came off that way. Many people immersed in traditional southern religion speak the same way. Hammer never interacted with the demons, never exhibited any unexplained behavior, and never seemed "out of his mind," other than those periods where he was high on crack. Rather, like most of the others, whether drug users or not, his explanations of the world tended to be framed by apocalyptic religious themes, characteristic of the South, especially the poorest parts of it.

We might compare this phenomenon to the use of hallucinogenic drugs by various indigenous populations in North and South America. Peyote- or mescaline-induced visions are not wholly the products of the drugs, but rather moments built on pervasive cultural ideologies and current social circumstances.[8] Religion has provided a sense of order to an ostensibly chaotic world, from volcanoes and hurricanes to the viciousness of European conquerors. Similarly, those on the street partly interpret the seemingly inexplicable inequality in society, of which they are the victims, by drawing on Judeo-Christian religious themes, spoken with an apocalyptic southern twang.

Hegemonic religious ideologies often do function to legitimate the condition of the homeless. But just as religious themes framed other aspects of life on the street, they also did so, somewhat ironically, for the issue of personal freedom and autonomy. We have previously described our attempt to integrate a new research partner into the field (see Chapter 2). This produced disaster when he took a proselytizing posture toward the men at Catchout. His most heated exchange was with L.A., the man who had been invited to speak to the city council about homelessness. He declined when he was told he would have only three minutes and noted that it would not do any good. The new researcher told him that he "still had to try," and L.A. responded quite angrily, "I ain't got to do nothing this week but make sure my kids get into school!" Notable here is that he went on to say, "You ain't gonna use that devil psychology on me." L.A. was particularly politically minded, and he clearly meant to condemn the ideology of the establishment, which he felt our novice was pressing on him. The use of the word *devil* is not coincidental, being freighted with a reference to an exploitative "white" way of thinking, and also clearly employs a decidedly religious metaphor. This was a typical way to construct those things, which those on the street conceived of as opposing their freedom.

* * *

Street homelessness is a life of both pain and joy, of simultaneous peace and unrest. The intellectual urge to explain and classify should not undermine those complexities. Those on the street sometimes are macho and stoic and at other times emotional and vulnerable. They speak of past joys and past regrets and of both happiness and sadness. Decidedly they are not a depressing group of people, but rather real, complex human beings in a situation that any of us would find depressing. It is a testament to their strength and resilience that they manage at all to find and appreciate the positive aspects of an existence that most of us could not even imagine.

Values and feelings often are overlooked in sociological assessments, or at least they are flattened into measurable attitudinal variables and thereby ironically stripped of feeling and affect. As sociology has become more positivistic, the study of abstract and ambiguous things such as feeling is seen as less tenable, and as a discipline we tend to focus on more ostensible factors such as demographic information and behavior. But we know also that in life, actions are predicated by beliefs, values, and feelings. So along with grasping various demographics, understanding street homelessness requires that we develop a good conceptual grasp of those admittedly ambiguous concepts. Our examination of these suggests that, as in so many other respects, those on the street are not much different than the rest of us, both in our virtues and our failings. Rather, like the rest of us, they tend to be variously or even simultaneously patriotically reverent and politically critical, open-minded and bigoted, joyful and pained. Those on the street ultimately reflect the culturally infused religious beliefs of their broader social context, and, most especially, like other Americans, they hold tight to the values of freedom, autonomy, and cowboy-style individualism.

Notes

1. Bourdieu, *The Logic of Practice.*
2. Freire, *Pedagogy of the Oppressed.*
3. It is interesting to note that the "us" and "them" dichotomy framed the perspectives of those on the street about others on the street; this echoes Snow and Anderson, "Identity Work Among the Homeless."
4. Freire, *Pedagogy of the Oppressed.*
5. LaGory et al. report, in *A Needs Assessment of the Homeless of Birmingham and Jefferson County*, that the general homeless population in Birmingham is 67.6 percent African American; we believe rates of the street homeless subpopulation to be even higher.
6. Arnold, *Homelessness, Citizenship and Identity.*
7. Department of Housing and Urban Development, *The Third Annual Homeless Assessment Report to Congress.*
8. See Baer et al., *Medical Anthropology and the World System*, 2nd ed; Becker, "History, Culture and Subjective Experience."

7

Street Identities
and Creative Resistance

Identity is a difficult concept to pin down. We all employ various identities in various situations. To draw on Erving Goffman's dramaturgical conceptualization, we act out different roles in the different plays in which we have been cast.[1] But not all roles are equal. We each have a master status; that is, one of our roles is more prominent than the others. Certain roles become more definitive components of who we are in the eyes of others, as well as one's own self-concept. Most of us have more than one prominent role, usually split across our most important social networks, such as, family, work, church, school, and so on. One will be, for example, a dad at home and a professor at work, a daughter at home and a student at school. But our statuses normally are rather benign and not terribly confining. There usually is nothing particularly bothersome about the roles of mother, artist, engineer, and so forth, save for the occasional missteps when shifting from one role to another.

When status goes hand-in-hand with stigma, however, one's entire life is permeated by an oppressive identity conception. Those who are homeless are in this latter situation. "Homeless" is a master status—an identity that permeates the entire life of the person who is homeless—and the negative judgments it carries become rigidly attached to understandings of who a person is, even sometimes in that person's own estimation.

But it would be wholly insufficient to allow the notion of "the role" to encapsulate a discussion of the concept of "self." We certainly do act out various generalized roles, drawing on various different identities. This notwithstanding, social scientists should not be content with the idea that one's "self" is just the combination of these generalized perspectives. In this section we describe ways in which identity plays out among those who are street homeless—for example, ways in which they manage imposed stigmas.[2] At the same time, we also discuss an underlying notion of the self, which we believe is not encapsulated by any combination of fixed identities but rather is an inherent, although often suppressed, function of human agency and creativity.

Those living on the street are centrally focused on the issue of freedom and autonomy. While the popular conception is that they are the most broken subgroup among a generally broken group of people, we will consider the possibility that resistance to shelters and other institutions might at least in some cases actually signify aspects of functionality. The capacity for creativity and assertion of will indicate laudable notions of self, or at least laudable aspects of it. This is not intended to romanticize homelessness, taking an inverted but equally simplistic perspective that being homeless is pervasively functional, happy, or liberating.[3] Rather, having a more complex perspective of homelessness allows us to break free of the usual, uniform conceptualization of it as social problem. Understanding the multidimensional nature of homelessness requires that we do not reduce it to misery and dysfunction, producing neat categories for the purposes of fostering science or funding service.

We first deal with the issue of mitigating stigma and the various strategies employed by those who are homeless to deal with negative judgments. This includes ways in which they hold on to a sense of normality and potency in the estimation of their own lives, as well as defending against the judgments of others. We then identify a common personality type as a salient quality of those who are street homeless, overlooked by academic research as a variable of interest but nonetheless highly relevant to their resistance to services. Insofar as those on the street tend to be extroverted and animated, they do not fit well into the cramped and confining quarters of homeless shelters. Finally, we examine the pervasive claim that those living on the street felt a "peace of mind" by living on the street. While service providers and social scientists tend to dismiss this report as machismo or the rationalization of addiction, more artistic perspectives explain how disengagement from social structures can be liberating in some respects, though that should imply no justification of oppressive features of the status quo. Rather than dismiss the claim of "peace of mind" in order to retain a neat categorization of homelessness as unadulterated misery, we find the claim valid, though still only one dimension of a highly complex and contradictory social world, where misery certainly is present.

Identity Management

We have previously discussed the importance of recognizing that homelessness represents only one period on the life trajectory of a person. It is one switch on a long track (see Chapter 5). It is a simple, but crucial, insight that those who are homeless have nonhomeless pasts. Becoming homeless represents an all-out assault on one's identity. One goes, often quite suddenly, from being a person with a set of socially acceptable identities, to being "homeless," an identity that trumps, if not obliterates, all others. Many of those on the street maintain contact with their families.[4] But beyond drawing social and, more rarely, financial support from family, maintaining these contacts can also be seen as an effort to retain one's prehomeless identity. More than anyone else, our family members form their identity conceptions of us from our more complete biographies rather than particular periods. Lockett gave a clear indication of the importance of family in the formation and maintenance of nonhomeless identity. "I've been out here a long time, but I never felt homeless until my Mama passed. I didn't stay with her, but I always felt like I had a home until she passed."

Others understood themselves and their homelessness in contradistinction to their families. Hammer had a wife and a home but spent relatively long stretches on the street when "things got to be too much." Potato Water had considered it more thoroughly. As noted, differences with his parents were the impetus of a brief period of homelessness when he was fourteen. While this did not launch his chronic stay on the street, which resulted from a complex of other factors, this sort of turmoil in his biography did contribute to his reflections about his situation. "You know, my parents, they would take me in. They've asked me to come stay with them before. But we just don't see eye-to-eye. Besides that, I'm a grown man, I'm not going to go stay with my parents." For Potato Water, staying on the street was a matter of retaining some notion of his own identity in contrast to his parents. This was partly a matter of disagreement with them, but also a matter of not sacrificing his pride or independence by accepting their help.

Another way in which one managed and resisted the stigmatic homeless identity was the practice of giving gifts. We brought many donations over the course of our research, and our participants were always appreciative. But they often quite consciously avoided being seen solely as takers. Of course, from our perspective, the knowledge that they shared with us was exchange enough. Many of them came to accept this, but others insisted on giving us things, taking pride when they did. When Wasserman had forgotten a hat on a particularly sunny day in the open field at Catchout, a sure way to get sunburned, a man nicknamed Knucklehead gave him one to wear. When we left, Wasserman went to return the hat, but Knucklehead insisted that he keep it. Over the next several years, Knucklehead asked on several occasions if he ever wore it; it clearly was an important gesture. During another stay in Matty and Potato Water's camp, hospitality came partly in the form of a parting gift for each of us. These gifts were not thrown-together afterthoughts, but rather had been set aside in anticipation of our departure and were presented to us as tokens with which to remember our visit.

Another time, a man we had met in the Second Avenue Camp, who had since gotten off the streets when his disability aid finally came through, was selling handcrafted games in Five Points, the local equivalent of a public square. He insisted that Clair accept one of the games as a gift, noting that we had been kind to him when he was homeless. Another particularly memorable instance occurred when we stopped at Catchout on our way to check into the shelter. Teasing us about how bad our shelter stay was going to be, Lockett went to the store and brought back two large bottles of water, saying that we would be glad we had them (he was right). When we tried to pay him for them, he refused our money, saying, "Just remember, that's Catchout water," making the gift a gesture on behalf of the entire community.

The connections between gift giving and identity run through a variety of US capitalist notions, particularly the stigma attached to receiving charity. There is a culturally induced guilt and shame attached to taking something that one did not perceptively earn. To the thinking of many of our participants, they did not earn our donations, although as we saw it, they earned more than we could give. Giving gifts was a way to return the balance, to stave off the feelings of shame associated with being a "charity case." This may be especially important among those on the street who place particular value on their individual ability to work and earn.

Finally, managing stigma and the demolition of one's sense of self was sometimes done at the expense of others. In Chapter 6 we described the way in which some of those on the street would invoke negative and even racist conceptions of others, even those of like race and condition to themselves.[5] In one sense this reflects the value ideals that they hold, expressed in those notions of choice and laziness directed at others but not at themselves. But in another sense, this was a means of separating oneself from a stigmatized group. This was the case with the man who claimed, "I'm not like those guys." The implication was that other people on the street were somehow morally corrupt in ways that did not apply to him.

Other examples of this sort of identity management were frequent. After some conflict with the others at Catchout, Lockett moved to another part of town. When we saw him later, he talked about how he was not like the other men at the Corner, whom he at that time characterized as violent and corrupt, offering that assessment as the reason that he left the area. Of course, this sentiment did not persist. As noted, after getting off the street, Lockett would return to Catchout to "hang out with the fellas." And while Lockett's negative remarks about Catchout are common to most one-sided presentations of an argument, they also reflect a discursive separating of his own character from that of those on the Corner. This type of distancing was a common means of validating one's identity in the face of the homeless stigma.

Characters (Not Caricatures)

Most of our participants living on the street could be accurately described as "characters." Here we mean to use the positive sense of the term and also feel inclined to note the crucial distinction between being a "character" and that of being a "caricature."[6] The latter is an objectified version of a person that usually conveys humor at the caricatured person's expense. The former, we use in a positive sense; a "character" is an upbeat, charismatic extrovert. As mentioned, those on the street tend to be great storytellers, funny, and charismatic. They are enmeshed in very difficult circumstances and certainly are not content with that condition. But neither are they wholly defeated by it. When we would show up in the field, we nearly always were met with a jovial welcome.

A foundational question for our research concerned why someone would stay on the street rather than in the shelter. At the outset, this was something we could not understand because it seemed so obvious that shelter is preferable to no shelter. While perhaps not much of an academic assessment, the fact that those on the street tend to be "characters" may be one of the best explanations of their resistance to the shelters, which has seemed inexplicable to many experts and service providers. To survive in the shelter, one must be subdued and introverted. Not keeping to oneself can be downright dangerous. During our stay in the shelter, when some of the other residents suspected Wasserman of being a cop, one of the primary reasons for their suspicion was his "looking around too much."

During a stay at Matty and Potato Water's camp, we had planned to eat dinner at a shelter with Wayne and another camp resident named Nick. In the midst of pleasant, jovial conversation, Wayne and Nick left the camp separately and without announcement. When we got through the line at the shelter and got our food, Wasserman went over to sit with Wayne, but noticed that he was no longer talkative. He kept his eyes on his bowl of stew and muttered one-word answers as Wasserman talked. We noticed also that Wayne and Nick did not sit together, and they walked up to and away from the shelter separately, rejoining each other around the corner to walk back to the camp.

Extroverts do not do well at the shelter. One is well advised to keep their eyes on their plate. Outgoing, talkative people will encounter resentment and get into conflicts. In those cramped conditions, a "character" is a nuisance. On the streets, proximity to others is voluntary. If someone is getting on another's nerves, they need only to separate. While there are sometimes mild conflicts, and more rarely serious ones, the freedom to be oneself without typically getting into conflict may be one of the most appealing aspects of staying on the street.

Perhaps it is not hard to imagine that a bunch of men with nicknames like Knucklehead, Potato Water, Waffle House, Black, Hammer, Pookie, and Motown are not well suited for life in a shelter. Their nicknames often directly reflect their personalities or pasts. Hammer is a strong, commanding presence; Potato Water, a vodka-loving, jovial, cutup. They are strong personalities who would not thrive in an environment that requires one to draw back. Big E stated unequivocally that one had to be humble when going through treatment. He discussed how getting along with others in such cramped conditions was a real test of personality and how much one is willing to "tone it down."

Mitchell Duneier and Harvey Molotch observed the way street vendors who were homeless in New York City used various tactics to engage passersby.[7] These included the same types of stylized, character-infused discourse that we saw among those on the street. For the street vendors, this was a strategy designed not only to pass the time but also to sell their wares. We suggest that while being a character often is a survival strategy, especially in particular endeavors, the street also "selects" these types of personalities. On the street a strong personality is required to survive. But the very aspects that enable one to survive on the street may make it impossible for them to survive in the shelter. The disconnect between those living on the street and service providers may simply be due to personalities of those who are street homeless tending to be square pegs in the round holes of the shelter.

Creativity and the Coexistence
of Freedom and Oppression

The concept of homelessness clearly has negative connotations. At this writing, the word *homeless* elicits notions of mentally ill and hopelessly drug-addicted people who plague city streets pushing shopping carts and sleeping on park benches in lieu of getting a job.[8] Although research demonstrates the multitude of insufficiencies with this image, or at least the complexities surrounding it, nearly all agree that homelessness is a condition of pain and misery, a problem to be solved. In this section we address a small but significant literature, which celebrates the freedom of being homeless. While some ethnographers have glimpsed the creativity that is in many ways endemic to a life on the street, others hold a deeper appreciation of it, and their artistic rather than scientistic approaches offer unique insight.[9]

It should be clear that finding positive aspects in homelessness, done properly, *in no way* attenuates the culpability of social inequality in producing involuntary and problematic conditions of homelessness. Nonetheless, there exists a salient paradox in street homelessness. Our participants living on the street all discussed the various obvious hardships, but they also talked about having a "peace of mind." A constant in our findings, perhaps the only one, is that social life is full of these "contradictions." At some point the complexity of social life is entirely resistant to the overly broad generalizations common to social science.[10] Moreover, the specifications common to social science do not just underreport the complexity of social phenomena, but also reflect biases in doing so. Those vested in a disease explanation of homelessness are well served to construct the choice of the streets as rationalization of addiction.[11] This buttresses the model of service on which they operate and on which they are funded (see Chapter 9).

Homelessness research seems often to seek *the* characterization in an effort to be concise and consistent. This is the type of neat and convenient thinking that is required to secure funding for policy interventions, but reducing such complexities often are more a matter of playing politics than of accurate depiction. Service providers and social scientists conclude, therefore, that homelessness is bad. This is not untrue, just incomplete and overly simplistic. It is no coincidence that alternative views are largely found in the political writings, biographical essays, and travelogues of small-press radical literature. These are especially worthy of inclusion because they fill in parts of the homelessness picture left obscure by academics. The artistic sense and presentation of these writers fits nicely with those like Adorno, who call on social science to transcend the grip of instrumental rationality.[12]

"Homeless by choice" is a concept typically invoked by those wishing to alleviate themselves and society of their sizable role in producing poverty and homelessness. The plain fact is that most people are not homeless by choice. However, drawing on images of homelessness rooted in the hobo-adventurer, some people still seek their own personal Walden Pond, often by riding the rails, hitchhiking the highways, and squatting in abandoned buildings and under bridges. While their experiences do not totally capture that of the average person who is homeless, they can help explain the peace-of-mind "paradox" that the tunnel vision of instrumentally rational social scientists cannot.[13]

Travelogues from modern-day wayfarers suggest an appealing life of freedom, creativity, self-reflection, and a conscious attempt to remove oneself from social structures deemed exploitative and unacceptable.[14] Two such authors, Hibickina and Kika, write:

> This is what it means to be an adventurer in our day: to give up creature comforts of the mind, to realize possibilities of imagination. Because everything around us says no you cannot do this, you cannot live without that, nothing is useful unless it's in service to money, to gain, to stability.
>
> The adventurer gives in to tides of chaos, trusts the world to support her—and in doing so turns back on the fear and obedience she has been taught. She rejects the indoctrination of impossibility.
>
> My adventure is a struggle for freedom.[15]

Captured here is the notion of not only adventure but of a life of self-reflection and peaceful freedom.[16] This contributes to our understanding of the assertion by those living on the street of a peace of mind, which often is discounted as a rationalization of their addiction or mental illness rather than a legitimate voice. The popular position is held as unassailable: The choice to stay on the streets is the result of sickness. These homeless artists eloquently call this into question and hold a mirror to our biased suppositions.[17]

While his literary demeanor suggests he does not see himself as an artist as much as someone who just likes to write, Lee Stringer presents his lived experience with homelessness in a style reminiscent of Kurt Vonnegut.[18] Stringer did not intentionally become homeless and was not seeking adventure, yet such themes are nonetheless present. About the unacceptable assault on his freedom at a shelter, he writes:

I didn't stay another night. I didn't like the karma of the place, for want of a better way to put it—the guards, the pat-downs, the food lines, the whole watch-your-back, watch-your-mouth, watch-out-for-number-one, jailhouse mentality. I figured I'd just as well take my chance on the street.[19]

In a poetic example, the anonymous author of the book *Evasion* takes the reader through his life as a dumpster diver, squatter, train hopper, and shoplifter, with romantic attention paid to the creative demands and artistic qualities of living outside the system.[20] On vacation in a neobohemian, artsy community (an irony noted by the author himself), he writes:

And when the artists doing Yoga in the park gasped as I stumbled from the bushes at 5 a.m., wet and scary, they might not recognize it as art, but they should. I wanted a little credit. Rooftop sonnets and moldy bagel blues. A novel is born each night in an unlocked U-haul. Yes, I would show them art.[21]

Even while they are not structurally similar, we can draw insights from the experiences of the homeless adventurer, which are applicable to a great many of those living on the street, even when they are displaced by political-economic structure. For example, it clearly takes a good deal of creative energy to survive on the periphery of society.[22] The systems we all utilize to create and structure our lives are stripped away from those who are homeless. At the same time, these systems and our complex bureaucracies also represent stressors for the average person. Respite from the stresses of daily life is sought by all of us as we take time out of the day to relax or take vacations to get away from it all. So it is not difficult to understand that while homelessness comes replete with its own set of stressors, there are aspects of living on the street that represent a reprieve from many of the pains of modern life. This was something we soon came to realize and felt, too, each time we headed into the field.

As with most other people, neither of us would have traded our relatively comfortable lives for homelessness, but our time on the streets with our participants certainly was in part an enjoyable reprieve from the demands of ordinary life. Even though staying in the camps was difficult, uncomfortable, and stressful in its own way, it was at the same time a break. Being on the street was a trying and at the same time relaxing experience—like going on vacation, which is on the one hand a break from one's daily life, but also brings with it other stressors such as airline delays and getting lost in unfamiliar places. This was an insight that occurred markedly when Wasserman returned from out of town on the morning of our first overnight outing. As he fought traffic that delayed his return and dealt with a variety of ordinary daily problems by phone on the way, he thought, "I can't wait to get to the Corner and relax." He saw the irony of the thought immediately, but the feeling was genuine and would continue to be part of the experience of our research.

To survive on the street requires an undeniable self-dependence and creative spirit. Kim Hopper touches on it:

> Settlements of homeless people are lumpen creations, wrested out of waste spaces and discarded materials in the precarious margins of our urban landscape. By an alchemy born of necessity, their proprietors— people with no property except what they scavenge—have turned these outlaw spaces into places of habitation, respite, and even hope.[23]

Ultimately, we ought not gloss the complexities of homelessness, or any social phenomenon for that matter. If nothing else, the conceptions of homelessness in the radical literature of authors such as Hopper should lead us to a deeper understanding and appreciation of the homeless condition, in all of its complexity, shedding some light on how those forced into the streets manage to retain some agency and freedom. Despite their abandonment by society, those on the street must live somewhere. They therefore creatively seek out sustaining habitats.[24] Leonard Feldman reminds us "that public policy should be oriented toward enabling dwelling, not criminalizing it or reducing it to the stripped-down client relationship of the shelter."[25]

Plato said, "Necessity is the mother of invention." Those living on the street have necessity in spades. The popular conception among the public is that those who are street homeless are broken and depraved, beggars with no initiative, bums who take and never give. However, as we spent time with those on the street in various camps and gathering spots, we found people who tended to be highly innovative, engineering solutions to myriad problems that would get the better of many of us.

One does not typically think of daily life as artistic expression. That is because for most of us, daily life is largely unconscious routine and ritual. There are standard procedures for everything—eating, working, moving from place to place, and getting a home. There is no standard procedure for the person living outside the system. For them, ordinary daily life is filled with creative acts.[26]

The very condition of living on the street essentially constitutes a creative act. Some are better at it than others, but all of those who live on the street must actively stake a claim to space. They must invent their own home. Whether it is a tract of land along the train tracks or a spot on the sidewalk, and whether it lasts for years or just for the night, the person living on the street must say to the world, "This is mine. It used to be yours, you think it still belongs to you, but I claim it for myself." Often they take this creative act to impressive lengths, not only claiming space but also developing infrastructure and amenities. Even more impressive is that this act emerges so directly from their individual will. They do not rely on banks and financing, on family, on a real estate agent, on Wal-Mart, on plumbers and electricians, on friends with housewarming gifts, or on the power company.

This is of course not to say that those on the street are transcendent personalities, but they do certainly respond to necessity in impressive ways that reflect the coexistence of laudable qualities along with all of their often-discussed shortcomings. Moreover, even though they have something borne out of necessity, rather than transcendent personality, those on the street rely more directly on themselves than perhaps anyone else in society. Despite this, society views them as thoroughly broken people. For such broken people, they can be remarkably creative and effective. Even a police officer we interviewed admitted—though in a backhanded and critical way regarding how those on the street know how to manipulate arrest procedures, by claiming to be suicidal, for example—"They're smart. They're not stupid." Most of us would be paralyzed if all the people and institutions we relied on to build and structure our lives were suddenly gone. Whether by necessity, personality, or both, those who live on the streets are stronger and more creative than most of us are willing to give them credit for.

* * *

In the end, the concept of self cannot be given adequate treatment by group-level focus such as we have presented here. Nonetheless, we hope to have countered the perception of those living on the street as corrupted individuals by giving examples of identity and creativity that cast a positive light, especially in such an often-dark environment. Our experiences with those who are street homeless have changed us in ways we could not have predicted.[27] Our sociological backgrounds predisposed us to examine the causal implications of things such as race and class, and so we did not have much difficulty moving beyond the individual pathology explanations of homelessness. But we did not expect to be so frequently and utterly impressed. We expected to meet people who had been beaten down by society, and we did. We did not expect to meet people who, in their own creative ways, were beating back. For all of the problematic aspects of street homeless life, the strength and inventiveness of it should not go unappreciated.[28] Most of us live lives facilitated by right of law and the ability to get financing, and without these, our gears would grind to a halt. People on the street, however, often must run on pure will and creativity.

Notes

1. Goffman, *The Presentation of Self in Everyday Life*.
2. Snow and Anderson, "Identity Work Among the Homeless."
3. We differ from Marin, for example, who suggests, in "Helping and Hating the Homeless," that those who are homeless are socially necessary rebels. While he seems to imply this in a very existential way, there is a risk of insinuating that everything is fine the way it is. We do not think this is the case.
4. In Pippert's *Road Dogs and Loners*, the more gregarious "road dogs" were noted as being more likely to retain contact with their families.
5. See also Snow and Anderson, "Identity Work Among the Homeless."
6. Liebow, *Tell Them Who I Am*.
7. Duneier and Molotch, "Talking City Trouble."
8. Liebow, *Tell Them Who I Am*; Phelan et al., "The Stigma of Homelessness"; see, for example, Jencks, *The Homeless*.
9. Examples of the former include Hopper, *Reckoning with the Homeless*; Rossi, *Down and Out in America*; Snow and Anderson, *Down on their Luck*.
10. See Blumer's classic statement in "Sociological Analysis and the Variable."
11. Hopper and Baumohl's notion of the homeless as "held in abeyance" is another interesting position on the real underlying motivations of the shelter systems as managing "surplus populations"; Wagner notes, in *What's Love Got To Do with It*, that social scientists have an interest in pathologizing a phenomenon in such a way that only they can solve it.
12. Adorno, *Negative Dialectics*; Adorno and Horkheimer, *Dialectics of Enlightenment*; Wilson et al., "Saving Society from Instrumental Rationality."
13. See Eighner's *Travels with Lizbeth*, where the author writes of his own homelessness and his relationship with his beloved dog. He notes clearly at the outset that his homelessness was qualitatively different from the popular conceptions and that he avoided both shelters and "hobo jungles."
14. Some examples include Duffy Littlejohn's *Hopping Freight Trains in America*, *Evasion* by Anonymous, and *Off the Map* by Hibickina and Kika.
15. Hibickina and Kika, *Off the Map*, p. 9.
16. Given the controversial and politicized nature of homelessness and homelessness research, we find it impossible to stress enough that finding our way conceptually to a positive version of homelessness, or at least positive aspects of it, does not in anyway justify its existence as a forced condition of economic deprivation. These divergent conceptions of homelessness turn on the notion of freedom. When chosen or utilized as a means of liberation, homeless-

ness can be positive. When forced on someone in direct opposition to human freedom, it is an unacceptable form of oppression.

17. See also Eighner, *Travels with Lizbeth.*

18. Stringer, *Grand Central Winter.*

19. Ibid., p. 42.

20. Anonymous, *Evasion.*

21. Ibid., p. 51.

22. See Dordick's discussion of homelessness as improvisation in *Something Left to Lose.*

23. Hopper, *Reckoning with the Homeless,* p. 191.

24. See Toth, *The Mole People.*

25. Feldman, *Citizens Without Shelter,* p. 147.

26. See also Dordick, *Something Left to Lose.*

27. Other homelessness researchers have had similar experiences—e.g., Snow and Anderson, *Down on Their Luck.*

28. See also Hopper, *Reckoning with the Homeless;* Snow and Anderson, *Down on Their Luck.*

8

Business, Politics, and the Moving Ghetto

As noted in Chapter 5, the urban landscape, particularly where it is being redeveloped for upper- and middle-class people tired of commuting from the suburbs, becomes highly contested space. Those on the street have little ability to resist encroachments into the areas they have developed. Rather, under the weight of an implicit manifest destiny, homeless camps are evacuated and razed. Their residents, often with a fatalism that reflects their belief in the inevitability of these street sweeps, usually carry what they can with them and establish new camps in less contested spaces.[1] But just like the glacial spread of suburban development after World War II, we have seen since the 1990s a glacial spread of urban redevelopment. Pushed out of certain areas of the city, the homeless move into the closest older, poorer sectors, but find that they become targets of complaint there as well. Moreover, the places to which those on the street relocate might presently be dilapidated and impoverished, and might simply be next in line for redevelopment. As gentrification spreads, the pressures on those who are poor work out from the city center to the surrounding areas. Complaints from businesses and residents start soft and grow louder until another round of sweeps comes down.

The notion of the ghetto is most readily attached to the Nazi quarantining of European Jews and the segregation of African Americans in poor neighborhoods in the United States. The former was enacted through political policies, the latter through a combination of those in the form of legal segregation but also and significantly by way of economic stratification. Segregation of those who are homeless is a feature of political and economic forces as well, where gentrification increases the value of urban space; local governments, in turn, protect its new-found value by enacting policy. People on the street, like those who are poor, generally are relegated to this or that space, but only as long as that space remains of little economic value. Those who are homeless are in large part shuffled around under the economic and political pressures of redevelopment. This is especially true of the many who more directly stake claims to space by building camps. The result is that those on the street live in moving ghettos. They are segregated to wasted spaces, but only until the wheels of citizen complaints become squeaky enough or until these spaces become valuable again.

Structuring the Legitimate Citizen

In feudal Europe poor people essentially were assigned to the servitude of noblemen.[2] Those unable to secure a life of servitude were largely excluded from the social system altogether and became vagrants.[3] "Poor laws" therefore began to arise around 650 A.D.[4] English common law served a distinctly noble class of property owners in the Middle Ages, but examination of US vagrancy laws shows not much has changed.

As described in Chapter 1, the late 1800s saw a formerly migratory group of workers become part of the urban landscape, and the resulting discomfort of the public soon was translated into legislation.[5] In a number of US cities, "ugly laws" in various incarnations prohibited public appearance by undesirable people. Ambiguity in the wording of the laws allowed for enforcement based on the will of public sentiment and the discretion of authorities. An early version appearing in Chicago in 1881 read, "It is hereby prohibited for any person, who is diseased, maimed, mutilated or deformed in any way, so as to be an unsightly or disgusting object, to expose himself to public view."[6] Not surprisingly, those who were homeless often were the targets of these sorts of policies. In fact, enforcement of an ugly law occurred at least as recently as 1974 in Nebraska, where a police officer arrested a man who was homeless for having "marks and scars on his body."[7]

By 1920, most ugly laws had been struck down by the courts. Even those that remained on the books had been forgotten (save by that zealous Nebraska policeman). But the 1980s saw both increases in homelessness and the reappearance of vagrancy laws. Most famously, New York City and then-mayor Ed Koch postured new policies of homeless roundups as in the best interest of those swept off the street. Arline Mathieu argues, however, "that officials were more concerned with removing homeless people from the public's view than assuring that homeless individuals—

mentally ill or not—would receive adequate housing and social services."[8] These efforts were undertaken despite a lack of adequate low-cost housing or shelter space, and the rhetoric focused on the visual burden borne by the general public and tourists to New York.[9] The implications of these sorts of attempts to manage vagrancy are that those who are homeless intrinsically are a public nuisance and that the "normal," propertied classes are victimized by the mere presence of others so undesirable and unsightly—not to mention some normally private activities that they are forced to perform in public, such as drinking and going to the bathroom.[10] We have already discussed how homelessness is conflated with mental illness (see Chapter 4). Mathieu shows how this characterization is utilized for political purposes to justify forcibly removing those who are homeless to jails and shelters on the grounds of their "best interests."[11] With their reporting, the media aided in this rhetoric by framing the policy as aimed at removing "dangerous" mentally ill people as a "homeless policy."[12] Other cities followed with similarly punitive policies, and by 1999 all fifty of the largest cities in the United States had enacted or reenacted vagrancy laws.[13]

Common to the discourse surrounding new vagrancy laws is the replication of us-them divisions and the conflict of "contested landscapes."[14] Waldron offers a convincing philosophical counter to arguments made in defense of protecting public sensibilities.[15] He argues that the public's distress in seeing those who are homeless should not count as a negative burden because it is distress caused by a true condition of society. In other words, the US economy operates systemically in a way that inherently disfranchises a portion of its citizens, while at the same time society cries foul at those who are the inherent product of its own structures and policies. Waldron is worth quoting at length on the issue:

This principle of the given-ness of community is quite rightly invoked by Ellickson, Teir, and others when they argue that street people too have responsibilities to the community—responsibilities, for example, for the condition and safety of the community's public spaces. Whether or not a homeless person has any choice about being on the street, the sheer fact of his being there means that he too has a duty to the community in that regard. This we can accept. What we cannot accept, however, is that the definition of communal responsibilities should proceed on a basis that takes no account of the predicament of the homeless person or of the particular nature of the stake that she may have in the way public spaces are regulated. If the norms for public spaces are to be observed *by* him, then the logic of genuine as opposed to cosmetic communitarianism requires that those norms be constructed in part *for* him as well. We are not entitled to insist that the homeless person abide by community norms or that those norms be enforced against her, if the norms are constructed in an image of community whose logic denies in effect that homelessness exists.[16]

Captured here also is the interesting irony under which vagrancy legislation proceeds. In the United States the comparative comfort of many, not to mention the incredible wealth of a few, is in part the product of a system with inherent inequality. Yet while the comfort of the privileged has been built on this inequality, at great financial, physical, and emotional cost to those who are poor, vagrancy legislation legitimates and institutionalizes complaints about their existence.

George L. Kelling and James Q. Wilson's theory of crime in "Broken Windows" became a quick classic, not so much among sociologists but certainly among city planners, politicians, and those employed in the criminal justice system.[17] The premise of the theory is that law enforcement against small crimes such as loitering and defacing with graffiti, promotes a reduction in more serious crimes by creating some etheric sense of order. But as is betrayed by the host of political policies enacted against their presence, those people who live on the street often are conceptualized as "broken windows" themselves.[18] More important, the idea that dramatic improvement in crime prevention can be made without addressing the fundamental social structures, such as poverty, that are its strongest correlates seems to trivialize economic influences—to suggest that addressing inequality is not as important as cleaning off graffiti when it comes to improving the community. Moreover, as noted, those who are homeless are more likely to be the victims of crime than to commit serious crimes (not counting vagrancy and the like, which they cannot really avoid). As one psychologist who does outreach work with those who are homeless remarked in our interview:

[The businesses] point to garbage that may be dropped in front of a building, or, I've even had pictures of human excrement pushed in my face, [and they say,] "This is what we're trying to get rid of." I know it's hard to run a business in any setting, but especially in a downtown setting that's not thriving, so I guess maybe there are some valid points in there, but what seems to always be missed in these discussions … is that homeless individuals are much more often victimized by other people. So you get this feeling that either someone believes or they want other people to believe that if you are in a setting where there are a lot of homeless people, it's very unsafe because they are going to … assault you, and that very rarely happens.

Most especially, what we have witnessed in the enforcement of the "broken windows" theory in the redeveloping downtown is that while social problems diminish in some areas, they worsen in others. This suggests that what is going on is not the elimination of social problems but a relocated concentration of them in social space.

Though less explicit than vagrancy legislation aimed specifically at those who are homeless, the very construction and delineation of public and private space seek to separate "us" and "them." Bickford observes, "The world is being constructed, quite literally, in ways that adversely affect how we regard politics and who we regard as fellow citizens."[19] Suburbs increasingly are guarded by gates and security personnel, and at this writing, planned communities have become replete with stores and restaurants of their own.[20] Moreover, local governments and businesses work together, not only on specific policies, but also in constructing exclusive spaces. When city zoning ordinances create areas designated for single purposes, such as retail, entire city blocks become places exclusively for consumers.[21] This means that those who are poor or homeless, who are not counted among those consumers, are effectively forbidden from entire areas of the city. Sometimes, even by entering those supposedly public spaces, they are violating the law. Lawton noted this practice in Birmingham:

> Because you are poor and homeless, you become a quality-of-life offense to somebody—middle-class people, businesspeople. So they pass all these ordinances to lock you up because you are infringing on somebody else's quality of life. And they have made it a crime to relieve yourself on the streets, but they did not provide a bathroom for you to go in. So what do you do? If you have to go, you have to go. So you relieve yourself, [and then] you are a criminal and they lock you up. [Did] you know if you do not have a dollar and eleven cents or some amount of money in your pocket, you are a vagrant, and [it's] against the law to be a vagrant? So if you do not have any money, you are breaking the law if you are standing around downtown Birmingham.

This is a clear example of the collusion of economics and politics in maintaining class segregation. In order to enforce the economic interests of proprietors and legitimate residents, a host of governmental ordinances are enacted to regulate who legitimately can enter this or that space.

Moreover, identifying someone as a consumer is not only a function of actual purchase, but incorporated core understandings about who is and is not a legitimate citizen. At its core, labeling theory tells us that what we observe in someone's behavior is fundamentally affected not just by what they actually are doing but also by who we think that person is.[22] In our research we found that those who were homeless were daily consumers at their neighborhood convenience stores. But despite the fact that they routinely were consumers by the behavioral definition of the term, they still were treated as nonconsumers. For example, one store owner put a three-minute time limit on their shopping, after which they would be asked to leave. Even though they were spending money at a business, this did not mean they were welcomed there.

On several outings we accompanied some of the men from Catchout to a nearby grocery store, where the scowls and shaking heads were palpable, despite the fact that they had come to make purchases just like the other customers. On other occasions we were given money to make purchases for particular people, who may have been given a temporary and even sometimes permanent ban from certain retailers. We also experienced the judgmental stares during our own stays sleeping on the streets, when we staggered into retailers, dirty, tired, hungry, dehydrated, with minimal funds and a wanting look, searching for some kind of relief.

Increasingly, there are attempts to extend a sense of the private further and further into public life. This is accommodated by political maneuvering and suburban development, which, in cyclical fashion, contributes to the legitimizing of an attitude of exclusion.[23] In Chapter 4 we noted that the conflation of homelessness with mental illness and addiction suggests that it is becoming increasingly a medicalized condition.[24] In this regard, service provision for those who are homeless takes up a treatment model, which we will discuss at length in the next chapter. But the legal approaches of local governments and business also employ a medicalized conception of homelessness, and they, too, react with a treatment model of sorts, although theirs is a quarantine approach characteristic of disease management strategies of the past.[25]

Prior to the domination of the germ theory as the guiding premise of professional medicine, illness sometimes was understood as the result of vapors, called miasmas, that emanated from undesirable places such as swamps or poor parts of town.[26] When coming in contact with undesirable people, wealthier individuals were known to spray perfume on a handkerchief and cover their nose and mouth so as not to breathe in the unsavory and diseased vapors.[27]

We might easily say that society views homelessness as a psychological miasma—a condition brought on by the sight of a homeless person, makes people feel *dis-ease*.[28] The general public is uncomfortable seeing those who are homeless, perhaps because their very presence calls into question the validity of their own lives and all the things that they have. To deal with public unease, vagrancy legislation in both the past and present attempts to forcibly remove the source of the discomfort.[29] We no longer cover our noses; we collectively cover our eyes. Vagrancy legislation is not an attempt at resolving homelessness but at hiding it to protect our sensibilities; it is an attempt to quarantine those who are homeless from the rest of "us."[30] And while quarantining likely does little even to make the problem invisible—common sense would tell us that the person sleeping on a bench in the park has probably run out of suitable places to go—it tells us a great deal about the general attitude society holds toward those who are homeless. It appears many view homeless people as constantly invading our space and spirits, interfering with our ability to achieve happiness and our notions of the good life. Of course, this logic holds only if we successfully ignore how poverty is a dialectical mandate of wealth in our economy.[31]

Cops and Shops: Quarantining Those Who Are Homeless in Birmingham

Businesses often feel victimized by the presence of those who are homeless. In Birmingham this is especially clear in Five Points South, a shopping, dining, and drinking district where the merchants association has argued that people who are homeless drive away customers by generally being a nuisance. The ire of Birmingham businesses especially in the Five Points area seems to be increasing, based on several factors, including a seemingly growing number of people living on the street and the redevelopment of business and entertainment districts in various other areas of the city.

Five Points is a trendy nightlife district but has faded in its popularity. In the center of Five Points is a rather bizarre fountain featuring a statue of a ram-headed man sitting atop a stone tree trunk reading from an undetermined book to a gathered circle of various entranced woodland animals. Until a 2007 renovation, "The Story Teller Fountain," as it is known, had fallen into a state of disrepair, and the streams of water that usually swirled around the animals had settled into a murky stagnant pool. Surrounding this centerpiece is a diverse array of business, from the highest-priced restaurants in town to hotdog stands and head shops. There is a wine and cheese bistro on one corner and across the street a dank, graffiti covered bar hidden away in the basement of an old hotel. In succession on one block there is a ritzy piano lounge, a Mexican restaurant that throws Latin dance parties, and a seedy pool hall. Down from another corner are a Thai restaurant, a vegetarian health food store, and a barbecue joint.

The diversity of businesses is paralleled by the diversity of people. Yuppies drink happy-hour wine on the patios of the nicer establishments, angst-ridden youth frequent the head shop and tattoo parlor, while college students go to the midpriced bars, and lawyers go to the expensive ones. Some meet after hours at the dance clubs. In the midst of all of this, those who are homeless punctuate the sidewalks of the area, particularly around the fountain and on the steps of the historical church right behind it.

But in recent years, other commercial pockets have been developed and the popularity of the Five Points area has declined. In what appears to be a direct correlation of this decline, the conflict between the businesses and those who are homeless has become more frequent. The Five Points Merchants Association proposed, for example, that the park benches in the area be removed so those who are homeless could not sit on them.[32] Clearly profit is the central concern for these businesses; few of them would deny this. They often framed the issue as a matter of community revitalization and quality of life, but these were only intermediate concerns between those who were homeless and the bottom line. The merchants' essential premise is that customer bases are negatively effected by the presence of homeless people. The owner of an expensive optical shop, for example, was quoted in the newspaper: "I would say there are people who don't want to come down here to do business with me because they don't want to contend with it."[33]

One key rhetorical attribute of the attempts to manage those who were street homeless in Five Points was an appeal to a sense of historical character. Five Points, it was said, was deteriorating, not because of economic competition, but rather because of the influx of negative social elements. Of course, it is questionable at best as to whether Five Points was ever the historical social utopia asserted by the merchants wanting to rid the streets of homeless people. Wasserman's memory from when he moved to Birmingham in 1994 is that Five Points was the edgy area that teenagers would sneak away to, congregating at the fountain for all sorts of deviance. Still, the rhetoric of one merchant presents a whitewashed "community of memory" clearly directed at vilifying those on the street.[34] One merchant lamented, "Five Points used to be viewed as 'the town within the city.' ... I'd like to see it regain that. Why can't Five Points be that town?"[35]

Those living on the street were are not the only targets of irritation by local residents and businesses. A variety of institutions that serve people who are homeless also have come under fire. Opposition to shelter programs and soup kitchens was equally strong from neighborhood associations of communities peppering the north and west sides of the city, where older, poorer neighborhoods experienced increases in homelessness and the influx of homeless services in the wake of suburban sprawl. One downtown mission was closed to make room for lofts and moved into one such area, while the expansion of the shelter programs by another was blocked by a local neighborhood association.

The church in the middle of Five Points had long served breakfast on its front lawn. The local newspaper reported how, as the agitation of merchants had grown, the church itself increasingly had become an object of disapproval:

> "[The church has] to understand that they don't operate in a vacuum," said Jeff Tenner, Five Points South Merchants Association president. "There's a large number of people who come in, get what they need and they leave. But there are a few who hang around and occasionally they drink and panhandle and they bother people. It diminishes the quality of life for merchants, residents, customers and tourists. If they want to minister to them, that's fine, but they can't allow them to use the front lawn as a home base all day and all night long."[36]

There is an irony in the merchants association agenda, particularly in light of the historical character of the community in the area. The diversity of Five Points has always been its trademark and extends not only to the types of people who coalesce there, but also to the businesses that serve them. The targeting of homeless people by local businesses in Five Points overlooks a notion of community that is not tied exclusively to considerations of the bottom line. This is representative of a broader phenomenon, whereby suburban expectations of living exclusively among people "just like us" are carried into diverse urban spaces. This expectation usually has negative consequences for those who are poor or otherwise undesirable. But it has consequences for the wider community as well, where spaces in which diverse people can interact among diverse enterprises are giving way to developing pockets of homogeneity. As Jeff, a radical community activist (a member of Food Not Bombs), put it:

> Here in my hometown, there's a place where people of all types have come for my entire life, since I can remember. They come to Five Points South, and they coexist. I've seen people become

friends down there of different ages and different classes, where
there normally is no place where they can all see each other.
We [need to] preserve that place, that very spot, because it is a
traditional place where community is created. And the guy from
Starbucks said, when they started their little group to oppose the
homeless down there, they wanted to "reclaim the neighborhood."
That's the guy from Starbucks! You can't *reclaim* that neighborhood
for *Starbucks!*

Reaction to the general deterioration of the area to which the business owners feel homeless people significantly contribute has taken several direct forms, including advising their patrons not to give money to
panhandlers and to deny those who are homeless access to their facilities. Signs are conspicuous in almost every storefront: "Restrooms are
for customers only." While we certainly can be sympathetic to a business not wanting to be the public restroom for the whole town, in Five
Points the rule is not uniformly applied. As a test, we walked into various restaurants and asked to use the restroom and were never denied.
This is not the case for those on the street. The idea is to keep undesirable elements away from customers and also to make the area as uncomfortable and uninviting as possible for those who are homeless. More
directly, in some businesses there are posters advising people not to give
money to those who are street homeless, specifically citing that they
will only use it to buy drugs and alcohol. One bar's entrance is adorned
with a large sign reading, "No bums, hobos, or transients allowed."
    These practices have only increased tensions and exacerbated prob-
lems. Those on the street note that there is nowhere to use the restroom,
since they are forbidden by the businesses and the city does not provide
any public facilities. To our knowledge there is only one public restroom
in the whole city, located in a park, but it remains locked unless there is
a scheduled park event, such as a softball tournament. As a result of this
overwhelming lack of public accommodation, one particular incident
has become legendary. Businesses, police officers, and even service
providers have all told various versions of a story about homeless person who defecated on the doorstep of an upscale Five Points business.
One police officer concluded his telling of it by suggesting that those
who are homeless should at least have enough self-respect to "go in the
bushes." This story is heralded as evidence of "the problem." In the estimation of the businesses and local government, it captures the way in
which those who are homeless are a constant nuisance, a threat to com-
merce, and simply disgusting. However, those on the street in the area

added some additional details to the story left out by local authorities and proprietors. According to their version, the homeless man was in a state of digestive emergency, went to the restaurant, and begged to use the bathroom, admitting to them that he understood it was against the rules and that he would not ask unless it was truly an emergency. The restaurant refused. Later, in an act of retaliation and protest, the man intentionally defecated on their doorstep.

Regardless of the veracity of either narrative or one's moral assessment of the act itself, the construction of the doorstep defecation legend clearly illustrates the agendas in conflict. The way in which businesses and city officials construct the story is a clear example of the way that their interests play out in narratives and also betrays their position on homelessness. The authorities' version leaves out information that casts the restaurant as rigid and heartless. The implication is that the manager and employees simply arrived one morning to find that someone had randomly defecated on their doorstep. With no other explanation, the insinuation is that those who are homeless simply are animalistic. The construction of the narrative by those on the street suggests a clear tension between themselves and the rest of the city, and the recognition of their own stigmatized position.

Because businesses possess institutional savvy and sociopolitical connections, they naturally turn to the city government for help. They complain to the police and the city council and push for the enactment of a variety of vagrancy laws. In the ways that local governments involve themselves in defending the economic interests of some in opposition to the civil rights of others, they betray the alignment of their interests with business. This alignment has been institutionalized by a host of city ordinances and public policies in Birmingham.

The connection between business and the local political structure is explicitly institutionalized in the form of a security force called City Action Partnership (CAP) that operates in the downtown district and is mostly funded by local businesses. While the force performs all sorts of services, such as helping stranded motorists and giving directions, it also acts as additional eyes and ears for the police, calling their attention to trouble. They also monitor those who are homeless, with an eye for any impact their actions might have on local businesses—for example, their sleeping in doorways, panhandling, and so on. The director was a former police captain and held negative views of those who were street homeless, views that were commensurate with those of other police officers we interviewed and observed. In her estimation, those on the street were seen as a public nuisance, and measures to remove them from public space were warranted. Of the three CAP officers we interviewed, two shared this same disposition, one adding repeatedly that street homeless people get complacent with their lot in life and lose all initiative.

But Bobby, the third CAP officer we interviewed, shocked us with his characterization of those on the street:

> Downtown, the general public sees a homeless person, [who is] maybe not cleanest shaven, the most well dressed, might not have all their teeth[,] … and they just try to pass them without looking them in the eye. I don't understand it. … How they can do that, being human? I figured everyone would understand that they've got feelings just like you and I.

In this book we mostly focus on how institutional positions tend to frame how a person comes to see the world they live in—for example, how service providers intellectually recognize the structural aspects of homelessness, but because of the agendas of the social programs they run, they come more implicitly to see homelessness through the lens of individual disease and deficiency (see Chapter 9). But Bobby serves as a reminder that a complex set of factors go into experiencing the world. While his experiences with those on the street likely were ostensibly the same as his colleagues', Bobby's way of seeing led him toward much different conclusions. As with so many other events, our interview with him stood out as a reminder about the complexity of social life and the dangers of categorical thinking, this time our own potential to think categorically about people from various institutions.

In Birmingham, specific vagrancy legislation began to reemerge in the late 1990s and has continued in an upswing to the time of this writing. The police and local government agencies continue to lay siege to homeless encampments, often literally bulldozing their entire contents, under the auspices of cleaning up the city.[37] Like other city initiatives, these homeless sweeps have been postured as being in the best interests of both those who are homeless and society at large.[38] In at least one instance, local shelters lent their residents to help sweep up the camps of those living on the street.

A 1999 "doorways ordinance" gave police the power to remove people on the street who were sleeping in the doorways of businesses. During our research an "urban camping initiative" was being discussed by the city council that would have made it illegal to "stay" on public property. This intentionally vague wording gives much latitude to the police who then would have the discretion to decide exactly what constitutes "staying," and it was an attempt at managing the presence of those who are homeless. The city councilman for the redeveloping downtown district said as much, though the wording of the proposal could not legally specify them as the target. The councilman ultimately was not reelected, but our interview with him was nonetheless illuminating, especially since similar proposals continue to float around the halls of city government.

"The parks are for everyone," the city councilman told us, "You should not be able to be in the park with your belongings scattered about, making someone else uncomfortable." This is clearly inconsistent. If the parks indeed are for everyone, this logically would include those who are homeless.[39] Being uncomfortable at another's mere presence does not justify an ethical claim for their removal. A racist white man, for example, cannot have an African American family banned from a public park because he is made uncomfortable by their presence. Still, this somehow was seen as a legitimate position when applied to those who were homeless. This is indicative of the pervasiveness of the homeless stigma and particularly the notion of homelessness as a choice. Legitimately applying this to those who are homeless, but not an ethnic group, would necessarily hinge on the notion that people choose to be homeless—that is, that they are somehow morally culpable for the condition whereas we do not choose our ethnicity. In essence, to legislate particularly against those on the street, one must hold that it is not morally legitimate to be street homeless. But since political and economic structures predict increases and decreases in homelessness (see Chapter 3), we can conclude that there are a significant number of people disfranchised by macrolevel forces. They therefore are not completely responsible for their condition, or at least it seems that society significantly shares in that responsibility.

As noted, because of its relative isolation from businesses, Catchout Corner receives less constant attention from the authorities. Police pressure there seems more intense but less frequent. For example, the men at Catchout are banned from the corner a few times a year, whereas in Five Points, those who are homeless are continuously harassed and arrested for minor "quality-of-life" offenses. Sweeps at Catchout are connected to local events such as the annual City Stages Music Festival, the Mercedes Marathon, the Crawfish Boil, or the occasional complaint from the few nearby businesses, but they are not dealt out on a daily or weekly basis. The most intense pressure came from one officer who works the Catchout area. The men just call him by his car unit number, #122, and dislike him intensely. They tell stories about him driving down the sidewalk where they sleep and arresting people simply for being on the "wrong side of the bridge." Of course, we could not verify these stories directly, but they were frequent and rather consistent between participants. Additionally, we were able to conduct a face-to-face interview with #122 and found him to be an archetype for the antihomeless approach that was playing out among businesses and the city council.

As with the city councilman we had interviewed, #122 constructed homelessness in Birmingham as significantly the result of people from out of town.[40] He commented:

> I mean other municipalities will actually put people on a bus because we do have so many shelters and the homeless people are actually treated quite well here. All the way from Atlanta, people will get off the bus, and we say, "How did you get here?" And they will be like, "Somebody bought us a ticket to Birmingham. They told us to come on down here—the shelters are great, food's great— you'll enjoy it there. ..." And I understand why the businesspeople are upset, because you got some guy sitting in your doorway when you start to open your business. He's defecated, urinated, creating a problem, pallets all over the place, stinks—you got customers wanting to come in. It is a problem.

In #122's estimation, those who are street homeless typically are animalistic addicts and beggars. Referring to our closest participants, he commented, "The guys at Catchout Corner would be the hard-core drug addicts." When asked what could be done about homelessness, he replied that there was "no hope" for people like them and that while one might occasionally get her or his life together, it was "rare." Though #122 explained that there was no way he could lock them all up, since the jails are overcrowded, he noted that he had to move them from one spot to another occasionally. He claimed also that charitable donations enabled homelessness in general and addictions in particular:[41]

> People think, oh this guy's just down on his luck, but they don't know where that money is really going. That guy will take that money and buy alcohol or crack, or they will sell the things people give them, blankets, whatever. They can sell pretty much anything.

Finally, #122 discussed how people who are homeless manipulate the system, for example, by saying they are suicidal so they can get an evaluation in a hospital, delaying their booking into the jail.

Suffice it to say, #122 holds a negative view of those who are homeless. At one point he mentioned, "I get up and go to work every day, so I don't see why they can't" (though he ironically noted in other parts of the interview that some of those who are homeless, those at Catchout in particular, do work). Similar statements were made by other police officers. At Food Not Bombs (FNB) picnics, police officers would harass both the people who were homeless and FNB volunteers.[42] As the FNB is a very political, protest-oriented group, sociopolitical arguments between FNB volunteers and the police officers were a window into their opposing dispositions. We discuss the FNB in more detail in Chapter 11. The police officers typically would reflect the same negative conceptualizations of those who are homeless that #122 embraced. In their estimation, most people chose to be homeless, many were criminals, and others were a nuisance at best.

The tumultuous relationship between those who are homeless, on the one hand, and businesses and government, on the other, reflects a deeper cultural problem. As Lawton noted in response to the proposed vagrancy laws, "You see, that's a symbol of our sickness. Someone's poverty should not offend you." Lawton railed against businesses that openly exploited those who were homeless, such as the plasma donation centers and temporary labor centers. He argued the city should shut them down, noting a particular irony in the fact that those who were homeless sold their blood but had very little access to health care themselves (see Chapter 4). Lawton contended that local businesses and the city council wanted to create a shopping island in the city of Birmingham, expelling all of those who were poor and homeless from the area. Their failure, as he saw it, was not addressing the systemic issues of poverty and attendant considerations such as public transportation. Lawton saw homelessness as an outgrowth of a "new economic Jim Crow" that plagues the country, and exclusionary political solutions such as vagrancy legislation were in his opinion only exacerbating the problem. As he observed:

> You are not going to solve homelessness with military solutions. You solve homelessness with justice. And the punishment, the exclusion, and [the] driving people out is not the solution. The solution is justice. So we will continue to give that witness and work for that, with whatever that requires.

Also keenly present in this excerpt is the extent to which Lawton's radicalism derived from his religious beliefs in a way that parallel liberation theologies.

A deeply religious man, Lawton was of the mind that Christianity was founded on ideals of love, inclusiveness, and liberation of the soul. For him, discussion of class conflict and structural oppression were always underpinned by deeper cultural problems concerning love and inclusiveness. "By and large wealthy people don't want to see homeless people. We don't have the capacity to love that way."

* * *

Vagrancy legislation and police harassment are the direct result, not of the general existence of homelessness, but of the immediate presence of people who are homeless. As we discussed earlier in this chapter, businesses would be happy with the quarantining of people who are homeless in this or that space, rather than the alleviation of homelessness. Storefronts are interested in keeping those who are homeless away. They may therefore support efforts to help people get off the streets, but they equally support subversive tactics designed to literally push people out of the merchants' part of town into another.

At a community forum an official from Operation New Birmingham, a city-funded group dedicated to the revitalization of downtown, described and supported an initiative called housing first, a philosophy that advocates providing subsidized housing in advance of enrolling those with substance-abuse or mental health problems in treatment programs. While this certainly may help get people off the street by removing many conditions that keep them out of service institutions, it does not address more fundamental problems of community and exclusion. Without conscious attention to those core questions about the nature of community itself, these "housing first" dwellings likely will be hidden away in barren sections of town and so will effect exclusion from job opportunities and, more generally, from participation in the community as a whole. The Operation New Birmingham representative contended that the financial interests of business and helping those who were homeless were not necessarily in conflict. But as long as the financial agenda of local businesses causes them to seek the mere removal of homeless people from public space, the functionary channels of exclusion that are at the heart of the political and economic disfranchisement of those who are homeless in the first place will only be exacerbated. Business support for a variety of service-providing strategies is consistent with entrepreneurs' economic motivation only because the strategies result in the exclusion of those who are homeless from public space. In the next chapter we address the service-provider industry in more detail.

Notes

1. See also Wagner, *Checkerboard Square*, for discussion of the shuffling around of those who are homeless.
2. Axelson and Dail, "The Changing Character of Homelessness in the United States."
3. Arnold, *Homelessness, Citizenship and Identity*; Axelson and Dail, "The Changing Character of Homelessness in the United States"; Kyle, *Contextualizing Homelessness*.
4. Axelson and Dail, "The Changing Character of Homelessness in the United States"; Phelan et al., "The Stigma of Homelessness"; Rossi, *Down and Out in America*.
5. Schweik, *The Ugly Laws*.
6. Quotes from Susan M. Schweik's *The Ugly Laws*, were taken from an early version of her manuscript, which she most graciously sent us years before the 2009 publication of her book.
7. Schweik, *The Ugly Laws*.
8. Mathieu, "The Medicalization of Homelessness and the Theater of Repression," p. 174.
9. Hopper, "Homeless Choose Streets over Inhuman 'Shelters'"; Marcus, *Where Have All the Homeless Gone?*; Mathieu, "The Medicalization of Homelessness and the Theater of Repression."
10. Gibson, *Securing the Spectacular City*; Waldron, "Homelessness and Community"; see Kyle, *Contextualizing Homelessness*, for an excellent treatment of the obsession with normalcy and its relationship to stigmas of homelessness.
11. Mathieu, "The Medicalization of Homelessness and the Theater of Repression."
12. Ibid.; also, Arnold, *Homelessness, Citizenship and Identity*.
13. Arnold, *Homelessness, Citizenship and Identity*; see also Gibson, *Securing the Spectacular City*, for a detailed account of those in Seattle.
14. Wright et al., *Beside the Golden Door*; see also Arnold, *Homelessness, Citizenship and Identity*; Gibson, *Securing the Spectacular City*; Kyle, *Contextualizing Homelessness*.
15. Waldron, "Homelessness and Community."
16. Ibid., p. 111, italics are in original.
17. Kelling and Wilson, "Broken Windows"; Gibson, *Securing the Spectacular City*.
18. Waldron, "Homelessness and Community."
19. Bickford, "Constructing Inequality," p. 356.
20. Ibid.
21. Ibid.
22. See Becker's classic, *The Outsiders*, on labeling; see also Rosenhan, "On Being Sane in Insane Places."
23. Bickford, "Constructing Inequality"; Kyle, *Contextualizing Homelessness*; see also Duneier and Molotch's discussion, in "Talking City Trouble," of the "urban interaction problem."
24. See Lyon-Callo, "Medicalizing Homelessness"; Lyon-Callo, *Inequality, Poverty, and Neoliberal Governance*; Mathieu, "The Medicalization of Homelessness and the Theater of Repression"; Phelan et al., "The Stigma of Homelessness."

25. See Foucault, *The Birth of the Clinic.*

26. Gallagher, "Public Health and Social Medicine."

27. Ibid.

28. Clair et al., *Experiencing the Life Cycle*, p. 165.

29. Zukin, in *Landscapes of Power*, has called this the "institutionalization of urban fear."

30. Arnold, *Homelessness, Citizenship and Identity*; Hopper, *Reckoning with the Homeless*; Hopper and Baumohl, "Held in Abeyance"; Kyle, *Contextualizing Homelessness*; Foucault's discussion of quarantining as an exercise of social control, in *The Birth of the Clinic*, also is relevant here.

31. See also Waldron, "Homelessness and Community."

32. Coman, "Merchants Group Pushes to Improve Area's Ambiance."

33. Coman, "Street Ministry Draws Complaints."

34. "Community of memory" comes from Bellah et al., *Habits of the Heart.*

35. Quoted in Coman, "Merchants Group Pushes to Improve Area's Ambiance."

36. Coman, "Street Ministry Draws Complaints."

37. Coman, "Homeless Camps Set for Removal."

38. Ibid.

39. This is the thrust of Waldron's argument in "Homelessness and Community."

40. See our discussion of this in Chapter 3.

41. We will return to the concept of "enabling" in the next chapter.

42. As we will discuss in more detail in chapter 11, the FNB is a radical group organized only by the ideology that food is a right and, especially in Birmingham, with the aim of reclaiming public spaces. They provide street meals (they call them picnics) at the fountain in Five Points.

9

Homeless Services:
Healing the Sick

The dominant model of homeless-service provision in the United States functions out of the dominant conceptions of homelessness (see Chapters 3 and 4). That is, service programs institutionalize concepts of homelessness as primarily a function of mental illness and addiction by mainly and sometimes exclusively offering services aimed at treating those conditions. While this approach confers all sorts of benefits on those for whom homelessness is a function of addiction and mental illness, it excludes a variety of other people for whom these are not significant factors. In this chapter we explore the problems of this medical model of homeless-service provision.

This is a difficult chapter to write. Homeless-service providers are nearly all good-hearted people who are highly educated on the issue of homelessness. They can tell you all about the structural inequalities that predicate homelessness, and they understand it as a complex issue by no means neatly reducible to mental illness and addiction. But despite often broad and rich understandings, service providers are enmeshed in an institutional framework wherein the scopes of service are heavily constrained. One of these key constraints has been the focus of service programs on treating homelessness as a disease.

While we are critical of the medical model of service provision, a few key observations are necessary at the outset. The medical model is manifest in a variety of ways at a variety of institutions, but there certainly is variation in homeless-service provision. None uniformly reflects the medical model. Our critique therefore is directed at the model itself, not at this or that service institution. Just as a regression line indicates a tendency among cases that often are significantly varied, we critique a tendency toward medicalization found among diverse service institutions.

Moreover, it should be clear that we are not denigrating the need for treatment per se. Certainly many people in general and many homeless individuals in particular need treatment, either because alcohol, drugs, or mental illness landed them on the streets or are keeping them there. Still, the disease conception of homelessness has promoted a rather exclusive service model, whereby those who do not need or want treatment have few other options. Those who are homeless, but who do not fit the vision and directive of the medical model are left in the lurch. Thus, our critique is aimed not at the value of treatment per se, but instead the exclusivity of medicalized conceptions of homelessness and the service model that emerges from them, something backed by particular interests and maintained by particular social powers.

The Medical Model and the Hegemony of Helping

Just as the nature of homelessness has varied across historical periods, homeless services also have changed, dramatically. Public policies influence the criteria for admitting people to the shelter, and the space available grows or shrinks accordingly as service institutions struggle to identify exactly what their role ought to be and who they are obliged to help.[1] Until the 1980s, when homelessness reemerged in the national spotlight, homeless shelters mostly provided emergency services. That is, service institutions were a place only to get food and shelter. The emergency shelter is a stopgap measure sometimes called, "three hots and a cot," because the focus simply is on providing the most basic of human necessities.

On the idea that the emergency shelter model does not address the problems seen as endemic to the homeless condition, the continuum-of-care model emerged as a new paradigm of homeless services.[2] Continuum-of-care facilities not only provided basic necessities such as food and shelter but also offered more comprehensive services, including treatment for mental illness and addiction.[3] Clients—the term itself particularly reflective of this paradigmatic shift—typically are treated in residential shelter programs, then helped with gaining employment, moved into transitional housing and, the hope is, gradually reassimilated into normal society as now-functioning individuals.

There is no doubt that a number of people have been helped back into housing by service institutions and particularly by those operating treatment-oriented continuum-of-care programs. However, high rates of recidivism and the stable, if not growing, number of those on the street who tend to resist these service institutions is evidence that homeless services are not entirely sufficient.[4] In itself, this is a rather uncontroversial claim. Many shelter directors themselves concede that homelessness is best addressed at a structural level, by correcting a lopsided opportunity structure that systematically disadvantages particular groups, those who tend to cycle in and out of homelessness. But despite this recognition by most providers, the services they offer still tend primarily to treat addiction and mental illness.[5]

Medicalization is a process by which nonmedical conditions become understood in a medical framework.[6] Insofar as homelessness is conflated with addiction and mental illness, both of which have come to be understood as disease, it is increasingly treated as a medical condition itself. The essential characteristic of homelessness is simply that one does not have a home. It does not necessitate any inherent pathology. However, the continuum-of-care model works off a conceptualization that folds other conditions into that of being homeless. According to the perspective of this dominant model, homelessness primarily is either caused by or at least inextricably linked to addiction and mental illness. This emphasis is made clear by the preponderance of treatment for these in lieu of other services and by the structure of services that make enrollment in treatment a prerequisite to accessing other services like job training and placement. Even where a broader spectrum of services is offered, treatment becomes the passkey to accessing them.

Continuum-of-care services do address some of the shortcomings of emergency shelters but contain their own problems. For one, medicalizing homelessness can mitigate discourse on those structural conditions that many suggest ought to be at the forefront of discussion.[7] Lyon-Callo writes that "focus on 'disease' within the discourses of 'helping' actually obliterates discussion of alternative explanations and thus hinders developments aimed at resolving homelessness through altering class, race, or gender dynamics."[8]

In addition to obscuring social structural causation, the medical model can also have negative consequences for the individuals wrapped up in it. Leonard Feldman describes the process of "shelterization" as, "isolating the individual homeless person ... for treatment and shelter."[9] Charles Hoch and Robert A. Slayton further argue that helping agencies foster dependency.[10] While continuum-of-care services confer some advantages over the simple food-and-shelter accommodations of the past, this model of provision contains other problematics, not the least of which is tending to individualize a problem that appears predominantly social.

Once admitted to the shelter, individuals are "helped" by way of diagnosis and treatment.[11] Diagnosis is a process in which one's sickness is labeled. This is not, however, a dispassionate scientific process, but rather is highly empirical and thus subject to a great deal of judgment, which is influenced by a variety of assumptions and predispositions. As homelessness often is understood as a function of illness, it is not difficult to understand how the diagnostic process of service programs readily utilizes this in the case management process. This is not to say that these conceptions are not ever appropriate, but instead to note that their application becomes a routine process that reflects biases toward addiction and mental illness diagnoses. The result is that diagnosis often locates the problem of homelessness within the person who is homeless, that is, as a disease that the person has. Treatment follows directly from this diagnosing process by focusing on what the individuals can do to fix themselves. Discussion of structural causes of homelessness is sometimes met with sympathy by treatment providers, but typically seen as outside the range of what they have the ability to address.

As mentioned, when broadly discussing the issue of homelessness, service providers' conceptions were far richer and more accurately complex than the constrained institutional structures in which they worked. Still, it appeared that this discourse was managed differently for us than for their clients who were homeless. That is, while they were willing to talk with us at length about structural inequalities and systemic explanations of homelessness, they seemed hesitant to do so with those who were homeless. This reflects a common sentiment of addiction recovery about "taking ownership" of the problem. While people are often cognizant about the social structural factors that contextualize individual experiences, both those who are in treatment and those who treat them approach structural factors cautiously for fear that they might be employed as excuses for continued substance use or relapse.[12]

Those who are homeless commonly internalize an individual-pathology understanding of their situation. Treatment in the service institution takes an Alcoholics Anonymous approach in that the first step is to admit that *you* have a problem. Without doing this, one cannot move on to other steps or get other services.[13] Lyon-Callo writes of a woman who after an unsuccessful two-month job search came to understand her homelessness as resulting from depression.[14] She was counseled that she did not interview for jobs well because she was depressed. Of course being homeless would likely be enough to cause depression in even the healthiest individual. Nonetheless, this woman came to understand her depression as the *cause* of her situation as opposed to the result of it. The process of forcing the acceptance of individual pathology concepts can be alienating and offensive to those who are homeless.

The resistance of those on the street to the shelters was reported to be in part related to this. Potato Water put it this way:

> You guys know me, I know where these shelters are [and] basically everybody who runs them, but I don't want to stay with 'em.
> I don't like their politics. When you are sitting there talking to this person [the case manager], I mean you're sitting there honestly actually asking for help, [but] you're sitting there getting looked down upon, degraded. Man, I'm a guy [that's] got three years college.

Service providers most often paradoxically seek to reassimilate those who are homeless into "normal" society while at the same time holding tight to the us-them dichotomy that is a necessary part of the treatment relationship.[15] Their rhetoric varies seamlessly and ironically by suggesting that those who are homeless are "just like us," on the one hand, but diseased and needy on the other. Kenneth Kyle notes that even when homeless advocates attempt to counter stigmas of homelessness they cannot help relying on notions of "normalcy and the ordinary."[16] As suggested before, at its core, there is an assumption in the reassimilation goal that being "like us" is a lofty aspiration in the first place. This certainly can be questioned by reference to any number of social problems and questionable values and practices that are endemic to the majority population.

The us-them division is fundamental to the power dynamics embedded in the traditional doctor-patient relationship, which service providers mirror in their own diagnostic and treatment processes. In his classic statement about the power differential necessary to the clinical relationship, Foucault writes:

> Can pain be a spectacle? Not only can it be, but it must be, by virtue of a subtle right that resides in the fact that no one is alone, the poor man less so than others, since he can obtain assistance only through the mediation of the rich. Since disease can be cured only if others intervene with their knowledge, their resources, their pity, since a patient can be cured only in society, it is just that the illnesses of some should be transformed into the experience of others.[17]

In the shelterization process, the otherwise unique and individual biographies and experiences of those who are homeless are transformed into the categorical designations familiar to the medicalized understandings employed by homeless-service providers.[18] Treatment is guided by the dispositions of the shelter authorities, not by those who are homeless themselves. The knowledge of homeless persons about their own life is legitimate only if it conforms to the a priori understandings of the institutions. Otherwise it is cast off as insanity, rationalization of addiction, or some other function of illness.

Critique of the continuum-of-care shelter model has additional theoretical roots in Gramsci's notion of hegemony and Freire's discussion of oppression in the form of "helping."[19] Well-intentioned advocates subtly impose particular conceptions of homelessness on the person who is homeless. These entail particular goals and courses of action not coincidentally reflective of the dominant social order. By either literally or effectively defining homelessness as a medical problem such as addiction or mental illness, one places the onus on those individuals who are homeless and tacitly obscures social conditions. Social inequalities therefore remain unaddressed and ultimately intact. The quintessential goal of the treatment model is to reassimilate the person who is homeless into normal society.[20] Making someone a functioning member of society means they must fit into the social order and also means they must take on its ideology and its logic. The purported inherent virtue of work, for example, attaches moral significance to behavior that not coincidentally serves the current economic structure, and ultimately bolsters the profits of those at the top of it.[21]

While those people who use shelters and other services have internalized the idea of homelessness as individual pathology, those living on the street are much less likely to do so. In the shelter, talk of political-economic structure is dangerous, and it may be seen as unwillingness to address the "you" problem.[22] "Being difficult" can itself become a diagnosis and might even result in that individual being kicked out of the program. Those on the street reported greater difficulty in dealing with this sort of regulating environment than those we interviewed in the shelter. As Randall described it:

> Everybody out here is basically a rebel. We're not going to go along. … I mean we're *nonconformist*. Most people out here are nonconformists. Most people out here do not like authority, do not like to be told what to do by other people. So now [the shelter is] telling people who as a group do not like to be told what to do, "Come here and let us tell you what to do. Don't do what you want—do what we tell you to do."

While sentiments such as this can and often are folded into the disease paradigm as mere rationalizations of addiction, the resistance of those on the street to the diagnosis and treatment of the shelter otherwise could be seen as a literal and often conscious struggle for individuality and freedom.

Freire contends that charity is oppressive.[23] He argues that in efforts to help the oppressed, the privileged replicate the structural power dynamics that are at the foundation of oppression. This is clearly characteristic of the dominant medical model. While the thrust of our research concerned those living on the street, their complaints of the shelters naturally led us to talk to the service providers. We used these contacts to pursue a comparison of those on the streets and those in the shelters as well as to delve into the complaints of those on the street about the shelters. Generally, the medical model relies on authority, something that the street homeless eschew, almost by definition. But this contentious relationship is maintained by reference to values embedded in Western culture and economy, primarily the logic of exchange and fairness that legitimizes the attachment of quid pro quo conditions to the act of helping.[24] Michael Rowe comments that while outreach workers from service institutions often see themselves as "allied with the poor against the soulless bureaucrats," their relationships with those who are homeless still are frequently characterized by exchange and guided by suppositions about the "price of help."[25]

As noted, homeless services underwent a significant shift throughout the twentieth century, from emergency shelters to a continuum-of-care model. The ideological roots of the continuum-of-care model are directly tied to notions of treatment, and especially treatment for individual problems such as addiction. Continuum-of-care is characterized by case management and enrollment in treatment for clients' problems, where they are counseled about the errant social and psychological experiences that sent them off course. It is a social programming model, and although that phrasing sounds odd and ominous, it is nonetheless accurate. After completing treatment programs, individuals ideally are provided with transitional housing, with the goal of reassimilation into society. Rules and restrictions become less stringent in transitional housing, and slowly autonomy is returned to the healing homeless person. But this autonomy is released to the individual only insofar as the individual demonstrates that his or her "choices" are consistent with social and institutional expectations. The continuum-of-care model reflects very clearly a disciplinary process of enforcing normative social standards.[26] That is, the heavy-handed regulation of early treatment slowly gives way to greater "freedoms," but only so long as individuals follow the rules on their own.

While they perform a variety of services, such as helping their clients get identification, job training, and life-skills coaching, their primary focus typically is addiction treatment and mental health counseling. Other services are supplementary, and given the preponderance of people enrolled in treatment programs relative to the total number of beds in the shelters, it is fair to say that in many shelters, access to these other types of services effectively is restricted to those enrolled in treatment programs. In other words, to get job training or transitional housing, one must first "go through the steps" of the addiction or mental health treatment program, or both. At a well-known shelter in Birmingham, estimates are as high as thirty out of forty-two beds given to those enrolled in treatment programs.

Those living on the street are quite conscious of the preference given to those enrolled in treatment. "You gotta be in the program to get a bed," said a man in Five Points, reflecting the common sentiment. His tone was irritated, containing a sense of alienation felt by those who, for whatever reason, are not willing to submit to treatment in order to get food, shelter, or the myriad of other addendum-benefits in these programs. Those who do use services without enrolling in programs are stigmatized by shelter workers and those already in treatment, a criticism summarized by the sanction-laden term *frequent flyers*.[27] Moreover, discrimination against those who want to use services without committing to treatment often is not just the latent effect of limited space or informal disdain, but institutionalized in the policies of some shelters that require payment from the person wishing to access a bed and food without committing to a program.[28]

It is not a coincidence that Lawton, the radical pastor, maintains an impeccable reputation among those who are homeless, particularly those on the street. Opinions about other service providers in the area vary from lukewarm to highly critical, but Lawton's reputation was exclusively positive. The common sentiment among those on the street in Birmingham was echoed by one of our participants: "He's the only one around that I've seen that actually does *real* things for homeless people." In the estimation of most of the street homeless persons, services offered at the shelters did not address their needs. As they saw it, the largest obstacles they faced were affronts from the businesses and related city sweeps, the police, and trying to get a job that paid a living wage. Lawton was keenly focused on these issues, and so he solidly had their respect. This also suggests that those on the street are not retreatists or pathological resistors of help, but that they specifically resist the kinds of help offered at most service institutions.[29]

Among the other service providers, Lawton is seen as something of an outsider. In the course of our research, we routinely asked people we encountered for recommendations on others to interview, and his name was rarely mentioned by the service providers (see Chapter 2). True to his own self-reflective inner radical, Steve was the only service provider to recommend him with any sort of enthusiasm; others spoke of him in a hushed tone. Lawton seems to be seen as an agitator whose structural approaches are viewed as peripheral, if not detrimental, to the treatment work of mainstream service providers.

Lawton is openly and vehemently critical of all sorts of social institutions, and he lets virtually no compromise slide. Yet at the same time, he carries a sincere ethos of togetherness, rooted in his religious and spiritual beliefs. This makes it difficult for the city government or local service providers to dismiss him, despite the fact that they are often the targets of his criticism. In a time where much service provider effort was directed at creating more shelter space, Lawton commented that more shelters were fine, but that they would not solve much as long as they operated as "night prisons." He seemed to mean this in two ways. First, when we asked him our standard question as to why someone would choose to stay on the street rather than in the shelter, he replied buoyantly, "I would! Have you ever been to one of those places? Ain't no way I'd stay in there." So partly his criticism of the currently offered services was that they alienated many of the very people they were supposed to help by the various ways in which they made themselves uninviting. But as in everything, Lawton also believed that only a radical restructuring of society replete with a rectification of economic inequality and the power dynamics that produce it, and, more important, a cultural, spiritual revolution in humanity's relationship with those disfranchised, would ultimately have any real effect on homelessness.

To see the way in which medicalized understandings of homelessness are endemic to the continuum-of-care model of homeless-service provision requires relatively little abstraction. As noted, we stayed overnight in one of the more progressive shelters in Birmingham. When we checked in, we were immediately given a needs assessment. Addiction and mental illness factored most prominently in the response sets to questions about why we were homeless. While we stayed only one night, had we stayed much longer, we would have been assigned to a case manager. As noted earlier, in order to ensure we did not take a bed from someone truly in need, Steve declared an "inclement weather day." Otherwise we may not have been let in at all, since a preponderance of beds were given to full-time residents in treatment rather than those "frequent flyers" such as ourselves. At dinner an eighteen-year-old man engaged Wasserman in conversation at one point, asking Wasserman if he had a drug problem. Attempting to stay as close to the truth as possible, Wasserman said he did not. The young man immediately responded, "You do now. They won't let you stay here if you don't. Tell them you're addicted to Klonopin. It's addictive as hell, and it can't be detected in your bloodstream." This young man said he had been homeless only six days, but had learned quickly that advantages were conferred to those who submitted to the program. While one might secure temporary shelter without entering the treatment program, lasting services required submission to it.

The institutional hierarchy of the shelter was palpable during our stay their; moreover, it was organized around the treatment model even when that organization was not *directly* related to treatment itself. That is, those who were enrolled in the treatment program were given all sorts of advantages and privileged positions. They assisted the shelter staff with intake, informally enforced the rules of the institution, and were treated much more personably than the "frequent flyers." To be clear, this is not necessarily motivated by a conscious assigning of value to those in treatment versus those not in treatment, but rather the natural outcome of the respective positions of those two groups vis-à-vis the institution. Those in treatment enjoy longer and more consistent stays in the shelter and develop closer relationships with the staff. They are therefore naturally trusted with privileged positions in the same way that any of us trusts someone we know more than someone we do not. Nonetheless, the organizational hierarchy that emerges from these natural processes reflects preference for those who submit to the medical model and conversely entails another means of alienating those who resist it.

The shelter that we stayed in had a relatively progressive mission, particularly when compared with other shelters in town, especially those that tended to be more intensively religious. Even so, a clear division and hierarchy remained. There were givers and takers in the shelter. The volunteers were privileged in all sorts of ways. One led a brief sermon intended to inspire the less fortunate in attendance. Others administered questionnaires upon check-in, frisking the "guests" and searching their bags for contraband. In the morning the staff assigned chores and generally enforced rules of a variety of kinds. The volunteers did not have bunk beds, each one enjoying privacy in her or his own cubicle, whereas their "clients" who were homeless slept literally on top of each other in bunk beds crammed into a single open room. As he went to sleep, Wasserman could hear the volunteers watching a movie through the wall that separated their spaces.

Reminiscent of Wasserman's experience at age ten (see Chapter 1), there was no doubt who was giving and who was taking, with higher status given to the volunteers. Many of these divisions have a rationale. For example, making volunteers comfortable helps bolster their willingness to volunteer in the future. Still, these divisions can easily have negative effects on the feelings of worth in those who are homeless. We felt denigrated in just one night, so it is reasonable to think that long-term exposure to the bottom end of the hierarchy may have significant and lasting psychological consequences.

Justice, Exchange, and the Insufficiency of Fairness

Critique of the now dominant continuum-of-care model has not only come from social scientists but also is emerging in competing models of service, which at the very least attempt to deprioritize the social control orientations of medicalized approaches to homelessness. "Wet shelters" have begun to take in intoxicated persons (the typical shelter requires at least the appearance of sobriety) and some even allow residents to drink alcohol, although typically restricted to designated areas.[30] Proponents suggest that it is preferable for all involved, including the general public, if those who are homeless are in shelters rather than out on the street, even if they are intoxicated.[31]

Housing first is a phrase touted by a variety of organizations with a variety of meanings. While some groups seemingly use it solely as a general call for more affordable housing, it also is the calling card of a new approach to homelessness.[32] The typical continuum-of-care model makes housing conditional on one's enrollment in a treatment program, but for housing-first programs, like Pathways to Housing Inc., "program founders decided not to require treatment participation or sobriety as a precondition to housing."[33] These programs are founded on considerations of housing as a right, rather than a privilege, and also on utilitarian trade-offs that assert the comparatively better personal and social safety of a home over that on the street, even for those drinking or doing drugs. Others add that this style of housing provision translates to saved dollars in terms of social services.[34]

A similar initiative to provide "hygiene centers" also has been hotly contested.[35] These alternative types of service often are opposed by government and businesses involved in urban renewal projects, at least when they are proposed to be located too close to the city center.[36] Additionally, response from most homeless-service providers toward these various new alternative services has been critical.[37] Providing housing without conditions, for example, is seen as enabling addiction. Though this argument cannot be rejected prima facie, it is reasonable to question how professional conflict and competition for funding might influence such attitudes. Indeed, we are witnessing more and more of what Wright, Rubin, and Devine describe as

> *the inevitable institutionalization* of the homeless problem[,] ... a vast cadre of shelter and soup kitchen operators, advocates, social workers, health care professionals, case managers, researchers, and others whose professional identities, job security, and personal values revolve around the homelessness issue. Already, we hear of turf battles between groups trying to protect their fiefdoms, sometimes even at the expense of the homeless people they are presumably trying to serve.[38]

Service providers largely write off homeless individuals who refuse their services.[39] While many service providers have mobile service programs in addition to those offered inside the shelter, there is an explicit aspect of these designed to persuade people to "come in." In their minds, they have created an opportunity structure in which people who are homeless can get help. The logic is this: since the opportunity structure exists, those not taking advantage of it are doing so by their own choice. Since those living on the street have opted out, their homelessness is their own problem; there is no remaining social obligation to help such people.[40] Service provision strategies become about creating and promoting the opportunity structure of particular social programs. As long as opportunity is provided, the rest is up to those who are homeless themselves.

Of course, this is familiar logic, and it resonates with our most basic notions of fairness. Americans, in fact, are fond of ascribing this logic to the problem of homelessness as a whole. In the land of opportunity, your fortune (or misfortune) is your own responsibility; equal opportunity is the obligation of society, and anything beyond that—any use of opportunity or outcome from it—are the responsibility of the individual. Service providers mostly recognize that no such equal opportunity structure broadly exists in US society, but they conceptualize their own projects with a remarkably similar logic. Moreover, the notion of "opportunity" here is overly general. The opportunity provided by service institutions is one primarily to get treatment for addiction and mental illness, which is only one possible service option among many.

This opportunity structure view is further characterized by exchange. Service providers frequently appeal to a "market logic" in rhetorical justifications of whom they include versus whom they exclude.[41] Using the opportunity structure is not free but requires some concession. For example, to use a bed at a shelter for any significant period of time may require that you enroll in a treatment program. Often those who are homeless significantly benefit from this treatment and the exchange is successful. Other times, they are able to manipulate this system by, for example, submitting to an addiction treatment program when they are not addicted (as suggested by Wasserman's eighteen-year-old shelter acquaintance). But occasionally these requirements keep people away.[42] This third outcome is our primary interest here, since those on the street are its most clear reflection. Those who benefit from services, either legitimately or by deception, are welcome as long as they make the proper concessions. But those who "stay away," if not totally, at least in spirit, are the ones service providers excuse, quite consciously, from their obligations.

We can again turn to the meeting about the no-strings-attached café to highlight the notions of fairness and exchange at the heart of the medical model (see Chapter 2). The meeting brought together an eclectic mix of people related to homeless-service provision in various ways and was therefore an explicit coming-together of service providers to discuss service provision. As such, it was highly informative about their conceptualizations of those who are homeless and how best to serve them.

The impetus for the café had been twofold. As noted, a local survey had "revealed" that 20 percent of people surveyed had listed food as one of their needs. But a second motivating factor was the growing hostility of local business toward those who were homeless. Many of the service providers, including Michelle, who was particularly fervent on the issue, thought this conflict was being exacerbated by street meals conducted by independent groups often from churches and frequently carried out in highly public places. Not surprisingly, centralized downtown locations for businesses also made nice spots for distributing food to those who were poor and homeless. While the café itself represented a rather progressive idea, there lurked in it the potential for quarantining homeless people by locating it out of sight, and therefore out of mind. Although not mentioned by name, the FNB (Food Not Bombs) group was at the forefront of this issue and had been previously contacted and criticized by some service providers.

Motives aside, the idea was quite progressive, particularly in this room. With the intentionally narrow goal simply of feeding people,

Chris explained that his vision was a place that was "warm and welcoming," where one did not have to be enrolled in a program or talk to a case manager in order to get food.[43] After his brief exposition, he opened the floor for suggestions, and his vision was subsequently bastardized and compromised in the most complete sense. Michelle, an archetype for the treatment mentality, immediately suggested that they staff the place with social workers and offer literature and program information, "even if it is not required." Several others made similar suggestions. While we had not anticipated speaking up, the group was clearly moving away from Chris's vision and in opposition to the dispositions of our participants on the street, and so we decided to attempt a reframing of the issue. This prompted Wasserman's suggestion that such things might be alienating, "even if they are not required." This comment was met with polite but firm rejection.

A number of subsequent remarks were noteworthy. The director of City Action Partnership (CAP) stated that most of these people were willing to listen to the sermons at street meals, and so they were obviously willing to do *something* in exchange for food. Of course, aside from questions about whether such an exchange is justified in itself, this argument rests on a quasi-empirical assessment biased by the fact that only those who *are* willing are sitting through such sermons; those that are not willing are not around to be counted. Another woman reacted more favorably, but worked Wasserman's comment into the treatment paradigm suggesting that his concern could be satisfied if volunteers and counselors at the café were properly trained to not put excessive pressure on those who would come to eat. One woman observed that the survey that had prompted the initiative was done at shelters and so the target group primarily was the service-using population that was not getting food on the weekends. She concluded, "So it's not necessarily about feeding *everyone*." This was affirmed when another shelter director nodded and said, "Good point." Later, when a woman who formerly was homeless talked about providing hope and spiritual food, Michelle immediately followed up with another comment about letting people know about treatment options; she seemed to operationalize "hope" as treatment programs.

For the present discussion, the key point is that everyone seemed to agree that by providing food, they accrued the right to make demands or place constraints on those who received it. To accept food was to become obligated to hear what the social worker had to say, to hear about treatment programs, to be talked to about one's problems. It is not coincidence that this reflects Parsons's "sick role" where quid pro quo conditions of seeking help entail obligations to try to get better and to follow the course prescribed by the authority, the doctor, in doing so.[44] More generally, this reflects a Westernized value of fairness, which underlies the logic of the exchange paradigm. The economic and political ideologies of our culture hold that we have no positive obligations to help, only negative obligations not to harm. We do not owe anyone anything other than the space to pursue their own happiness, but we do not have to actively help them in seeking it. As long as we do not impede on the rights of others, we live ethically.

Welfare is a positive act of giving and is therefore difficult to reconcile with the dominant political-economic logic rooted in John Locke and bestowed on the United States by Thomas Jefferson. Homeless service constitutes such a positive action of helping. In order to be folded into the exchange logic of our culture, to be consistent with our notions of fairness, giving must not be an end in itself, but must produce a reciprocal obligation. After all, it would not be fair for someone to simply get food and not give something in return.

Obviously, there is another way to approach the issue. It certainly feels odd to suggest that the principle of fairness is not a good guiding principle—what kind of person is against fairness?—but this is exactly what we suggest in regard to helping those who are homeless. There is nothing beyond cultural ideology that necessitates a reciprocal obligation when helping another. This does not preclude offering the very same types of treatment programs that currently exist. Rather, it calls into question the idea that the rejection of these programs warrants the exclusion of a group of people from the general scope of helping.

Clearly many service providers do react with exclusion, and it is understandable. They care very much and work hard to set up and run these programs and are then rejected by a certain subsection of the very people they intend to help. It is not difficult to understand how this can be taken as insulting or how service providers might then reject new ideas about how to interact with those who are homeless—new ideas such as those of the FNB or a no-strings-attached café. After all, their prior efforts went unappreciated. Besides that, no one thinks they owe anyone this help in the first place; they have lived up to the universal principle of fairness and nothing ethically compels them to act beyond that. But as understandable as this reaction is, if the ultimate goal is to offer help, appealing to a principle of fairness fundamentally is irrelevant and counterproductive.

There is no reason to think that a café whose sole purpose is to give food unconditionally is an insufficient service, particularly if the criteria for sufficiency, like the inclusion of social workers and treatment programs, negatively affect this goal. There is a fundamental difference between charity and exchange that is seemingly eroding. Ideally, charity is a pure act of giving, free from expectation and even from questions of who deserves to receive it.[45] Increasingly, however, charity is an exchange act where, by giving, we receive commodities such as bracelets, buttons, bumper stickers, or our name on a plaque. Similarly, if "charity work" becomes largely about *work*, then it flirts dangerously close to the exchange paradigm; "giving" becomes "working for," and recipients become "clients." The blurring of this distinction facilitates mental blocks to types of homeless-service provision that reject the exclusion of those who refuse to reciprocate.

Ultimately the question facing service providers should not be whether they have a right to expect particular behavior in exchange for their services. Evolving out of such a mindset opens up fundamentally different and needed approaches to service provision. Moreover, it is not necessary to reject exchange altogether, but to relegate it to one of many models for interaction. One certainly could take the more moderate position that providing food does create a reciprocal obligation, but nonetheless conclude that even without reciprocity, giving is better than not giving. By taking this stance, one would see reciprocal exchange as ideal yet recognize the value that remains in a nonreciprocal exchange. Regardless of whether one rejects the condition of reciprocity altogether, or subverts it for utilitarian considerations, this much seems clear: as long as the notions of fairness and exchange embedded in US capitalism continue fundamentally to guide the provision of services, those on the street will continue to be alienated.

Power vs. Empowerment:
The Maintenance of the Medical Model

While most of those who work in shelters are savvy enough to understand the structural economic conditions that predicate homelessness, generally they do not focus their efforts at rectifying structural problems. Steve was a particularly compelling example. A highly progressive individual, and extremely sympathetic to the structural explanations of homelessness, he was in an interesting position. He noted that the real solution was prevention. "People shouldn't be coming to me; we need to keep them from becoming homeless. [The shelter] should be a last resort." Moreover, Steve was sympathetic to the complaints about the shelters—being crowded, dangerous, and so on—and over the course of several years and multiple interviews, he was working on the creation of a new facility that rectified many of these immediate problems. Still, despite his recognition of social structural inequalities, as a shelter director, he seemed to feel confined to working on individual pathology problems, and his shelter program predominantly focused on the treatment of addiction.

Steve's inner conflicts were made particularly clear in the meeting discussion about the no-strings-attached café. Our comment—about how the alienating nature of social programs might work at cross-purposes with a café having the narrower goal of providing food—had been fairly thoroughly dismissed. But while this was the common response, Steve's was the exception. With a characteristically troubled and introspective manner, he witnessed to the group of his peers:

> I think that we [service providers] need to hear some of those
> things and think about the ways we can improve. It's hard
> because we've been doing certain things for so long, and there's
> good reason for some of them, but we can question those things
> and make improvements.

As noted at the outset of this chapter, individually speaking, nearly all the service providers we interviewed seemed conscious of the broader complexities of homelessness in the United States, but when acting out their professional roles in their respective service institutions, this broader vision was narrowed to fit the institutional constraints of the medical model. Steve illustrated this best of all because he seemed more conscious of the conflict between his personal feelings and the directives of his job. While he is not personally disposed to the individual pathology explanation of homelessness, he nonetheless directs a shelter whose primary focus is on the treatment of those conditions. He always appeared to have an inner struggle over this, but he also faced explicit institutional conflicts related to the constraints of the treatment model versus other notions of service more broadly defined. Steve mentioned, for example, several instances where his attempts at community advocacy, such as when he had vocalized opposition to the city sweeps of homeless camps, had been met with hesitation and discomfort by the shelter's board of directors. In essence, Steve and the shelter he directs can be seen as the most difficult test case for the medical model. A disease conception of homelessness exists there despite conscious recognition of its shortcomings.

Homelessness predominantly is an offshoot of poverty, where poor people become even poorer. As such, it is broadly a problem of stratification, of severe economic inequality. In more egalitarian societies, homelessness does not exist, or at least not in a socially significant form (e.g., in Canada, Sweden, and so on). That addressing individual pathology remains the focus of service providers suggests that many of these services are little more than a cyclical Band-Aid. This is particularly highlighted by research that notes that these individual pathologies often are the result, not cause, of homelessness.[46] Max, a more radical advocate for homeless people whom we interviewed, remarked that despite all of the institutional programs created to provide services to those who are homeless over the last several decades, homelessness has gotten worse, not better. Steve himself noted similar limitations when he suggested that prevention, not service provision, was far more effective in combating homelessness. The question then becomes, "How can such an unsuccessful model become so entrenched?"

Of course, our critique of the continuum-of-care model should not be overly simplistic. The shelters do have their successes. As we have observed it, those who are successful tend to have been homeless for only a short period of time, who retain various social ties, and who generally are more institutionally savvy. The service model dominant in the early 2000s has also had success with those for whom homelessness *is* the direct result of addiction. Our discussion of Big E is a good example. He always defined his homelessness as related to addiction or mental illness, even when he was living on the street. He therefore fit well into the shelter and was successful in using the treatment model to get off the streets.

This suggests that the failures of the dominant service model are not simply the failures of individuals who are homeless, but rather that services address only certain types of homelessness and that an entire subset of those whose homelessness is not essentially related to an individual pathology will not be successful in utilizing those services. This is a systemic problem with the rigid constitution of the service model, not a failing of the person who is homeless. That is to say, exclusion from services is categorical not random.

The way in which the medical model is maintained is related, as well, to the vested interest of service providers. A significant portion of federal funding for shelters is based on enrollment in treatment programs. Rowe notes that a shelter in his study was required to enroll at least one hundred people per year to keep their funding.[47] The director of a women's shelter in our study noted, for example:

There is more tension, in a way, from the federal government; there is more funding for programs that address homelessness and related homelessness, other supported services, but then in another way, there is almost a homeless bureaucracy—that didn't used to exist; it used to be that a couple of churches or some people from some other organizations, some organizations just opened up their doors and did this or that, and today there are a lot of rules and you have to have certain forms and homeless people have to certify that they're homeless in order to get services that are funded by this or that, so I think some of the attention in health we have gotten can come with making us less hospitable than we would like to be.

Early in our research we heard the accusation made by those on the street that the shelters were "a racket" and largely dismissed it as untrue. However, the way in which the treatment programs of the medical model are effectively mandated by the funding channels from the federal level down adds legitimacy to this position. The existence of the shelter depends on funding, and funding depends on compliance with disease perspectives of homelessness.

Second, entire careers are built on providing services within the continuum-of-care paradigm for those who are homeless. It would be quite a personal feat for someone to subvert the very orientation by which she or he is employed. Max summed this up: "I was in New York at a conference, and we were getting coffee, and I heard someone say that [a university] was offering a master's degree in homeless-service provision. And I thought, that's it … it's over." The implication was that by generating such sophisticated institutional infrastructures around providing for those who were homeless, there was a diminished incentive to actually eliminate homelessness as a social problem. Doing so would uproot the foundations on which those institutions are built and in which a large number of people are employed. It should be added that we do not wish to suggest that those with vested financial interests in the dominant model consciously celebrate the existence of homelessness. They nearly all are sincere in their efforts. Nonetheless, as social scientists, we cannot ignore the way in which certain approaches to homelessness are reinforced by financial interests at both an institutional and personal level.

It also is no coincidence that Lawton's church receives no funding from the government. This adds support to the idea that particular approaches are financially mandated. Free from those constraints, Lawton is able to confront systemic issues and to openly call into question dominant approaches toward homelessness in society. Steve made this especially clear when he recommended Lawton to us, noting, "He can say things that I can't."

Moreover, while financial investment in the medical model may not serve as a *conscious* impetus for its maintenance, service providers do engage in other justifications of the status quo. This is not surprising, since we all tend to defend our own work more often than we are willing to step outside of it and be critically reflexive of that in which we invest so much time and energy. As mentioned, several service providers in our study expressed a great deal of concern and irritation with various independent groups who feed those who are homeless on the streets. This includes a variety of church groups and also the FNB. Shortly after they began to hold their picnics, the FNB was approached by these service providers and asked to cease and desist. They were told that they were angering local businesses because their (once-weekly) picnics supposedly were contributing to the congregation of people who were homeless in the Five Points area. Additionally, it was noted that these types of street meals "enabled" people to stay on the streets, and the service providers routinely referred to meals provided by groups like the FNB as "drive-by feedings."

The concept of "enabling" comes not by coincidence directly from the addiction literature, which tends to take a view of addiction as disease. The critique suggests that this sort of giving without condition makes it significantly easier to stay on the street. In our research we have also been confronted with the enabling criticism because we bring toothpaste, food, and socks to our research participants. Steve described enabling:

> We get accused of enabling too. ... I think you can make it easy
> for someone to have a comfortable lifestyle. That's part of what
> enabling is. Regardless of the situation you can enable an
> alcoholic by continuing to provide them with alcohol. You can
> enable a drug addict by providing them with drugs, or making it
> easy for them. ... [Addicts] thrive on being able to manipulate
> people. As that relates to homelessness ... individuals often times
> want to stay outside because of mental illness. Lots of times there's
> a part of addiction there. Often times people think it's their right to
> be able to stay on public property. ... I [actually] think it
> *is* their right to be able to stay on public property as long as we as
> a society do not offer them alternatives. And so we need to provide
> alternatives. So if you make it easy for someone to get their drugs
> for instance, then they are going to continue that lifestyle until
> you make [them] uncomfortable.

It is notable that service providers get criticized by others in the community, particularly those who see those who are homeless as a detriment to business and local quality of life (see Chapter 8). This criticism likely varies in direct proportion to how many unconditional services they offer and how close they are located to redeveloping areas of downtown. Still, service providers also leveled the enabling critique at others whose relationships with those who were homeless they viewed as problematic impediments to "hitting bottom," which is the point at which those who are homeless become desperate enough to ask for help. While sympathetic to those living on the street, Steve's sympathy is contextualized by a lack of "alternatives," namely, the lack of shelter space (as he clarified this at another point in the interview). But once the opportunity for treatment was made available, then the practice of living on the street becomes less acceptable. Of course, the presupposition is that the help those who are homeless need is available at the shelters, though, as mentioned, the shelters offer certain kinds of help and not others.

Additionally, the enabling argument, as it applies to those on the street, rests on the quite questionable premise that giving someone food or toothpaste makes it significantly easier to live on the streets. Our various three-day stints on the street made it clear to us that this is by no means the case. There is nothing easy about living on the streets, regardless of how much toothpaste or how many pairs of socks one has.

The terms *enabling* and *drive-by feedings* are notable rhetorical constructions.[48] They imply that alternative, independent services like the FNB impede the "real solution." As a play on the phrase "drive-by shooting," the "drive-by feeding" reference goes so far as to rhetorically equate feeding people with shooting people. The director of the service provider coalition in Birmingham said, "I'm tired of people saying bad things about *my* homeless people." She blamed "drive-by feedings" for fanning the flames of this hatred, particularly by making businesses angry. The service providers largely desired to appease the complaints of business and the city. This, of course, is likely tied at least implicitly to funding they receive from these institutions. While the city of Birmingham has not yet done so, other cities have passed laws against street meals, and people have literally been jailed for giving food to those who are homeless.[49] The rhetoric itself and, even more clearly, the policies enacted based on it suggest a right and wrong way to serve those who are homeless, putting the dominant paradigm on the preferable side of that line. But this certainly is questionable, since homelessness has "gotten worse and not better," as Max pointed out, despite the institutional structures that have been built to deal with it.

Homeless-service provision is a social institution guided by professional service providers. As such, its concerns extend into broader social, political, and economic arenas. Self-regulation is an essential feature of a profession.[50] Not just anyone can be a physician; there are sets of professional and legal requirements that regulate who can legitimately practice that profession. Homeless-service provision has these same characteristics, including governmental recognition of the service profession with increasing legal prohibitions against those who would provide services without the appropriate credentials. Of course, the self-regulation of a profession has the effect of promoting certain conceptions over others. The American Medical Association (AMA) subverted homeopathic medicine to the extent that, in the past, AMA physicians were prohibited from conferring with "irregulars."[51]

As homeless-service provision is ever-more institutionalized, it increasingly exercises power to delineate what kinds of services are appropriate for those who are homeless and what kinds are not. Insofar as it privileges particular conceptions of homelessness over others, this will likely have serious consequences, including the increased alienation of homeless individuals who refuse to conform to the standard diagnoses. Professional boundaries are reinforced and perpetuated by financial interests, rhetorical domination, and social and legal coercion. The medical model of homeless-service provision is a growing profession, replete with all of these characteristics.

The social sciences also hold significant culpability in maintaining the medical model.[52] Not only has there been a tendency toward medicalization in a variety of fields, including psychology, which factors particularly heavily into homeless-service provision, other social science disciplines, such as sociology, also are guilty. Through an obsession with neatly delineated variables and high degrees of correlation-sans-causality, population-level approaches of the social sciences have backed the medical model.[53] We have unreflexively promoted the finding of high rates of mental illness and addiction among the population of those who are homeless, largely sidestepping methodological questions about sample selection and causality that make otherwise conveniently neat statistics quite messy and convoluted. We then have passed along these population tendencies to those planning social programs in a way that, again unreflexively, promotes a highly suspect detection and treatment process, but without also supplying a pedagogy for working with the idiosyncratic qualities of individual human beings.

The result is the routine objectification of actual people into cases, codified as sets of variables. While perhaps appropriate for discerning aggregate tendencies of a population, it is an entirely inappropriate and antihuman thing to do to an actual person. Despite the lip service paid to this problem in the form of warnings against the reductionist fallacy (where aggregate population tendencies are applied to individual people), the social sciences have supplied little else to homeless-service providers by way of a plan for working fluidly and dynamically with actual persons, in a manner that can be attentive and respectful to their individuality.

This is made clear in implementation of homeless management information systems, where funding, particularly from HUD (Housing and Urban Development), is contingent on analysis of data collected by cities and particular institutions.[54] Services are assessed by quantifying problems in a population and also particular outcomes (i.e., numbers enrolled in treatment programs, numbers moved to transitional housing posttreatment, and so on). What this amounts to is placing value on a limited set of particular, predetermined outcomes, especially those easiest to quantify, like numbers enrolled in treatment. Things such as empowerment, happiness, the achievement of self-determined goals are difficult to quantify and thus are considerations subverted to the easier data. Thus, the same sorts of practices for detecting tendencies in a group are used to assess and treat homeless individuals in the case-management process of the shelter. In the end, even those service providers inclined toward more humanistic approaches are supplied with little means of enacting them in their service institution.

* * *

Working within a medicalized conception of homelessness, service providers rely on their authority to diagnose and treat those who are homeless, and inversely on the submission of those who are homeless to the individual pathology conceptualizations of their own homelessness. More generally, in this paradigm those who are homeless are situated as the problem, which naturally implies that service programs, and the medical model on which they frequently are structured, are a solution. Even when shelter directors and workers consciously reject individual pathology conceptions of homelessness, they often reinforce them as they act out their professional roles. This institutional model emerges not only from popular conceptualizations of homelessness, but also is influenced by a notion of fairness embedded in US capitalism and the way in which vested financial interests serve to maintain it even when it clearly is insufficient. Ultimately, this calls into question whether a condition that results from inequality can be addressed by an institution that replicates and perpetuates inequality in its hierarchical constitution.

The problem-solution dichotomy that is juxtaposed over the homelessness/service-provision roles is insufficient.[55] The conceptualization of those who are homeless as "the problem" is the shared foundation of both political (Chapter 8) and treatment approaches and ultimately is the reason they both are oppressive. To define a group as "the problem" legitimizes stripping them of power and autonomy. Defining and dealing with homelessness then becomes the rightful domain of everyone except for those who are homeless themselves. Business, local governments, police, and service providers all assert their authority over the lives of those who are homeless. They therefore ironically reflect and perpetuate the very same power dynamics at the root of homelessness.

Notes

1. That is, help involves providing physical shelter and reforming and reassimilating homeless people; see Culhane, "The Quandaries of Shelter Reform."

2. Axelson and Dail, "The Changing Character of Homelessness in the United States"; Goetz and Schmiege, "From Marginalized to Mainstreamed"; Lyon-Callo, "Medicalizing Homelessness"; Lyon-Callo, *Inequality, Poverty, and Neoliberal Governance.*

3. Lyon-Callo, "Medicalizing Homelessness"; Lyon-Callo, *Inequality, Poverty, and Neoliberal Governance.*

4. Hopper, in *Reckoning with the Homeless*, has a similar conclusion; see also Feldman, *Citizens Without Shelter.*

5. Lyon-Callo, "Medicalizing Homelessness."

6. Conrad, The Medicalization of Society; Conrad and Schneider, *Medicalization and Deviance*; Clair, Karp, and Yoels, *Experiencing the Life Cycle.*

7. Arnold, *Homelessness, Citizenship and Identity*; Baer et al., *Medical Anthropology and the World System*, 2nd ed.; Hopper, *Reckoning with the Homeless*; Lyon-Callo, "Medicalizing Homelessness"; Lyon-Callo, *Inequality, Poverty, and Neoliberal Governance*; Mathieu, "The Medicalization of Homelessness and the Theater of Repression"; Snow et al., "The Myth of Pervasive Mental Illness Among the Homeless."

8. Lyon-Callo, "Medicalizing Homelessness," p. 330.

9. Feldman, *Citizens Without Shelter*, p. 147; see also Grunberg and Eagle, "Shelterization."

10. Hoch and Slayton, *New Homeless and Old.*

11. Lyon-Callo, "Medicalizing Homelessness"; Lyon-Callo, *Inequality, Poverty, and Neoliberal Governance.*

12. Lyon-Callo, in "Medicalizing Homelessness," observed a similar disconnect between understandings of social structural factors and the willingness to allow those into treatment discourse.

13. This is somewhat oversimplistic. Although this linear, hierarchical process is characteristic of the medical model, Rowe describes, in *Crossing the Border*, how shelter outreach workers provide a variety of commodities to those who are homeless, even those rejecting enrollment in a treatment program. The process he describes, and consistent with our experience, however, is that these commodities are given in an anticipated exchange whereby they are tools designed to persuade those on the street to submit to treatment. Rowe's description of the client selection process whereby good and bad candidates are delineated buttresses such an assessment.

14. Lyon-Callo, "Medicalizing Homelessness."

15. Desjarlais, "The Office of Reason"; Kyle, *Contextualizing Homelessness*; see Hoffman and Coffey, "Dignity and Indignation," on complaints about the shelters as objectifying and infantilizing; the goal of reassimilation is something to which we will return.

16. Kyle, *Contextualizing Homelessness*, p. 24.

17. Foucault, *Madness and Civilization*, p. 84.

18. Grunberg and Eagle, "Shelterization," p. 552.

19. Gramsci, *Selections from a Prison Notebook*; Freire, *Pedagogy of the Oppressed*.

20. Kyle, *Contextualizing Homelessness*; for an example, see Goetz and Schmiege, "From Marginalized to Mainstreamed."

21. Wagner notes, in *Checkerboard Square*, that work is a virtue imposed on the poor, while the wealthy spend a great deal of time and money seeking leisure.

22. Lyon-Callo, "Medicalizing Homelessness"; Lyon-Callo, *Inequality, Poverty, and Neoliberal Governance*.

23. Freire, *Pedagogy of the Oppressed*; see also Wagner, who suggests, in *What's Love Got to Do with It*, that the virtue ascribed to charity masks the social injustices that make it necessary in the first place.

24. See also Lyon-Callo, *Inequality, Poverty, and Neoliberal Governance*.

25. Rowe, *Crossing the Border*, p. 76.

26. See Foucault, *Discipline and Punish*.

27. See also Lyon-Callo, *Inequality, Poverty, and Neoliberal Governance*, on cooperative versus uncooperative guests.

28. For example, in Birmingham one shelter granted seven free nights a month and then charged seven dollars a night after that; see also Culhane, "The Quandaries of Shelter Reform."

29. Though some certainly are "loners"; see Pippert, *Road Dogs and Loners*.

30. Cat Le, "Sobriety Won't Be Rule at New Shelter"; Crane and Warnes, "Wet Day Centres in the United Kingdom"; Silberner, "A Homeless Shelter for Alcoholics."

31. Ibid.

32. For example, www.housingfirst.net seems to take the former position, whereas Eckholm takes the latter, in "New Campaign Shows Progress for Homeless."

33. Pathways to Housing Inc., "Providing Housing First and Recovery Services for Homeless Adults with Severe Mental Illness," p. 1303.

34. For example, hospital care, incarceration; Eckholm, "New Campaign Shows Progress for Homeless"; Pathways to Housing Inc., "Providing Housing

First and Recovery Services for Homeless Adults with Severe Mental Illness"; Sadowski et al., in "Effect of a Housing and Case Management Program on Emergency Department Visits and Hospitalizations Among Chronically Ill Homeless Adults," provide empirical evidence for lower costs of medical care; Kertesz and Weiner, in "Housing the Chronically Homeless," suggest similar savings but note that the results for addicted users is still tentative.

35. See Gibson, *Securing the Spectacular City*, for an account of one such debate in Seattle.

36. Their opposition seems primarily to turn on where such services will be located. As noted at the end of Chapter 8, a representative of downtown redevelopment in Birmingham was fully supportive of housing-first initiatives, arguing this would be good for both those on the street and the businesses operating in the city center. While location of this housing was not explicitly discussed at the community forum where the representative spoke, in other cities opposition to housing-first projects and hygiene centers has emerged when these services are located in the city center as opposed to outside of it. Opposition seems mitigated when such services are located in poor and dilapidated areas, seemingly on the hope that these will draw those who are homeless out of town.

37. Cat Le, "Sobriety Won't Be Rule at New Shelter."

38. Wright et al., *Beside the Golden Door*, p. 213.

39. See also Hopper, *Reckoning with the Homeless*.

40. As a Libertarian, Tanner takes such a position in "Housing Is Not a Human Right."

41. See Boltanski and Thévenot, *On Justification*; see Lyon-Callo, *Inequality, Poverty, and Neoliberal Governance*, for discussion of the market-based model of services that emerged in the 1990s.

42. Again, we are oversimplifying here. Most of the time, service providers offer some unconditional services and other conditional services. For example, a shelter might offer lunch to anyone but dinner for residents only. Also, most homeless people use *some* services. In our conceptual scheme, nonservice users represent a disposition away from only some services rather than a total rejection of them.

43. Some other cities have seen the opening of such places; see, for example, Little, "Homeless Cafés Serve Self-Help."

44. Parsons, *The Social System*.

45. It should be kept in mind that we agree with Wagner, in *What's Love Got to Do with It*, that even these more altruistic versions of charity can obscure the social injustices that predicate them.

46. For example, Conley, "Getting It Together."

47. Rowe, *Crossing the Border*.

48. See Mathieu, "The Medicalization of Homelessness and the Theater of Repression," for an additional discussion of the nature and impact of medicalization rhetoric.

49. See McKay, "Homeless-Meal Clash Still Simmers"; Pratt, "Critics Say Regional Plan Won't Solve Homelessness."

50. Goode, "Community Within a Community"; Starr, *The Social Transformation of American Medicine*.

51. See Baker, "Physician Licensure Laws in the United States, 1865–1915"; Duffy, *From Humors to Medical Science*.

52. See Wagner, *Checkerboard Square*.

53. See also Hoffman and Coffey's discussion, in "Dignity and Indignation," of quantitative research as promoting discriminatory accountability practices of homeless-service agencies)

54. See Hoffman and Coffey, "Dignity and Indignation"; this is also mentioned, though uncritically, by the National Alliance to End Homelessness in an April 2009 publication titled "Homelessness Prevention and Re-Housing: Key Partnerships."

55. See also Hopper and Baumohl, in "Held in Abeyance," for a discussion of the political interests served by the "crisis trope" attached to homelessness.

10

Religious Approaches: Saving Souls

There is little attention paid to the ways religious groups factor into homelessness and service provision. This is odd because these organizations easily make up the majority of those people running, staffing, and supplying homeless-service organizations, not to mention the sizable number of church groups conducting street meals and religious outreach. Even those service institutions without official religious ties commonly are supported by donations from church groups, who not only give food, clothing, and other materials, but also often operate as a volunteer staff or sponsor meals. Yet in the academic literature, religion is hardly mentioned in connection to social engagement with those who are homeless.

Perhaps one explanation for the relative dearth of literature here is that religious groups are not easily subsumed under a common theme. In the United States, for example, Christianity has so many variants that the term itself gives little definition to any one person or group invoking it. So while countless members of Christian groups engage in homeless services and outreach, that broad religious identification tells us very little about the beliefs under which they operate.

Some religious groups parallel the medical model of homeless service, employing the concept of sin in the same way that other service providers employ the concept of sickness. Likewise, exchange often is at the heart of their methods. One common approach is to use food and shelter in exchange for the opportunity to witness.[1] Lured by charity, those who are homeless sometimes become a captive audience for religious lectures. While it is worth mentioning that many resist this captivity, the nature of the homeless condition often makes promises of heavenly intervention highly appealing. Of course, these cosmic "plans" can easily distract from the rectification of problematic worldly conditions. Moreover, the degree to which coercion with food and other donations is successful varies inversely to circumstances on the street. The harder things are—that is, the less work, the more sweeps, the colder it is—the more those who are homeless may have to concede to sermons in exchange for sustenance. As noted earlier, however, this is not only a criticism directed at others; we worried about this in regard to the relationship between our own agenda as researchers and the donations we supplied our participants.

Other religious groups, however, reflect a more classic notion of Christian charity, acting out of obligations to the poor, based on thematic extrapolations from the Bible. These groups tended to be less judgmental, but they, too, reflected and replicated the us-them dichotomy, playing the role of the virtuous saviors and in an often implicit while nonetheless patronizing way, conceptualizing those who were poor and homeless as "the meek." Finally, there are those who take radical approaches to homelessness, which emerge directly from their religious orientations. These groups parallel the liberation theology of some religious activists, particularly in some inner-city African American churches and in impoverished areas of countries in Central and South America. In Birmingham the pastor Lawton focuses his attention on structural problems and social inequality. He directly opposes the notion of those who are homeless as spiritually corrupt, stating in an interview, "That is what everybody tells the homeless, that they are a problem and they are sinners. Well[,] ... that only bashes them down further. ... In other words, makes religion contribute to the oppression." This radical perspective is something of an anomaly in the region where we conducted our research; moreover, there is a paradigmatic disconnect between that perspective and myriad others, which may employ different strategies and rhetoric but hold fundamentally similar views of those who are homeless. We therefore focus here on the way in which religious groups mirror the problematics of political and treatment approaches to homelessness. That is, many of these groups employ, to varying extents, judgment and separatist rhetoric while attempting to spiritually heal those who are homeless.

We wish to make it clear from the outset that our critiques of some of these groups, like those of the service providers, should not be taken as an indictment of their individual character, but rather the ideological structures under which they tend to operate. The diversity of their perspectives and intervention programs means any analysis will flirt with oversimplification. Still, it seems important to offer some insights, even if they are sweeping, since this area is so grossly underrepresented in the literature.

In what follows, we identify two general faith-based approaches under the broad rubric of Christianity. One is somewhat malignant in its judgments and fiery rhetoric. The other is comparatively kind in its approach, but still replicates divisions that subvert the humanity of those who are homeless and "create dependencies."[2] As such, these two variants parallel the political and treatment approaches we already have discussed in Chapters 8 and 9.

Jesus, Physician of the Sinner

Like political or business groups (Chapter 8), religious groups often utilize what can be termed the "punishment paradigm," standing in explicit accusation of those who are homeless as morally corrupt and impoverished by their own free will. In addition to informing a general cosmology through which all sorts of worldly affairs, including homelessness, are understood, the wages of sin become tools for motivation, an approach to controlling human behavior. "Don't do X or you'll go to Hell," it goes. Of course this assumes an entire order of the universe and the existence of unseen parts of it that is beyond the scope of this project. For our purposes, a core assumption of the punishment paradigm is that humans need to be compelled by external motivations to act ethically.

It seems that human beings, particularly those socialized in Western cultures, are susceptible to the punishment paradigm. After all, some of our earliest life lessons revolve around internalizing the costs and benefits for following the rules of our families. Foucault notes that the process of disciplining a person often begins with enforcement through very immediate, physical consequences but that over time these are folded into the disciplined person's way of being, such that they act "properly" without such external threats.[3] This suggests, we think correctly, that we are culturally very sensitive, although not always consciously, to the idea that we might "get in trouble" at any moment.[4] Punishment is a very culturally powerful concept because we learn it very early in life. Even as we grow out of such beliefs that bad behavior will cause Santa Clause to skip our house at Christmas, or even as some eschew belief in cosmic threats of damnation, the threat of punishment nonetheless remains very salient in our cognitive processes. Punishments, as well as rewards, therefore have a potent effect on getting us to behave according to social norms, and both punishment and reward are frequently used as incentives for good behavior. There is an endless list of ordinary social processes that reflect as much: promotions at work, incarceration for crime, good or bad grades for school performance, and so forth. But the wages of sin are perhaps the greatest threat of all in a culture highly influenced by Protestantism. Eternal, insufferable, and impossible to falsify, the threat of damnation is a formidable psychosocial tool for motivating behavior. Religious groups often quite explicitly employ sin as a cosmic threat, and those who are homeless are quite openly addressed on such terms.

The specific implication that those who are homeless need the motivation of punishment to coerce them to live more virtuous lives betrays other presuppositions made by these judgmental religious groups. It suggests at the outset that homelessness is a wage of sin, and if sin is the free-will choice of the individual sinner, the logical conclusion is that people choose to be homeless. Additionally, the religious punishment paradigm approach presupposes that those who are homeless, by definition, are not leading virtuous lives. Of course, religious groups are not immune to cultural notions of homelessness as a function of addiction or mental illness. The former can easily be constructed as evidence of immorality. As for the latter, the history of "madness" suggests a lineage of equating mental illness with moral corruption and even satanic forces.[5]

Despite the fact that homelessness is, strictly speaking, simply the condition of being without a home, Western culture has a long history of counting poverty as evidence of immorality, and in approaching homelessness, Christianity often adds its own religious flavor to this evaluation. The director of a religiously oriented homeless shelter illuminated clearly the connection between being homeless and having a corrupted spirit, tying together religious and governmental initiatives in the process:

> The greatest problem that we see across the board, whether it be working with social services or juvenile delinquents, or anything like that, is that when a change needs to take place in someone's life, and the government's beginning to realize this, not only city and state, but the federal government especially, are beginning to realize that the only programs that work are faith-based programs. You can change all of the outside that you want to. You can put new clothes on 'em, you can feed 'em, you can give 'em a place to live, but if on the inside they haven't developed a new spirit and a new attitude and a new viewpoint on life, they're eventually gonna fall away and have nothing to gain strength from.

Notable here is that the problems of homelessness are linked to a lack of strength in the person who is homeless. Moreover, presumption is that faith in God not only is lacking but additionally is an essential part to getting off the street. As such, it is postured as not just a matter of the personal experience of the individual who is homeless, but also an integral part of social programs, even those run or supported by the government.

The connections between those who are homeless and Western cultural notions of immorality perhaps are best explicated for the Christian context by Weber's notion of the Protestant ethic.[6] In particular ascetic Protestant sects such as Calvinism and Puritanism, the seed of predestination grew into cultural notions about the inherent value of work. While Marx could explain labor only in terms of earning money, Weber adds to Marxist materialism the notion of substantive rationality, or what we might call semiconscious cultural tradition. According to Weber's analysis, efforts to show oneself to be a member of the elect, the group preordained to go to heaven, leads the Protestant to work hard for work's sake.[7] The Puritan saying "Idle hands are the devil's workshop" captures this religious prescript. As this practice is repeated in communities and across generations, it becomes separate from any initial impetus and comes to rest as a given cultural way of life, which we might simply call tradition. The development of this tradition in Protestant culture explained for Weber why Protestants were more successful in industrial, capitalist economies. Our experience suggests this view still resonates with Christian groups such as the Pentecostals. Generally, this religious ethos connects work and subsequent ownership of property to virtue and therefore categorically denies virtue to those who have little property, that is, those who are homeless.[8]

Perhaps our description of religious judgment and coercion of those who are homeless by means of the punishment paradigm seems heavy-handed. We would have thought so, too, until we encountered Mama Reatha. One of the joys of doing grounded theory is that if you are open to it, the research experience can significantly transform preconceptions and undermine expectations. Mama Reatha pulled up to Catchout Corner in her car yelling, "I brought food!" She got out, conspicuously empty-handed, introduced herself, and began to witness to the men. Throughout the course of her lecture, she told them that Jesus had come for the poor and that if they accepted him, he would cure them of their "wicked ways." As her presentation came to a close, she pointed to Motown and recounted her last visit: "This guy will tell you. Last time I was here, I told the guys if they prayed, that Jesus would provide the rest. So we all prayed, and a little while later a van pulled up with food." This is what she had meant when she had promised food upon her arrival. She had brought the power of prayer and salvation—spiritual food—but God apparently was going to bring the actual food some other time.

Mama Reatha later got into an argument with Knucklehead when she told him that he obviously had not repented because he was still on the street:

Knucklehead:	You think I don't want to get off these streets?
Mama Reatha:	But you need to accept Jesus.
Knucklehead:	I've accepted God.
Mama Reatha:	Then why haven't you gotten up [off the streets]?
Knucklehead:	God's got a plan for everybody.
Mama Reatha:	But he gives you a choice, son. He gives you a choice to turn from your drinking and your crack cocaine.
Knucklehead:	[shocked] Who say I do crack cocaine?
Mama Reatha:	I am because I see it. I said I love you. … God has a gift for you that you can receive today. That's the spirit in me.
Knucklehead:	God bless you—you understand what I'm saying.
Mama Reatha:	And he gives you a spirit of discernment. I can look at you and see the drugs all over you. This is the ministry.
Knucklehead:	You must be psychic, Sweetie.
Mama Reatha:	No, I'm not; this is the ministry that God gave me. How can I not see? Your eyes are the mirror to your soul. I can look at your eyes and see that you're not sober.
Knucklehead:	I am sober.
Mama Reatha:	Are you sober?
Knucklehead:	I promise I'm sober.
Mama Reatha:	If you take this gift I'm offering you through Jesus Christ, you will sober up, immediately. Do you believe that?
Knucklehead:	Sure I believe that. I trust in God; you know what I'm saying. That's what feeds me and takes care of me every day of my life; you know what I'm saying. I'm 51 years old; you know what I'm saying. I didn't get 51 years old on my own.
Mama Reatha:	Are you 51 years old?

Knucklehead: A good 51 years old. I'm blessed by God.
Mama Reatha: Do you like being out here and being miserable
                and not—
Knucklehead: I'm not miserable. I'm not miserable.
Mama Reatha: The Devil has got you deceived.
Knucklehead: No. No.

Indicated clearly in this excerpt is the connection between sin and homelessness and the idea that the Christian notion of free will illuminates homelessness as the choice of the person who is homeless. For Mama Reatha, divining the sins of those on the Corner probably was less of a heavenly power and more a matter of constructing homelessness as, by definition, the result of wicked ways. She presumes at the outset, for example, that Knucklehead is on crack, suggesting that she folds the connection between homelessness and addiction that exists broadly in the culture into her specifically religious framework.

There are many other similar stories. Lockett told of a preacher who used to serve meals along with a lambasting about how they were sinners. "I bet there wouldn't be this kind of line if I was givin' away Bibles!" Lockett quoted one of the man's harangues. Potato Water remarked that while the shelter we had stayed in was "not real bad about it," other shelters could be extremely religiously judgmental. "[That shelter's] the worst. Got some guy up there [screaming], 'You're gonna burn in hell!' You know, a bunch of shenanigans."

In Chapter 2 we noted the significance of being a constantly judged spectacle. People openly gawk at those on the street, shake their heads in disgust without even an attempt at discretion. The religious, whether in the shelters or on the street, make similar implicit judgments, entailed in the very act of approaching someone with religious prescriptions. There is an assumption built into the didactic act of witnessing that presumes the one witnessing is enlightened and the one witnessed to lacks such righteous knowledge. We felt this judgment ourselves when on the streets we found ourselves approached with the "good news." Wasserman was doing fieldwork at a Food Not Bomb's picnic when a man came and sat next to him and said, "I can tell by looking at you that everything's not all right in your life." Wasserman was surprised by this, especially since he did not feel like things were going especially badly. His immediate reaction was to say as much, but, later, irritation set in as he came to feel that he had been strongly and negatively judged by the man. This is a common experience for those on the street, who are approached routinely with such judgments. Because they are seen as in dire need of spiritual witness and typically stay in public spaces, there is no personal or spatial privacy to protect them against such intrusions.[9]

What the "sinners" explanation suggests is that nothing will have an impact on homelessness except the willingness of those who are homeless themselves to reestablish a relationship with God. From this perspective, the condition of being homeless is just punishment for their sins, and getting off the street a reward for "getting right with God." This of course conveniently alleviates social responsibility. The punishment-reward paradigm was made shockingly clear as Mama Reatha was debating Knucklehead, "Don't you want to have life and have it more abundantly? I accepted God, and I can have whatever I want." Knucklehead responded by asking her why, if in fact she could have whatever she wanted, she was driving such a shoddy car. She told him, "I choose to drive that car. I can have whatever car I want." "You choose to drive *that* car?" Knucklehead laughingly exclaimed. Knucklehead's jokes aside, the punishment-reward paradigm for Mama Reatha was particularly explicit, tied not only to reward in heaven but also to real things on earth.

Weber's evaluation ascribes the Protestant ethic to Calvinism and other ascetic Protestant sects that upheld the virtue of economic pursuits, but by the time Weber wrote, the religious foundations of this practice had given way to a similar, but secular cultural ethos that he called the "spirit of capitalism."[10] But connections between explicitly religious Protestant virtue and economic success still are plentiful. Pentecostalism is a more modern sect that believes as much. Mama Reatha's rhetoric fit closely with Pentecostal notions about the connection of belief in God to happiness on earth, including that which comes from material success. In her explicit conception, poverty was just punishment for laziness and moral corruption, and "turning from [their] wicked ways" would not just garner spiritual reward but distinctly material payoffs as well. She was zealously repetitious on the point that they could "have life and have it more abundantly."

The punishment paradigm is not exclusive to those with a judgmental religious orientation. The latter employs exactly the same notions found in the exchange logic of the service institution, where submission to the program garners the reward of shelter services. While the religious include invisible cosmic punishments for moral nonconformity (though Mama Reatha makes clear this is often in addition to the purported material punishment of poverty on earth), the quid pro quo structure of these religious programs directly mirrors broader cultural trends toward charity as reciprocal exchange. In the end, even the extremities of religion reflect fairly ordinary cultural logics. The reciprocal logic of homeless services is not very different from the logic that Mama Reatha used that day at Catchout Corner. Submission begets reward; resistance begets punishment.

Connections between sin and sickness betray an additional link between these religious approaches and the medical model of homeless-service provision. The process of diagnosis in the shelter is of a similar character to religious judgments of sin, where the focus of both is on individual deficiency. Mama Reatha supplied an explicit example of the link between religious approaches and those of the medical model:

> This one right here [pointing at Hammer]—you can see Jesus on this guy's face, right here. But you know, he's come out here and gotten out in the wilderness. But you know something? Jesus had a wilderness experience, too. And guess what happened after he went and had his wilderness experience? The angels came and ministered to him. And then what did he do? He went out and started *healing the sick*, you know, and causing the blind to see, 'cause he went out and started preaching, didn't he? And he preached to people just like ya'll. [She points her finger and pans it across the crowd.] And he wasn't for the upper class; he was for the ones that needed the *physician*. He said *those that are sick need the physician*, not them that are well. And these are the kind of people ya'll are [another sweeping point] that Jesus went walking about and ministering to when he was here on earth.

In her mind, the connection between sin and sickness was markedly clear. Jesus was a physician for sinners. The problematics of the medicalization of homelessness (Chapter 9) carry over into the metaphor that sin is a type of sickness—a metaphor obviously taken quite literally in some cases. That is, whether sick minds or sick souls are the focus, both the secular and religious medicalization of homelessness maintains structures that privilege some people over others. Specifically, people other than those who are homeless themselves are empowered to define and deal with homelessness.

Mama Reatha finished with a group prayer and rendition of "Amazing Grace." She tried to wake up Lockett, who appeared to have been sleeping in a chair through the whole thing, though he kept opening his eyes and subtly shaking his head in dismay at her more extreme statements. He made a swatting motion and muttered, "Go on … leave me alone." This was particularly interesting because at other times, Lockett had exuded the highly religious worldview common to those on the street. When asked in an interview once how things were going, he replied, "I can't complain, you know. God is good." After Mama Reatha left, Lockett "woke up" and clarified:

> People come out here all the time and try to get you to pray. When I pray, it's between me and God, God and me. I learned a long time ago, I pray when I want to; I don't pray because they want me to. If I go to heaven or I go to hell ... it's between me and God. I don't mean no harm, but that's how I do with all of them. Everybody wants you to pray.

Here we see a great deal about the religiosity of homeless individuals. As noted in Chapter 6, those who are homeless, generally, and those on the street, in particular, tend to be very religious. They commonly use religious concepts to construct their understandings of the world and their often tremendously difficult circumstances. For example, they often have fatalistic notions about God's control of the universe, and these are related to their belief in the impotency of political solutions, discussed previously. But as religious as they are themselves, they still directly resist the control of religious institutions and other religious people.

It may seem contradictory that those on the street have deeply fatalistic religious beliefs, but at the same time an intensely autonomous spirit (see Chapter 7). There are several ways to drive this toward consistency. For example, it's not difficult to understand resistance to the control mechanisms of religious people and a belief in the validity and righteousness of God's own hand. But conversely, not all contradictions need to be resolved. As the reader knows by now, a central premise of this work is that human life is full of irreconcilable contradiction and irreducible complexity.

Religious Charity:
Kindly Putting the Meek in Their Place

Most service programs are supported, if not governed and staffed, by religious organizations. During all of our visits to shelters, church groups served the meals, always prefaced with prayer. While not typically of the hell-fire orientation, these prayers nonetheless suggested that all power for change lay in the hands of God. Religious belief among those who are homeless parallels, historically, that of the poor. When Marx said, "Religion is the opiate of the masses," he meant that the belief that God is wholly good and in total control of the universe manifested as acceptance of human-caused economic injustice among the poor.[11] Poverty and homelessness in the fatalistic world are given reason and meaning by the idea that they must result from God's will and infinite wisdom.

Several times at street meals and also during a stay in the shelter, we watched as "the clients" were led in a religious cheer by an enthusiastic volunteer, "God is Good, and he's good all the time!" This mantra was repeated often when we visited shelters and meals and sometimes on the street, though there it was often truncated to just "God is good."

In various service programs this idea was explicitly reinforced and in particularly interesting ways. While waiting on a spot to open up in a transitional housing program after successfully completing a twenty-eight-day treatment program, Big E described his achievement:

> With the help of the program, with the help of the professionals, you know, things are looking better for me, you know—one day at a time. If anyone want to see things get better, just give it a try. That's all you can do is try. Just give it all to God, and he will do the rest. He will send people in your life that can and will help you. You just have to let go of those that's still in trouble; there is help, and it comes from above.

Though this comment has some similarities with the fiery rhetoric of Mama Reatha, particularly in the notion of God's power over life, appeal to religion in the treatment-oriented service institution does not usually aim explicitly to shame a person onto a more righteous path. Rather, proponents quite sincerely intend to use religion to inspire and uplift the person who is homeless. But they often were unsuccessful at doing so, and closer analysis of their espoused ideologies suggests that they replicate stratification in ways similar to that of the medical model. That is, these more kindly religious approaches still tend to repress rather than empower the person who is homeless.

While homeless individuals themselves often espoused the mantra that "God is good, and he's good all the time," when led in the cheer by volunteers, their enthusiasm was lacking. They would murmur the refrains, but clearly lacked the heartfelt energy the religious volunteers were looking for. The idea that God is always good may imply a world-view that sees every life circumstance and event as legitimate and just. To follow this line of thinking would mean that inequality is not the result of systemic power, but rather the righteous will of God. Poverty, death, suffering, and misery all are good because God is always good and in control. We saw this worldview among those who were homeless, although notably more so in the shelters than on the street.

A logic that suggests that homelessness ultimately is God's choice, or the natural order of things, implies that challenging the structures of political economy is at best secondary to calling on a higher power. Thus, in addition to the aforementioned demoralizing phenomenon of city sweeps and other often insurmountable political and economic barriers, the fatalism of those on the street can be understood as influenced partly by these religious assertions that implicitly justify the status quo as God's plan. These notions of religious fatalism involve the same aforementioned deduction, thus betraying the irony that treatment is at best secondary to calling on a higher power, despite the fact that such espousals were fixtures of even the most treatment-oriented service institutions. While intending to uplift those who were down on their luck, these religious mantras may subconsciously produce fatalism by suggesting that the status quo is produced by and consistent with God's will.

The judgmental nature of Mama Reatha's ideology and preaching would likely appall many other Christian groups who employ less fiery concepts, such as the biblical notion that "whatever you did for one of the least of these brothers of mine, you did for me."[12] This classic version of Christian charity certainly is less offensive than the idea of saving the souls of the wicked. But closer examination suggests that notions of helping "the meek" replicate problematic judgments of those who are homeless in the same way as did both Mama Reatha and the medical model of service provision. While less accusatory, the concept of Christian charity still rests on the idea of helping the less fortunate. This does little to empower them as agents in their own lives, but rather suggests they are inevitably dependent on those who are not so meek.

Both the judgmental and the kindly religious perspectives locate the problems of homelessness in those who are homeless themselves, either as sinners or the helpless meek, and so establish hierarchical relationships that make saving those who are homeless the calling of righteous others. The status of the givers and takers remains intact, and thus the structural social arrangements that predicate homelessness, and oppression in general, continue unmitigated. The meek remain meek, and salvation is irrevocably managed by the privileged.

Status differences between givers and takers manifest in very clear ways at the shelters and street meals. As already noted (Chapter 9), space in the shelter often reflects the hierarchical social divisions between staff and volunteers, on the one hand, and "clients," on the other. The spatial organization of religious street meals tended to be very similar. Volunteers served the food line from behind tables and led prayers from behind a microphone. When we attended an Easter street meal conducted by a number of churches, the video camera we brought immediately gave away that we were not among those who were homeless. While we were not trying to be taken as homeless, neither had we expected the radically different treatment that emerged from the recognition we were not. Without even asking, Wasserman was approached with a name tag that served to credential him as not-homeless. He was told that with that he could "go behind the line"; that is, as not-homeless, he was allowed into privileged spaces. This sort of hierarchical organization might seem to be an inevitable feature of the street meal activity itself, but groups who consciously subvert such manifestations of status hierarchies illustrate that it is not.[13] Moreover, we do not intend to suggest that this organization was intentionally exclusive, but simply that it was a very visible manifestation of the us-them dichotomy, one that made the differences between givers and takers very clear.

As with service institutions, religious groups tend to evaluate success based on the extent to which those who are homeless are able to reassimilate into "normal" society. This may not be consistent with a purely religious notion of Christian charity, but religion is not immune to influences from wider social contexts. In any society, social spheres overlap each other. It is not a coincidence that societies with democratic political systems tend to have capitalist economies, as both of these employ individualist cultural ideologies. Likewise, charitable religious approaches to homelessness are not immune to influences from polity, economy, and culture. Charity often must be understood as exchange in order to remain consistent with the logic of capitalist economy. So even when driven primarily by religion, charity still can be conceptualized, or at least evaluated, on the extent to which it satisfies expectations of reciprocity.

This is best summed up for the present discussion by the statement of a religious volunteer who, when hearing that a man who supposedly had come to the Easter street meal five years before had gotten a job and gotten off the street, commented, "That makes it all worth it." This was a casual utterance on his part, but it betrays that the underlying quid pro quo requirements of charity were colored by Western culture even when explicitly premised on Christian values. Would having given him a meal not been worth it if the man was still homeless? Failure to reciprocate might not cause these groups to end their charitable programs, since they frequently still do have roots in more classical, duty-oriented notions of Christian charity. All this suggests is that multiple, even opposing logics of justification can coexist within single people or single institutions.[14] This notwithstanding, the evaluation of "successful" giving falls in line to a significant extent with the exchange logic of the economy. As it turned out, the man who had made "it all worth it" had come to another street meal conducted by the same churches a few months prior and was still homeless, though he had recently gotten a job.

* * *

The same dynamics that underlie the political and treatment approaches to homelessness also influence both the judgmental and charitable religious perspectives of it. There, too, the problem of homelessness is located in the person who is homeless rather than in the structure of society. Whether the problem of homelessness is conceptualized as nuisance behaviors (political), mental illness or addiction (treatment), sin (judgmental religion), or meekness (charitable religion), these all are assertions of problems of character with the person who is homeless and take no account of the structural arrangements that contribute to homelessness. These "varied" perspectives ultimately have more in common than they do differences.

Notes

1. Lyon-Callo makes a brief comment about this, in "Medicalizing Homelessness"; see Rowe, *Crossing the Border*, for discussion of how Christian notions of redemption color the perspective of outreach workers even when they espouse no conscious religious ideology; we observed this in two shelters and also at multiple street meals conducted by religious groups.
2. Hoch and Slayton, *New Homeless and Old*.
3. Foucault, *Discipline and Punish*.
4. The Milgram experiments, conducted at Yale University in the 1960s, provide a classic empirical justification of a human disposition to obedience.
5. See Foucault, *Madness and Civilization*.
6. Weber, *The Protestant Ethic and the Spirit of Capitalism*.
7. Ibid.

8. While it is true in fact that most of the homeless, especially the street homeless, do work, in the perceptions of the general public—which overlap with these religious groups—laziness is endemic to the homeless condition.

9. This echoes Goffman, in *Behavior in Public Places*, regarding his concept of "open persons."

10. Weber, *The Protestant Ethic and the Spirit of Capitalism.*

11. Marx, *A Contribution to the Critique of Hegel's Philosophy of Right.*

12. Matthew 25:40.

13. See the discussion of Food Not Bombs's picnic model in Chapter 11.

14. See Boltanski and Thévenot, *On Justification.*

11

Conclusion: Improving Research, Improving Policy

For all the work done to understand and solve homelessness, conditions do not seem to have gotten much better. This comes as no surprise to jaded social scientists like us. Little we do seems to make much of an observable difference, especially when it comes to the big picture. Our participants who lived on the street knew it, too. "At best it'll be a drop in the ocean," one once said in his brutally honest assessment of what we were doing. But not everyone felt that way. The night we were politely surmised as a drop in the ocean, Potato Water stumbled into our tent at the Second Avenue Camp and lay down next to Clair. He took a deep breath and said with the utmost concern, "I don't care what anyone says, Professor; you guys are more than a drop in the ocean." On the one hand, it seemed like the sort of cliché thing that nice people say. But Potato Water's consolation also had a ring to it that suggested that perhaps we had become, at the very least, important to him. We had become friends.

For researchers to admit friendships with participants is somewhat taboo. How can one be fair and dispassionate in analyzing one's friends? But this underestimates the natural social developments that attend longitudinal, in-depth research like ours. As we see it, the question is not how the ethnographic researcher becomes friends with some participants, but rather how can they avoid it? Moreover friendship does not so much color one's judgments as one's judgments fund friendships. In an equally "unscientific" admission, let us go ahead and state the considerably unremarkable fact that we met plenty of people, including those on the street, we disliked as well. This is unremarkable because it simply is unhuman to spend a great deal of time with people and not form judgments about them, to develop affinities or aversions.

The survey researcher can do this because they do not get to know their subjects to any expansive degree, focusing rather on this or that piece of information. Once those tidbits are collected, everyone goes their separate ways. We are not troubled professionally by the notion that we have become friends with some of our participants. As with most friendships, we learned about the participants first and came to like them second. Our affinities largely developed from our judgments, not the other way around.[1]

After four years of research, we found it hard to "go our separate ways." Wasserman left Birmingham for a job in Texas, but even when he returns, visits to the streets are as natural to his agenda as seeing friends and family. Clair also visits the streets, though keeping up with people as they move around is difficult and time produces waning numbers of old contacts.

Our discussion of friendship might have ended as a mere admission of a study limitation, replete with the typical defenses about how in the end it is not so problematic, like the one above. But the notion of friendship has deeper implications. Social science, public policy, service programs, and US culture all tend to approach homelessness with a rigidity fueled by fear of difference and uncertainty. For the public, this is a fear caused by the violation of social norms and probably a subconscious worry that poverty could happen to them. For public policies and service programs, it is a fear that human difference is chaotic and unmanageable and therefore is the enemy of social and institutional order. Western culture pervasively believes that when left to their own devices, human beings are nasty, decadent, and dangerous.[2] Difference, therefore, must be controlled and should seep through the control mechanisms only in manageable ways and in very small amounts.

Social science fears difference, too. Difference is the enemy of discerning a healthy sociological tendency, for which one needs a small amount of difference—just enough variation but not too much. A lot of blood, sweat, and tears are poured into controlling for outliers. This amounts to more than math. While aggregate tendencies are interesting and often useful, social science lacks a methodological way to understand too much variation. In the end, individualism is a very sick concept in the social sciences. As a discipline, we have constructed our search for social truth as a matter of rooting out complexities often by aspiring to increasingly abstract levels of aggregation. But the real truth is that our world is a complex and diverse place, and in looking at any subject, one would do well to aspire to an equally complex vision of it.

Derrida wrote:

> The friends of the *perhaps* are the friends of truth. But the friends of
> truth are not, by definition, *in* the truth; they are not installed there as
> in the padlocked security of a dogma and the stable reliability of an
> opinion. If there is some truth in the *perhaps*, it can only be that of
> which friends are friends. Only friends. The friends of truth are with-
> out the truth, even if friends cannot function without truth. The truth
> … it is impossible to *be it, to be there, to have it*; one must only be
> its friend.[3]

The concept of friendship can teach us much about our relationship with
those who are homeless, what is (and is not) wrong with homelessness,
and how we might make that relationship better. Friendship is an inherently fluid relationship that requires accepting the individuality of your
friends and interacting with them collaboratively, not solely on your
terms or theirs. Friends engage in voluntary association, and their activities and discourse emerge naturally from their identities and the equality
of their status. Friendships are not governed by formalized rules or
authoritarian demands and cannot be sustained with heartless judgments
or callous disregard. And it is by way of their informality, fluidity, and
inherent respect that the good friendship can shed much light on the
good society.

As a society, we arrogantly advance all sorts of social solutions to
phenomena that we insolently label as social problems. There is prima
facie, though suspect, evidence to support such judgments. As a matter
of course, we fear difference, and *they* are not like *us*. Case closed. But
while there is no doubt that there are things in society that need to be
made better, we ought to make proper preparations, lest we dive head-
long into a pool we have not yet checked for water.

We cannot "fix" homelessness if we do not know those who are
homeless. Those who know them as friends also know that boasting of a
"fix" is a grotesque and judgmental assertion of authority built on supposed wisdom from a distanced relationship with very little historical
success.[4] It seems that rather than cling to our implicit sense that *we* can
fix *the problem*, implying in the process that *we* could not possibly *be*
the problem, we must in politics, service programs, social science, and
throughout the public square, learn first to be the friends of those who
are homeless. More than that, we must learn to be the friends of *homelessness* as a concept in the same way Derrida calls us to be friends of
truth. We must recognize that the immense complexity, fluidity, and
individuation within that concept mean we can only have the type of

organic relationship with it by which "friends are friends." In concluding this book, we examine some insights born in us through submission to the seemingly simple and ordinary notion of friendship.

On Knowing Homelessness

There has been much written on homelessness yet comparatively little on the social construction of defining the concept itself or deconstructing the judgments that attend it. One can glean some of this from various historical accounts in which it is made clear that the meaning of homelessness has changed dramatically over time. The hobo lifestyle was a homeless existence but certainly not the same as homelessness in twenty-first-century United States.[5] But less attention has been paid to the wide range of meanings that homelessness still retains. Discussions of this sort lurk in questions about "who counts" (literally) when organizations attempt to enumerate the population (see Chapter 3). But this only skims the deep differences in the meaning of homelessness, even for those individuals who are most decidedly homeless according to popular perception, such as those on the street.

On the street it is not uncommon to hear someone say something like, "I'm not homeless. I can go home anytime I want." A statement like this might easily come from a person who has lived under a bridge for several years, and so the claim immediately butts up against what we "know." So we quickly determine this "I'm not homeless" stuff to be patently ridiculous and ripe for the rationalization machine that is the academic mind. We rewrite it as machismo, an ego trip that is skewing an accurate perception of self. Explanations of this sort are easy, particularly if we simply hold the "I'm not homeless" notion up against the fact that said person sleeps outside in the city. But this does little to help us penetrate the meaning of the statement.

Recall Lockett's observation about having been on the streets a long time, but never feeling homeless until his mother died. Place yourself in J. K.'s frame of mind, growing up in a house with a dirt floor and no running water and then later living under a bridge, but with access to a working bathroom at the neighboring stone company. The meaning of homelessness does not change only across human history, it also changes across each human experience. From the standpoint of meaning, homelessness is to a significant degree a state of mind, not a sickness and not even a lack of a legal address. Wasserman once asked a Kenyan colleague if people living in homemade shacks would be considered homeless in her home country. "No, we would count them in the census," she replied.

It is clear that homelessness, like all other judgments of deviance, ultimately is measured only in terms of distance from the norm. But "the norm" is something of an illusive creature. It changes from time to time, culture to culture, and person to person. Knowing homelessness, then, is not such a simple process, not something that can be understood with routine appeals to normative standards. Here, as suggested by Derrida, it is of great benefit to "know" homelessness from the perspective of "perhaps." That is, if we want to know it, we must listen to it as we would a confidant and allow it to change and grow as we would a friend. At least to any significant depth, we can be only friends of homelessness.

On Solving Homelessness

Arrogant people make bad friends. A quick way to end a friendship before it starts is to lay a bunch of "oughts" on someone you do not know very well. Tell someone whom you have just met what he or she ought to do with his or her life, and see if you are not shown the metaphorical door. We have some permission to meddle caringly and gingerly in the lives of our friends, but trying to do it with a stranger usually goes poorly. This is no less the case for all the people who "know" how to "fix" homelessness, and it is as true interpersonally as it is for public policy.

Recall, for example, when we brought a new colleague into the field. From the very beginning of his first visit, he pontificated about what different men at Catchout ought to be doing (Chapter 2). The problem is not so much about what he said as it was that he had not organically developed a friendship and instead approached them as a proselytizing outsider. His "oughts" were met with hostile reaction and, ironically, since he was African American, tagged as the "devil psychology" of the white man. Both of the authors had commonly made statements similar to his, engaging in discussions about even sensitive topics like drugs and religion. As friends, we were allowed to do so. Once a man at Catchout was having health problems. Clair told him, "You need to lay off the drugs and go to the hospital to get your kidneys checked out." He received this warmly, with the caring and concern it was intended, and took the advice seriously. But the same statement from a stranger, rather than a friend, likely would have been met with hostility or dismissal, as were so many of the moral prescriptions preached at the Corner by the various strangers who were always dropping by.

So much public policy gives in to this same fallacy. The armchair proclamations of experts and politicians about how to deal with homelessness are routinely dismissed by those on the street with the notion "They don't know us." And they are right. Those policies rarely take into account how those on the street see themselves and understand their homelessness. Yet these experts and politicians pontificate about what homeless people need to do and how they need to live.

From the beginning of our research, we learned a great deal about how to be friends of homelessness, both from those on the street themselves and from those who had in their own lives learned similar lessons. We are thankful to have interviewed Ralph, the radical homeless advocate, early in our project, since at the time, we were ourselves enmeshed in the more arrogant modes of thinking. "What can be done to help get people off the streets?" we asked him. His characteristic reply subverted the assumptions of our question from the outset:

> I'm not so sure that there needs to be a steadfast decision to get people off the streets. I think perhaps there needs to be some green areas in all cities where people might want to live. I don't even know if the goal is to get them off the streets. If that is what they so choose, then there needs to be those opportunities in terms of shelters, different kinds of ideas of shelters, and that sort of thing sure should be made available. But for someone that because of a diagnosis can't quite at most times of the year, or some times of the year … live in 90-degree walls made of cheap cardboard, which is what this office is, surrounded by brick with no wind, I might add, and very little sunshine … I start thinking maybe they've really got it right and we don't.

The fluid reflexivity is evident even in the way he speaks. Ralph was a friend to homelessness and therefore did not attach a priori rules and judgments to it. Approaching this radical idea from the dominant way of thinking not only about homelessness itself but also from our cultural sense of truth in general, it is easily dismissed as the wacky idea of an ex-hippie. If we are not able to be friends of homelessness, then ideas such as this are seen as just cheap utterances of blindly critical nonsense. The chorus of experts might even be offended at the suggestion that the existence of those who are homeless has advantages over those who are housed. They almost certainly will see it as a dangerous justification of an illegitimate way of life, of rationalizing addiction, laziness, and so on. We have openly worried about such a response related to our discussion of "peace of mind" (see Chapter 7). But such a knee-jerk reaction would betray that these experts operate from uniform visions of homelessness as a social problem and make clear that in constructing such simplified perspectives, they have not learned much from those who are homeless or have interacted with them in very selective ways that produce such biases (e.g., at addiction treatment centers).

To make the sort of intrusions into homelessness that "fixing it" requires, we must prepare ourselves to deal with the diversity and complexity that are part of it. Further, to be so fluid and flexible, it seems best to start with every idea "on the table." The notion of "green areas," suggested to us by Ralph is one such radical idea among others, such as no-strings-attached cafés, no-questions-asked hygiene centers with showers and lockers for storing one's possessions so they do not get stolen, and housing-first initiatives that do away with the exclusionary criteria of the treatment model. None of these is without problems and potential pitfalls, just as the medical model offers some advantages but also carries some problems. "Green zones" and housing-first programs risk further ghettoizing those who are homeless, quarantining them to what effectively become internment camps.[6] One can imagine the segregationist justifications made possible by designating such spaces for those on the street: "This space is for *us*. That space is for *them*." Whether this is a problem inherent to these ideas or could be avoided through proper planning and implementation remains to be seen.

For the purposes here, such proposals serve a much simpler insight. In approaching the diversity of homelessness, we must be open to a diversity of ideas and to their coexistence in a complex social reality, even when they are oppositional as abstract ideologies. Similarly, though we have been critical of the treatment model, we hope to have made it clear that our critique centers on its exclusionary practices, not the treatment itself. Many people need treatment and should be able to engage in the treatment process. But rather than punishing those who do not need treatment or will not engage in the process, there ought to be other alternative approaches. While from the dominant mode of thinking alternatives are easily written off as "enabling," we might also consider that all together they simply are varied responses to a varied group of people.

To deal with homelessness, one must first know it. But the best way to know homelessness is to be its friend, and this means letting go of the idea that it is something to be solved. We do not approach friends as their saviors but from concern and caring that manifests as a listening ear, friendly advice, and the standing offer of assistance that is accessed freely, rather than thrust on them.

Social Science and Friendship

As a discipline that is uncomfortable with the sort of uncertainty that attends the notion of friendship, social science has exacerbated problems of the various approaches to homelessness. While its positivistic sectors decry a relationship with truth grounded on the fluid notion of "perhaps," the interpretivist sectors do no better by devaluing the real knowledge afforded by it. Rigid notions of homelessness feed inflexible ways of working with those who are homeless. Nihilistic notions of homelessness suggest that all understanding is hopeless. Although both positivism and relativism are strongly influential threads of social science, neither is very appealing. As we befriended people who were homeless, and then ultimately the concept of homelessness itself, we learned a great deal about the flawed relationship of social science to social problems.

The problem partly is methodological. The linear models of social science rarely explain more than 30 percent of the variance in a population. Rather than developing more complex models that could better explain the complexity of the world, social scientists remain comfortable calling the other 70 percent of human behavior "error." But not only has social science not been able to develop methodological techniques equal to the complexity of social life, we have also rarely participated in the development of practices for working with individuals as active, creative participants rather than objectified cases to be acted on. The social sciences have done little to build pedagogies for working with those who are homeless in any way that respects their individual diversity. We have preferred instead to produce the aggregate tendencies of most significance and then fed these to those seeking to solve homelessness, thereby promoting conformity to a selected set of supposedly likely causes.

In their instant classic *Habits of the Heart*, Robert Bellah and colleagues give a sociophilosophical account of American culture and the problematics that underlie the prima facie opposition between individualist ideology and the demands of social order.[7] This is a dialectic that has characterized political philosophy for centuries. How do we divide yet integrate? How can society be at the same time free and orderly? While there have been countless perspectives delineating the line between liberty and law, nearly all of them have assumed that order must be enforced as a set of external propositions to which individuals should be made to conform. But underlying this is an assumption of human behavior as inherently antagonistic. Debating the innate qualities of the human animal is beyond the scope of this discussion, but the concept of friendship at the very least calls us to recognize our capacity to develop free and natural associations founded on caring and respect. Friendships are not legislated; they grow out of the inherent qualities of the friends and into a relationship, rather than from external rules that are imposed on the individual friends. It is ironic that this concept of free association that grows out of organic connections among individuals, and that is so natural to ordinary social life, runs counter to the sociological perspective that takes formal or informal social controls to be not only inevitable but also pervasive.

The opening pages of *Habits of the Heart* chronicle four representative American perspectives lying on the spectrum between individualism and community. The fourth position comes from a man named Wayne, a community organizer who works mostly for the rights of tenants in low-income housing. After grounding his sociopolitical dispositions in his biography and showing how these manifest in his current work as an activist, Bellah and colleagues proceed to explicate ambiguities and contradictions as they have for the first three emblematic participants, Brian, Joe, and Margaret. While Wayne purports to work with disfranchised people and help them accomplish their goals, the authors criticize the fact that he cannot clearly state what those goals are. According to Bellah and coauthors, the problem with Wayne's perspective is that it is not grounded in any wider framework; it is not guided by any overarching value system. From another perspective, however, this critique of Wayne tells us more about problematic presuppositions of the authors— and social science in general—than it does about shortcomings of Wayne's radicalism.

Wayne's goals are to help empower disfranchised people so that they can achieve *their* goals. For him to presume what those goals ought to be is in direct opposition to the very character of his activism, since it would require bringing to bear his values on a group of people he hopes to enable to be self-determined. Because such value presumptions are the ideological structures at the heart of oppression, Wayne is uncomfortable and downright unwilling to say what goals ought to be worked toward because it is exactly that presumption that leads to oppression.[8] We might say Wayne approaches those he works with as a friend, not as an expert or a savior.

Bellah and his colleagues' criticism of Wayne highlights the extent to which sociophilosophical thinking in our culture is lost in the tension between freedom and order.[9] Working from the assumption that any reasonable philosophy must include external universal principles that limit the number of possible goals of activism, the authors can only conclude that Wayne's philosophy is ambiguous and incomplete.[10] In their defense, Wayne does seem to have difficulty articulating the idea that listing legitimate goals in advance would itself be contradictory to his goal of empowerment. He seems simply to *feel* that prefabricating values for others is wrongheaded, but since he apparently has not philosophized about it, he has a difficult time explaining the reasoning of it all. Paulo Freire had no such difficulty.[11]

In *Pedagogy of the Oppressed*, Freire critiques the epistemic direction of traditional education and presents an alternative. More important, in doing so, he suggests an alternative way of approaching social problems, if not the discipline of social science itself. Traditional education operates from the top down, whereby experts convey a body of knowledge to students, whose job is to passively consume that knowledge. Freire calls this the "banking concept of education." At its core, this model assumes that there is a particular and definite set of things that ought to be learned. But this ignores entirely the fact that the worldviews of the students and the teacher might be very different. Because any representation of the world includes ontological assumptions about the nature and order of things, representing only one way of seeing to the exclusion of others alienates entire sets of students from the process. The banking model of education risks therefore the reinforcement of dominant conceptions of the world and thus elite interests. For example, the idea that competition is virtuous or at least socially beneficial is a value orientation that underlies and promotes the free-market economies in which the wealthy have prospered tremendously.

Thinkers such as John Locke or Adam Smith represent the virtue of competition not just as a driving force of markets but also as something inherent in the character of human beings. The self-interested nature of the human being, then, when presented as knowledge in the traditional banking model of education as merely a fact about the world, reinforces the interests of the wealthy by excluding critical questions about whether human beings are in fact inherently competitive. This ontological assumption becomes the disposition of the poor as much as the wealthy, even though the former ostensibly are oppressed by that very belief and the economic system that grows out of it.

Alternatively, Freire offers dialogical collaboration as another way to proceed with education. Dialogical collaboration operates in an entirely different direction than the traditional banking model. Rather than presuming a definite and particular body of knowledge, and all the value assumptions that go with it, dialogical collaboration begins by seeking to understand the worldview of the student. And instead of assuming a singular, universal knowledge that is then projected onto the student in a top-down direction, collaboration works from particular relationships between the teacher and student and builds up a body of knowledge grounded on the coming together of their perspectives. One might easily say that Freire calls on the relationship of the student and the teacher to be grounded on friendship.

Freire's pedagogy speaks directly to our critiques of homeless-service institutions and how they might otherwise be structured. The relation of service providers to their "clients," particularly in the medical model, mirrors that of the authoritarian teacher and the passive student. Since the service providers tend primarily and sometimes exclusively to address mental illness and addiction, these become the core of the body of knowledge that explains homelessness and treating these becomes the near-exclusive way services are provided. This is incongruent with the ontological disposition of a great many of those who are homeless, particularly those on the street, and so they are alienated from the process in the same way that those with ontologically different views of the world are alienated from traditional education. When forced into the medicalized paradigm of services, those who are street homeless gain little because the shelter discourse does not resonate with the way they understand the world. While those on the street do not ignore mental illness or addiction as problematic conditions, they are much less likely to understand these to be the core explanations of their homelessness (see Chapter 4).

Those who are street homeless tend to retain a central place for the notion of structural injustice such as the inability to get a job or to make a living wage even if they can secure work. As noted, refusing to locate oneself as the central problem can manifest as "troublemaking" from the perspective of shelter staff.[12] Refusing to accept the view of homelessness as strictly a function of individual sickness, those on the street remain outside the service institution, either literally or in spirit (i.e., they might go for help, but they likely will not accept much of what is said and do not get much out of the process).

In our study, Matty highlights clearly the shortcomings of authoritarian models and the promise of dialogical collaboration to restructure the concept of service. As a highly creative person, Matty had carved out of "wasted space" a relatively comfortable existence.[13] He built a two-room wooden structure in his camp, which also boasted a kitchen area and dishwashing station, a separate tent for dry storage, a fire pit, and a makeshift driving range on the roof of his house (see Chapter 5).

As such, Matty was not particularly motivated to seek out shelter services, feeling that trading freedom and self-determination for a sturdier roof and central heat and air was not a good bargain. Moreover, Matty did not conceive of his homelessness as a function of mental illness or addiction and therefore thought that the types of services offered were not for him. But if the service institutions were disposed toward working with Matty in a free collaboration, there might have been any number of plans that could have improved his life, but in ways consistent with his own perspective. For example, they might have tried to get the city to donate a small patch of unused land on which Matty could grow vegetables. This would have been more in keeping with Matty's autonomous, self-reliant identity, and while such a plan might never have gotten him into an apartment or a "legitimate" job, it certainly could have made his life better. Without the service providers' ability to shelve their a priori goals and work with particular individuals in a dialogical collaboration, a variety of creative possibilities remain obscure and entire sets of those who are homeless remain alienated from service institutions.

In the most fundamental sense, the disconnect between those who are street homeless and service providers results from the posture of the latter as "expert." This creates a relationship of unequal power and legitimacy and therefore obscures the ability of either party to listen sincerely to the other. At the heart of the relation of the expert to the person who is homeless lies the issue of freedom and the degree to which that person can shape the character of his or her own life. Service providers presume that they know best what sorts of goals are worth pursuit and what sorts of plans of action are legitimate (usually, housing and work are to be pursued through a treatment process). Those who are homeless certainly engage in all sorts of rationalizations of problematic behaviors, such as addiction, although they frequently just admit them, and such rationalizations can stand in the way of self-awareness. But this is equally true of service institutions in which a single-minded focus on particular values and goals obscures the way in which they exercise power vis-à-vis the disfranchisement of groups of people whose worldviews simply are not congruent with service program prerequisites. Ralph, a credentialed expert in his own right, suggested something similar:

> I don't believe experts. I believe that people, a majority of the time, have the ability to communicate what their wants and desires are and also need that incredible freedom to have a choice. We have to think differently than we have in the past.

Service Without Power: The Food Not Bombs Example

We think it is no coincidence that the most insightful and novel approaches to homelessness often have come from the least credentialed. We might count ourselves among them. Despite our degrees and social science training, we fell rather haphazardly into the issue of homelessness (see Chapter 1). But we attempted to take advantage of this, and, by so doing, hope at least to challenge the wisdom of experts with some new ideas. But other modes of thinking have informed other novel approaches to homelessness.

Food Not Bombs (FNB) holds open community picnics in public spaces where they distribute free food. As is commonly the case, in Birmingham, FNB quickly becomes the target of criticism as well as cease and desist threats from not only local businesses but also homeless-service providers. The Birmingham group held their picnics in the heart of Five Points (see Chapter 8). While a large portion of those who attend FNB picnics are homeless, someone claiming, "FNB feeds the homeless," will be quickly and decisively corrected. "We'll feed anyone," they put it succinctly. Consistent with its radical ideology, FNB is a worldwide "nonorganization"; in the Birmingham FNB group, for example, there is no official membership, but rather a collection of people loosely organized on the premise that food is a right.

FNB directly counters the problematic concepts of community that are rampant in the United States and exacerbated by conflicts of urban redevelopment (see Chapters 5 and 8). While the original idea for a no-strings-attached café (see Chapter 9) itself had been somewhat progressive, there lurked within it the danger of contributing to the quarantining of those who are homeless, particularly since its partial impetus had been complaints about the homeless by the local businesses. FNB saw this as directly antithetical to their agenda of "reclaiming public space." Jeff from Birmingham's FNB contingent observed, about proponents of the café idea, "They conveniently wanted to be out of the areas where they might bother the yuppie businesspeople," adding later, "I want people to see [our picnics]. I want it to be right in their face, to challenge them." Reminiscent of Waldron's critiques of the false sense of community and social inequality that underlies vagrancy legislation (see Chapter 8), FNB was taking action on those illusions by conducting their business in highly visible locations.[14]

FNB's model of operation also suggests new concepts of service that avoid the institutionalizing of social problems in general and homelessness in particular. They are funded by food donations from individuals, local restaurants, and the farmers' market, as well as from their own pockets. A woman once tried to give money to the group, but her charity was met with polite refusal:

> We don't take money, not because we don't want it, but we really don't have any structure to deal with it. We'd rather you just cook something vegetarian and bring it down on Sunday. Or if you can't cook, just come and eat.

Because most ways of approaching homelessness end up institutionalizing it (see Chapter 9), FNB's inherent fluidity and resistance to institutional rule-making is highly instructive. Its refusal of the monetary donation was not because the group did not appreciate the offer. Rather, they were inherently resistant to institutionalizing their activities. Establishing a bank account for the organization and electing a leader or a treasurer to handle money were things that compromised the kind of structure FNB participants wanted their group to have. They did not want anyone to be in charge or in a privileged position. Everyone had equal voice and no responsibilities other than what they themselves wanted to give to the process. There are a minimal number of requirements that stem directly from their underlying antiviolence stance (e.g., food must be vegetarian), but insofar as institutionalization necessitates establishing formal procedures and obligations, the FNB wanted nothing to do with it. Additionally, the short quote above exemplifies that they resisted the quid pro quo logic at the heart of other institutionalized charities (see Chapter 9). That is, they invited the philanthropic woman to bring some food to the picnic, but then became immediately concerned that this might be interpreted as some sort of requirement and so added that she did not have to do so, but could simply come and eat.

FNB's model of operation was built implicitly on the same concept of friendship to which Derrida calls our attention. As Lacinda of the Birmingham FNB group put it:

> I think there is a difference, though [between us and the shelters]. The shelters want to fix homelessness. They want to fix these people who they think are broken. And we're not trying to fix homelessness. We're [only] saying, "Hey look, you're hungry. What we're providing you [with] is a meal. We think that the system that got you in this place is oppressive, and we think that the shelters are oppressive as well. And we're trying really hard

to not be oppressive. So come eat with us, come bring something vegetarian if you have it. Just come hang out. We're not asking anything of people other than what they want to give.

This is not only a different model of service, but also and more important, it employs different assumptions about how organizations must operate. FNB participants did not make orders or demands on one another or the people who came to eat. Everyone participated in whatever way they wanted, and yet everything still seemed to work. This is a mystery to Western philosophy, which usually holds that organizations require rules and that order requires the authoritative management of people. The irony is that most people are members of these sorts of organizations. Though we do not usually call them "organizations," because we have reserved that term for formalized institutions, we all participate in groups of friends that despite lacking institutional rules nonetheless manage to organize events and sustain relationships.

A variety of cultural, us-them assumptions colored the public's sense of what FNB was doing. A man passing by once sarcastically approached the table while his companions snickered as if he was playing a joke. "What do you guys got to eat here?" "Red beans and rice, collard greens, vegetarian lasagna, corn bread, and a variety of cookies. Would you like a plate?" He was shocked at the offer, and it was clear from the change in his facial expression that his joke had been turned upside down. "No thanks, I already ate." "How about some dessert then?" an FNB volunteer pointed at the cookie tray. He was hesitant but replied, "Umm, okay sure." He took two on a napkin and ate them as he walked away. He had assumed that like most organizations, there was some set of rules that separated him from those entitled to the food. But friendships are not governed by such rules, and FNB was looking only for friends, not for clients.

More than that, street meals and soup kitchens nearly always reified the divisions between givers and takers by organizing space to keep them distinct (see Chapters 9 and 10). FNB consciously disorganized their space to avoid this. All of the volunteers ate alongside those who simply came to eat. In short order, the division of givers and takers dissolved into a brilliantly chaotic milieu. This had a real consequence on the perspective of those on the street. At FNB picnics, one could routinely hear things like, "You know the food's good because they're eating it, too." People openly expressed appreciation for the fact that there was no quid pro quo requirement and, without it, no judgments about being homeless. Everyone at the picnic felt like a member of the group not a charity case. When the FNB participants who brought the food arrived, nearly everyone around would participate in helping set things up, carry things from the cars, clean up afterward, and so forth.

Solving homelessness is the goal of governmental and charitable institutions that are willing to make rules delineating the legitimacy of this or that case. But this institutionalizes all sorts of exclusionary judgments and practices that only replicate the power dynamics that force people into bad situations. If power fundamentally is the problem, then any solutions that rely on it will only produce other problems. Power-driven approaches to homelessness certainly may work for any number of persons who are homeless, those who are deemed service worthy and who enthusiastically participate in the programs made available to them. But "fixing" homelessness with power also will inevitably exclude and subjugate others.

* * *

It is difficult to bring to a close an issue as diverse and complex as homelessness. While academic works usually labor under the goal of giving clarity to a topic, in some sense, we have seen our task as the opposite. Because giving clarity often entails the artificial paring down of highly complex phenomena, we hope to have worked to subvert overly simplistic approaches to homelessness emerging from a variety of sectors of society: if they would just get a job; if they would just go somewhere else; if they would just admit they are sick and get treatment; if they would just ask for God's forgiveness.

If there is a singular conclusion to draw out of our experience, perhaps it is that at the core of society's broken relationship with those who are homeless, and at the heart of any number of social problems more generally, is a broken concept of self that makes no room for real individuality or creative freedom. There are few well-articulated alternatives. Those, for example, who take the more radical perspective, both those on the street and activists working on their behalf, like Ralph, Lawton, and FNB, seem to operate out of feeling. Despite their varied specific opinions, they seem to share a subconscious sense that social controls exercised on people, especially those who are disfranchised, at best are inherently suspect and mostly—if not inevitably—oppressive and unconscionable.

In the early 2000s, when our research began, experts from the social sciences and service sectors were saying things to us like, "We've only just now gotten to the point where we can end homelessness over the next ten years." In fairness they have five more years from this writing to make good. But the statement (a loose but accurate quotation) betrays a total lack of social awareness. We are good at criticizing the past, yet despite how wrong we think it was, we have an indomitable spirit of "now we know."[15] We will make no such assertions here. We will not suggest how to end homelessness because we are not willing to homogenize it as something to be ended. The truth is that there are lots of good approaches and no great one. There are many things that will work for many different people to improve their lives, but no magic bullets that will work for everyone. Instead, we will suggest not how to end homelessness, but how to begin with it.

The Mexican Zapatistas have a saying of "one no, many yeses."[16] As a movement, they fight not for this or that ideology, but for the freedom to have diverse beliefs, social institutions, and personal lives. We would do well to learn this lesson in our society, where public discourse is a contest for dominance between opposing groups with opposing ideas. But the diversity of the world means that dominance by one idea, one group, or one model of service can never work for all people. Those who suggest they have *the* answer inevitably will respond to a narrow sliver of those who fit in and exclude those who do not. And then, if history is any guide, they will fall back on rhetoric that blames those excluded for their nonconformity, rather than examining the inevitably partial nature of any single position. So to begin working with the concept of homelessness, to begin to be its friend, we must abandon first our presuppositions about what it is, what it means, how to fix it, and that it is something to be fixed. The diversity of those who are homeless means that we must be diverse in how we think about it and equally diverse in developing relationships with it. Only then can we avoid the oppression that comes with *the* idea, and actually speak to all people who are homeless, to help them improve their own lives on their own terms. Only then can we be the friends of homelessness.

Notes

1. This, too, admittedly is an oversimplification, since observations and judgments naturally occur in the human mind constantly and in an evolving dynamic.

2. This cultural perspective has its clearest roots in the political philosophy of Thomas Hobbes, who suggested in *The Leviathan*, that without the regulation of the state, human life would be "nasty, brutish, and short." Additionally, one need look no further than Durkheim's *The Rules of the Sociological Method* to

see that this idea is strongly rooted, even in a social scientific vision. His classic notion of "homoduplex" is a process of human nature in need of social regulation, where individual egoistic tendencies are controlled to lessen the potential struggles of integrating an imposed conscience collective.

3. Derrida, *The Politics of Friendship*, p. 43.

4. See also Wagner, *Checkerboard Square*.

5. Nonetheless, that existence still has lessons to teach us about today, as discussed in Chapter 7, and persists in a small subculture.

6. See Hopper and Baumohl's legitimate worry about creating an "anthropological zoo" in "Held in Abeyance."

7. Bellah et al., *Habits of the Heart*.

8. In the footnotes to the second edition of *Habits of the Heart*, Bellah et al. note that since the time of the first publication, Wayne has formalized many of his ideas and has a more concrete idea about what goals and values should guide his interventions. The authors see this as a step in the right direction, but we would question whether the new structure of Wayne's activism, insofar as it resembles the top-down direction of repression, is not far more problematic than the mild ambiguity of his original position.

9. Bellah et al., *Habits of the Heart*.

10. Ibid.

11. Freire, *Pedagogy of the Oppressed*.

12. Lyon-Callo, "Medicalizing Homelessness"; Lyon-Callo, *Inequality, Poverty, and Neoliberal Governance*.

13. Hopper, *Reckoning with the Homeless*.

14. Waldron, "Homelessness and Community."

15. See quote in Chapter 2 from Ravindra Svarupa Dasa with Shelter, audio recording, track 12, *Attaining the Supreme*, Equal Vision Records, 1993.

16. See also Kingsnorth, *One No, Many Yeses*.

References

Adler, P. A., P. Adler, and E. B. Rochford, Jr. 1986. "The Politics of Participation in Field Research." *Urban Life* 14: 363–376.

Adorno, T. W. 1973. *Negative Dialectics*. London: Routledge.

Adorno, T. W., and M. Horkheimer. 1977. *Dialectics of Enlightenment*. London: Verso.

Atkinson, P., and D. Silverman. 1997. "Kundera's 'Immortality': The Interview Society and the Invention of the Self." *Qualitative Inquiry* 3: 304–325.

Alabama Governor's Statewide Interagency Council on Homelessness. 2007. *Homelessness in Alabama: Statewide Data Report*. www.servealabama .gov, retrieved April 21, 2009.

Anderson, E. 1999. *Code of the Street: Decency, Violence, and the Moral Life of the Inner City*. New York: W. W. Norton.

Anderson, N. 1923. *The Hobo: The Sociology of the Homeless Man*. Chicago: University of Chicago Press.

Anonymous. 2003. *Evasion*. Atlanta, GA: CrimethInc.

Arhem, K. 1993. "Millennium Among the Makuna: An Anthropological Film Adventure in the Northwest Amazon." *Anthropology Today* 9: 3–8.

Arnold, K. 2004. *Homelessness, Citizenship and Identity*. Albany: State University of New York Press.

Axelson, L. J., and P. W. Dail. 1988. "The Changing Character of Homelessness in the United States." *Family Relations* 37: 463–469.

Baer, H. A., M. Singer, and I. Susser. 2003. *Medical Anthropology and the World System*, 2nd ed. Westport, CT: Praeger.

Bahr, H. M. 1967. "The Gradual Disappearance of Skid Row." *Social Problems* 15: 41–45.

Baker, S. L. 1984. "Physician Licensure Laws in the United States, 1865–1915." *Journal of the History of Medicine and Allied Sciences* 39: 173–197.

Ballard, J. G. 1973. *Concrete Island: A Novel*. New York: Picador.

Becker, H. S. 1963 [1997]. *The Outsiders*. New York: Free Press.

Becker, H. S. 1967. "History, Culture and Subjective Experience: An Exploration of the Social Bases of Drug-Induced Experiences." *Journal of Health and Social Behavior* 8: 163–176.

Bellah, R. N., et al. 1996. *Habits of the Heart: Individualism and Commitment in American Life,* 2nd ed. Berkeley: University of California Press.

Bernstein, J. 2006. "Wages Picture: January 31, 2006." *Economic Policy Institute.* www.epi.org, retrieved April 25, 2006.

Bickford, S. 2000. "Constructing Inequality: City Spaces and the Architecture of Citizenship." *Political Theory* 28: 355–376.

Blumer, H. 1956. "Sociological Analysis and the Variable." *American Sociological Review* 21: 683–690.

Boltanski, L., and L. Thévenot. 2006. *On Justification: Economies of Worth.* Translated by C. Porter. Princeton, NJ: Princeton University Press.

Bourdieu, P. 1990. *The Logic of Practice.* Cambridge, UK: Polity Press.

Burt, M. R. 1992. *Over the Edge: The Growth of Homelessness in the 1980s.* New York: Russell Sage.

Cat Le, P. 2002. "Sobriety Won't Be Rule at New Shelter." *Seattle Post-Intelligencer.* March 26.

Charmaz, K. 2006. *Constructing Grounded Theory: A Practical Guide Through Qualitative Analysis.* Thousand Oaks, CA: Sage.

Clair, J. M. 1990. "Regressive Intervention: The Discourse of Medicine During Terminal Encounters." *Advances in Medical Sociology Research Annual* 1: 57–97.

Clair, J. M., D. Karp, and W. Yoels. 1993. *Experiencing the Life Cycle: A Social Psychology of Aging.* Chicago: Thomas.

Clair, J. M., and R. M Allman (eds.). 1993. *Sociomedical Perspectives on Patient Care.* Lexington: University Press of Kentucky.

Clarke, A. 2005. *Situational Analysis: Grounded Theory After the Postmodern Turn.* Thousand Oaks, CA: Sage.

Cohen, D., and B. Crabtree. 2006. "Qualitative Research Guidelines Project." http://www.qualres.org, retrieved May 6, 2008.

Coleman, J. S. 1958. "Relational Analysis: The Study of Social Organization with Survey Methods." *Human Organization* 17: 28–36.

Coman, V. L. 2006a. "Merchants Group Pushes to Improve Area's Ambiance." *Birmingham News.* September 13.

Coman, V. L. 2006b. "Street Ministry Draws Complaints." *Birmingham News.* November 15.

Coman, V. L. 2007. "Homeless Camps Set for Removal: City Says Makeshift Shelters Pose Health and Safety Risks." *Birmingham News.* May 4.

Conley, D. C. 1996. "Getting It Together: Social and Institutional Obstacles to Getting off the Streets." *Sociological Forum* 11: 25–40.

Conrad, P. 2007. *The Medicalization of Society: On the Transformation of Human Conditions into Treatable Disorders.* Baltimore: Johns Hopkins University Press.

Conrad, P., and J. Schneider. 1992. *Medicalization and Deviance: From Badness to Sickness.* Philadelphia: Temple University Press.

Crane, M., and A. M. Warnes. 2004. "Wet Day Centres in the United Kingdom: A Research Report and Manual." Sheffield Institute for Studies on Ageing, commissioned by the King's Fund and Homeless Directorate.

Culhane, D. P. 1992. "The Quandaries of Shelter Reform: An Appraisal of Efforts to 'Manage' Homelessness." *Social Science Review* 66: 428–440.

Department of Housing and Urban Development. 2008. *The Third Annual Homeless Assessment Report to Congress.* www.hud.gov, retrieved May 8, 2009.

Depastino, T. 2003. *Citizen Hobo: How a Century of Homelessness Shaped America.* Chicago: University of Chicago Press.

Derrida, J. 2006. *The Politics of Friendship.* London: Verso.

Desjarlais, R. 1996. "The Office of Reason: On the Politics of Language and Agency in a Shelter for 'The Homeless Mentally Ill.'" *American Ethnologist* 23: 880–900.

Dey, I. 1999. *Grounding Grounded Theory: Guidelines for Qualitative Inquiry.* Burlington, MA: Academic Press.

Dordick, G. 1997. *Something Left to Lose: Personal Relations and Survival Among New York's Homeless.* Philadelphia: Temple University Press.

Duany, A., E. Plater-Zyberk, and J. Speck. 2000. *The Rise of Sprawl and the Decline of Nation.* New York: North Point Press.

Duffy, J. 1993. *From Humors to Medical Science: A History of American Medicine.* Champaign: University of Illinois Press.

Duneier, M. 1999. *Sidewalk.* New York: Farrar, Straus, and Giroux.

Duneier, M., and H. Molotch. 1999. "Talking City Trouble: Interactional Vandalism, Social Inequality, and the 'Urban Interaction Problem.'" *American Journal of Sociology* 5: 1263–1295.

Durkheim, É. 1895 [1982]. *The Rules of the Sociological Method.* New York: Free Press of Glencoe.

Eckholm, E. 2006. "New Campaign Shows Progress for Homeless." *New York Times.* June 7.

Eighner, L. 1993. *Travels with Lizbeth.* New York: St. Martin's Press.

Ellin, N. 1999. *Postmodern Urbanism,* rev. ed. Princeton, NJ: Princeton University Press.

Erikson, K. T. 1967. "A Comment on Disguised Observation in Sociology." *Social Problems* 14: 366–373.

Eskew, G. T. 1997. *But for Birmingham: The Local and National Movements in the Civil Rights Struggle.* Chapel Hill: University of North Carolina Press.

Failer, J. L. 2002. *Who Qualifies for Rights? Homelessness, Mental Illness, and Civil Commitment.* Ithaca: Cornell University Press.

Fallin, W., Jr. 1997. *The African American Church in Birmingham, Alabama, 1815–1963: A Shelter in the Storm.* New York: Garland.

Feldman, L. 2004. *Citizens Without Shelter: Homelessness, Democracy, and Political Exclusion.* Ithaca: Cornell University Press.

Fine, G. A. 1993. "Ten Lies of Ethnography: Moral Dilemmas of Field Research." *Journal of Contemporary Ethnography* 22: 267–294.

Fine, M., et al. 2003. "For Whom? Qualitative Research, Representations and Social Responsibilities." Pp. 107–133 in *The Landscape of Qualitative Research: Theories and Issues,* 2nd ed., edited by N. K. Denzin and Y. S. Lincoln. Thousand Oaks, CA: Sage.

Foucault, M. 1963 [1994]. *The Birth of the Clinic: An Archaeology of Medical Perception.* New York: Vintage.

Foucault, M. 1965 [1988]. *Madness and Civilization: A History of Insanity in the Age of Reason*. New York: Vintage.

Foucault, M. 1978 [1995]. *Discipline and Punish: The Birth of the Prison*. New York: Vintage.

Franklin, J. L. 1989. *Back to Birmingham: Richard Arrington, Jr., and His Times*. Tuscaloosa: University of Alabama Press.

Freire, P. 1994. *Pedagogy of the Oppressed*. New York: Continuum.

Frey, R. G. 2005. "Intending and Causing." *The Journal of Ethics* 9: 456–474.

Gallagher, N. 1994. "Public Health and Social Medicine: The Historical Legacy of the English Plague Experience." *University of Vermont History Review* 6 (December).

Geertz, C. 2000. *Available Light*. Princeton, NJ: Princeton University Press.

Gerdes, L. I. (ed.). 2007. *The Homeless*. Detroit: Greenhaven Press.

Gibson, T. 2004. *Securing the Spectacular City: The Politics of Revitalization and Homelessness in Downtown Seattle*. New York: Lexington.

Gladwell, M. 2002. *The Tipping Point: How Little Things Make a Big Difference*. Boston: Back Bay.

Glaser, B. G., and A. Strauss. 1967. *The Discovery of Grounded Theory: Strategies for Qualitative Research*. Chicago: Aldine.

Goetz, K. W., and C. J. Schmiege. 1996. "From Marginalized to Mainstreamed: The HEART Project Empowers the Homeless." *Family Relations* 45: 375–379.

Goffman, E. 1959. *The Presentation of Self in Everyday Life*. New York: Doubleday.

Goffman, E. 1963a. *Stigma: Notes on the Management of Spoiled Identity*. Englewood Cliffs, NJ: Prentice Hall.

Goffman, E. 1963b. *Behavior in Public Places: Notes on the Social Organization of Gatherings*. New York: Free Press.

Goode, W. J. 1957. "Community Within a Community." *American Sociological Review* 22: 194–200.

Gramsci, A. 1971. *Selections from a Prison Notebook*. New York: International.

Grunberg, J., and P. Eagle. 1990. "Shelterization: How the Homeless Adapt to Shelter Living." *Hospital and Community Psychiatry*. 41: 522–524.

Guard, G. 2007. "Programs That Focus on Chronic Homelessness Will Hurt Homeless Families." Pp. 142–146 in *The Homeless*, edited by L. I. Gerdes. Detroit: Greenhaven Press.

Hall, P. 1988. *Cities of Tomorrow*. Oxford: Basil Blackwell.

Harrington, B. 2003. "The Social Psychology of Access in Ethnographic Research." *Journal of Contemporary Ethnography* 32: 592–625.

Hibickina and Kika. 2003. *Off the Map*. Atlanta, GA: CrimethInc.

Hoch, C., and R. Slayton. 1990. *New Homeless and Old: Community and the Skid Row Hotel (Conflicts in Urban and Regional Development)*. Philadelphia: Temple University Press.

Hoffman, L., and B. Coffey. 2008. "Dignity and Indignation: How People Experiencing Homelessness View Services and Providers." *The Social Science Journal* 45: 207–222.

Hogg, M. A., and D. Abrams. 1990. *Social Identity Theory: Constructive and Critical Advances*. New York: Harvester Wheatsheaf.

Holstein, J. A., and J. Gubrium. 1995. *The Active Interview*. Thousand Oaks, CA: Sage.

Hopper, K. 1987. "Homeless Choose Streets over Inhuman 'Shelters.'" *Guardian*. November 11.

Hopper, K. 2003. *Reckoning with the Homeless*. Ithaca, NY: Cornell University Press.

Hopper, K., and Baumohl, J. 1994. "Held in Abeyance: Rethinking Homelessness and Advocacy." *The American Behavioral Scientist* 37: 522–553.

Horowitz, R. 1986. "Remaining an Outsider: Membership as a Threat to Research Rapport." *Urban Life* 14: 409–430.

Horwitz, A. V. 2002. *Creating Mental Illness*. Chicago: University of Chicago Press.

Jacobs, J. 1961. *The Death and Life of Great American Cities*. New York: Vintage.

Jencks, C. 1994. *The Homeless*. Cambridge: Harvard University Press.

Kelling, G. L., and J. Q. Wilson. 1982. "Broken Windows." *Atlantic Monthly*, March.

Kertesz, S. G., and S. J. Weiner. 2009. "Housing the Chronically Homeless: High Hopes, Complex Realities." *JAMA* 301: 1822–1824.

Kingsnorth, P. 2003. *One No, Many Yeses*. London: Free Press.

Kusmer, K. L. 2002. *Down and Out on the Road: The Homeless in American History*. Oxford: Oxford University Press.

Kyle, K. 2005. *Contextualizing Homelessness: Critical Theory, Homelessness, and Federal Policy Addressing the Homeless*. New York: Routledge.

LaGory, M., F. J. Ritchey, and J. Mullis. 1990. "Depression Among the Homeless." *Journal of Health and Social Behavior* 31: 87–102.

LaGory, M., et al. 2005. *A Needs Assessment of the Homeless of Birmingham and Jefferson County*. Report submitted to City of Birmingham, Office of Community Development, and to Jefferson County, Community Development Department.

LaMonte, E. S. 1995. *Politics and Welfare in Birmingham, 1900–1975*. Tuscaloosa: University of Alabama Press.

Lee, B. A., C. R. Farrell, and B. G. Link. 2004. "Revisiting the Contact Hypothesis: The Case of Public Exposure to Homelessness." *American Sociological Review* 69: 40–63.

Lesher, S. 1995. *George Wallace: American Populist*. Cambridge, MA: Da Capo Press.

Liebow, E. 1993. *Tell Them Who I Am: The Lives of Homeless Women*. New York: Free Press.

Little, J. B. 1997. "Homeless Cafés Serve Self-Help." http://www.villagelife .org, retrieved April 16, 2009.

Littlejohn, D. 1993. *Hopping Freight Trains in America*. Los Osos, CA: Sand River Press.

Lofland, J., et al. 2005. *Analyzing Social Settings: A Guide to Qualitative Observation and Analysis*, 3rd ed. Belmont, CA: Wadsworth.

Lyon-Callo, V. 2000. "Medicalizing Homelessness: The Production of Self-Blame and Self-Governing Within Homeless Shelters." *Medical Anthropology Quarterly* 14: 328–345.

Lyon-Callo, V. 2004. *Inequality, Poverty, and Neoliberal Governance: Activist Ethnography in the Homeless Sheltering Industry.* Ontario, Canada: Broadview Press.

Maharidge, D., and M. Williamson. 1993. *The Last Great American Hobo.* Rocklin, CA: Prima.

Mahoney, D. 2007. "Substance Abuse Contributes to Homelessness." Pp. 74–78 in *The Homeless*, edited by L. I. Gerdes. Detroit: Greenhaven Press.

Manis, A. M. 1999. *A Fire You Can't Put Out: The Civil Rights Life of Birmingham's Fred Shuttlesworth.* Tuscaloosa: University of Alabama Press.

Marcus, A. 2006. *Where Have All the Homeless Gone? The Making and Unmaking of a Crisis.* New York: Berghahn.

Marin, P. 1988. "Helping and Hating the Homeless." *Harper's* (January): 39–49.

Marx, K. 1843 [1977]. *A Contribution to the Critique of Hegel's Philosophy of Right.* Edited by J. O'Malley. Cambridge: Cambridge University Press.

Mathieu, A. 1993. "The Medicalization of Homelessness and the Theater of Repression." *Medical Anthropology Quarterly* 7: 170–184.

McKay, R. 2006. "Homeless-Meal Clash Still Simmers." *Orlando Sentinel.* August 2.

McKiven, H. M., Jr. 1995. *Iron and Steel: Class, Race, and Community in Birmingham, 1875–1920.* Chapel Hill: University of North Carolina Press.

McWilliams, T. S. 2007. *New Lights in the Valley: The Emergence of UAB.* Tuscaloosa: University of Alabama Press.

Moore, C. H., D. W. Sink, and P. Hoban-Moore. 1988. "The Politics of Homelessness." *PS: Political Science and Politics* 21: 57–63.

Morris, D. E. 2005. *It's a Sprawl World After All: The Human Cost of Unplanned Growth—and Visions for a Better Future.* Gabriola, British Columbia, Canada: New Society.

Mossman, D. 1997. "Deinstitutionalization, Homelessness, and the Myth of Psychiatric Abandonment: A Structural Anthropology Perspective." *Social Science and Medicine* 44: 71–83.

Newman, K. 1999. *No Shame in My Game: The Working Poor in the Inner City.* New York: Russell Sage.

Nunez, R., and C. Fox. 1999. "A Snapshot of Family Homelessness Across America." *Political Science Quarterly* 114: 298–307.

Parsons, T. 1951. *The Social System.* New York: Free Press.

Passaro, J. 1996. *The Unequal Homeless: Men on the Streets, Women in Their Place.* New York: Routledge.

Pathways to Housing Inc. 2005. "Providing Housing First and Recovery Services for Homeless Adults with Severe Mental Illness." *Psychiatric Services* 56: 1303–1305.

Peterson, P. E. (ed.). 1985. *The New Urban Reality.* Washington, DC: Brookings Institution.

Phelan, J., et al. 1997. "The Stigma of Homelessness: The Impact of the Label 'Homeless' on Attitudes Toward Poor Persons." *Social Psychology Quarterly* 60: 323–337.

Pippert, T. D. 2007. *Road Dogs and Loners: Family Relationships Among Homeless Men.* Lanham, MD: Lexington.

Podmore, J. 1998. "(Re)Reading the 'Loft Living' Habitus in Montreal's Inner City." *International Journal of Urban and Regional Research* 22: 283–302.

Pratt, T. 2005. "Critics Say Regional Plan Won't Solve Homelessness." *Las Vegas Sun*. August 13.

Putnam, R. D. 2000. *Bowling Alone: The Collapse and Revival of the American Community*. New York: Simon and Schuster.

Ritchey, F. J., M. LaGory, and K. Fitzpatrick. 1995. Raw Homeless Data Set from a Population in Birmingham, AL.

Rosen, M. 2007. "The Problem of Homelessness Is Exaggerated." Pp. 26–29 in *The Homeless*, edited by L. I. Gerdes. Detroit: Greenhaven Press.

Rosenhan, D. L. 1973. "On Being Sane in Insane Places." *Science* 179: 250–258.

Rossi, P. H. 1989. *Down and Out in America: The Origins of Homelessness*. Chicago: University of Chicago Press.

Rossi, P. H. 1999. "Half Truths with Real Consequences: Journalism, Research, and Public Policy." *Contemporary Sociology* 28: 1–5.

Rossi, P. H., G. A. Fisher, and G. Willis. 1986. *The Condition of the Homeless in Chicago*. A report prepared by the Social and Demographic Research Institute, University of Massachusetts, and by the National Opinion Research Center, University of Chicago.

Rossi, P. H., J. D. Wright, G. A. Fisher, G. Willis. 1987. "The Urban Homeless: Estimating Composition and Size." *Science* 235: 1336–1341.

Roth, J. 1962. "Comments on 'Secret Observation.'" *Social Problems* 9: 283–284.

Rowe, M. 1999. *Crossing the Border: Encounters Between Homeless People and Outreach Workers*. Berkeley: University of California Press.

Sadowski, L. S., et al. 2009. "Effect of a Housing and Case Management Program on Emergency Department Visits and Hospitalizations Among Chronically Ill Homeless Adults: A Randomized Trial." *JAMA* 301: 1771–1778.

Sahlins, M. D. 1972. *Stone Age Economics*. New York: Rinehart.

Salganik, M., and D. Heckathorn. 2004. "Sampling and Estimation in Hidden Populations Using Respondent-Driven Sampling." *Sociological Methodology* 34: 193–239.

Schiller, F. 1795 [1965]. *On the Aesthetic Education of Man: In a Series of Letters*. New York: Frederick Ungar.

Schweik, S. 2009. *The Ugly Laws: Disability in Public*. New York: New York University Press.

Scribner, C. M. 2002. *Renewing Birmingham: Federal Funding and the Promise of Change, 1929–1979*. Athens: University of Georgia Press.

Shlay, A. B., and P. H. Rossi. 1992. "Social Science Research and Contemporary Studies of Homelessness." *Annual Review of Sociology* 18: 129–160.

Silberner, J. 2003. "A Homeless Shelter for Alcoholics: Getting Chronic Drunks off Deadly Cold Streets." National Public Radio. July 21.

Snow, D. A., and L. Anderson. 1987. "Identity Work Among the Homeless: The Verbal Construction and Avowal of Personal Identities." *American Journal of Sociology* 92: 1336–1371.

Snow, D. A., and L. Anderson. 1993. *Down on Their Luck: A Study of Homeless Street People*. Berkeley: University of California Press.

Snow, D. A., et al. 1986. "The Myth of Pervasive Mental Illness Among the Homeless." *Social Problems* 33: 407–423.

Starr, P. 1982. *The Social Transformation of American Medicine.* New York: Basic Books.

Stringer, L. 1998. *Grand Central Winter: Stories from the Street.* New York: Washington Square Press.

Sutherland, E. H., and H. J. Locke. 1936. *Twenty Thousand Homeless Men.* Chicago: J. B. Lippincott.

Szasz, T. 1998. *Cruel Compassion: Psychiatric Control of Society's Unwanted.* Syracuse: Syracuse University Press.

Tanner, M. 2007. "Housing Is Not a Human Right." Pp. 116–118 in *The Homeless,* edited by L. I. Gerdes. Detroit: Greenhaven Press.

Tewksbury, R., and P. Gagne. 1996. "Assumed and Presumed Identities: Problems of Self-Presentation in Field Research." *Sociological Spectrum* 17: 127–155.

Thorne, B. 1980. "'You Still Takin' Notes?': Fieldwork and Problems of Informed Consent." *Social Problems* 27: 284–297.

Toth, J. 1993. *The Mole People: Life in the Tunnels Beneath New York City.* Chicago: Chicago Review Press.

Wacquant, L. 2002. "Scrutinizing the Street: Poverty, Morality, and the Pitfalls of Urban Ethnography." *American Journal of Sociology* 107: 1468–1532.

Wacquant, L. J. D., and W. J. Wilson. 1989. "The Cost of Racial and Class Exclusion in the Inner City." *Annals of the American Academy of Political and Social Sciences* 501: 8–25.

Wagner, D. 1993. *Checkerboard Square: Culture and Resistance in a Homeless Community.* Boulder, CO: Westview Press.

Wagner, D. 2000. *What's Love Got to Do with It: A Critical Look at American Charity.* New York: New Press.

Waldron, J. 2000. "Homelessness and Community." *University of Toronto Law Journal* 50: 371–406.

Wasserman, J. A., J. M. Clair, and K. L. Wilson. 2008. "Problematics of Grounded Theory: Innovations for Developing a More Rigorous Qualitative Method." *Qualitative Research* 9: 355–381.

Wax, M. 1980. "Paradoxes of 'Consent' to the Practice of Fieldwork." *Social Problems* 27: 272–283.

Weber, M. 1930 [2002]. *The Protestant Ethic and the Spirit of Capitalism.* Oxford: Blackwell.

Wejnert, C., and D. Heckathorn. 2008. "Web-Based Network Sampling: Efficiency and Efficacy of Respondent-Driven Sampling for Online Research." *Sociological Methods and Research* 37: 105–134.

Whyte, Jr., W. H. 1963. *Man and the Modern City.* Pittsburgh: University of Pittsburgh Press.

Wilson, K. L., J. A. Wasserman, and F. Lowndes. 2008. "Saving Society from Instrumental Rationality: A Study of Mahler and Homeless Research in the Spirit of Adorno's Critical Musicology." *Journal of Music and Meaning* 7 (Fall/Winter).

Wilson, W. J. 1987. *The Truly Disadvantaged: The Inner City, the Underclass and Public Policy."* Chicago: University of Chicago Press.

Wright, J., B. Rubin, and J. Devine. 1998. *Beside the Golden Door: Policy, Politics and the Homeless*. New York: Aldine de Gruyter.

Wright, T. 1997. *Out of Place: Homeless Mobilization, Sub-Cities, and Contested Landscapes*. Albany, NY: SUNY Press.

Zukin, S. 1982. *Loft Living: Culture and Capital in Urban Change*. Baltimore: Johns Hopkins Press.

Zukin, S. 1991. *Landscapes of Power: From Detroit to Disneyland*. Berkeley: University of California Press.

Index

About the Book

In their compelling examination of what it means to be truly at home on the street, Jason Wasserman and Jeffrey Clair argue that programs and policies addressing homeless people too often serve only to alienate them.

Wasserman and Clair delve into the complex realities of homelessness to paint a gripping picture of individuals—not cases or pathologies—living on the street and of their strategies for daily survival. By exploring the private spaces that those who are homeless create for themselves, as well as their prevailing social mores, the authors explain how well-intentioned policies and programs often only widen the gap between the indigent and mainstream society. The result is an unvarnished look at the culture of long-term homelessness and a fresh approach to reaching this resurgent population.

To view a documentary featuring the people written about in the book, visit the authors' website, www.athomeonthestreet.com.

Jason Adam Wasserman is assistant professor of sociology at Texas Tech University. **Jeffrey Michael Clair** is associate professor of sociology at the University of Alabama at Birmingham.